WITHDRAWN

Xaver Scharwenka

Sounds from My Life

Reminiscences of a Musician

Xaver Scharwenka

Translated by
William E. Petig

Introduction by
Robert S. Feigelson

THE SCARECROW PRESS, INC.
Lanham, Maryland • Toronto • Plymouth, UK
2007

SCARECROW PRESS, INC.

Published in the United States of America
by Scarecrow Press, Inc.
A wholly owned subsidiary of
The Rowman & Littlefield Publishing Group, Inc.
4501 Forbes Boulevard, Suite 200, Lanham, Maryland 20706
www.scarecrowpress.com

Estover Road
Plymouth PL6 7PY
United Kingdom

British Library Cataloguing in Publication Information Available

Library of Congress Cataloging-in-Publication Data

Scharwenka, Xaver, 1850–1924.
  [Klänge aus meinem Leben. English]
  Xaver Scharwenka : Sounds from my life : reminiscences of a musician / Xaver
Scharwenka ; translated by William E. Petig ; introduction by Robert S. Feigelson.
    p. cm.
  Includes bibliographical references (p.), discographies (p.), and index.
  ISBN-13: 978-0-8108-5669-1 (hardcover : alk. paper)
  ISBN-10: 0-8108-5669-7 (hardcover : alk. paper)
  1. Scharwenka, Xaver, 1850–1924. 2. Composers—Germany—Biography.
3. Pianists—Germany—Biography. I. Petig, William E., 1942– II. Title. III. Title:
Sounds from my life.

ML410.S235A313 2007
786.2092—dc22
[B]   2006037448

Contents

~

Introduction

Robert S. Feigelson

(Franz) Xaver Scharwenka was one of the most prominent and beloved musicians in Europe and North America from the 1870s until the early twentieth century. He was one of the finest piano virtuosos of that time and a composer of numerous highly regarded compositions, including an opera, a symphony, four piano concertos, chamber works, and a large number of piano compositions. Many important musicians and composers, including Liszt, Brahms, and Bruch, socialized with him. He devoted a large part of his life to teaching, school administration, and helping musicians get fair financial and professional treatment throughout Germany. In addition he was a kind, well-educated individual with a keen sense of wit, but serious in his musical endeavors—even those that express his humorous, playful personality. During his lifetime critical comments about his playing and musical compositions were highly complimentary. Current-day critics reviewing his music (now revived in both the concert hall and on recordings) have been, for the most part, enthusiastic as well.

I first discovered Scharwenka's music when I was a young piano student circa 1950. I often rummaged around used record stores and dusty bookshops in lower Manhattan after school when one day I stumbled across the sheet music of his once famous Polish Dance. Although first impressed by his exotic name, which brought to mind far-off, mysterious places, I subsequently found the score itself very appealing. At that moment I had no idea how popular this piece had been. I spent many hours practicing, particularly enjoying the dramatic opening chords, before bringing it to my piano teacher to ask if we could include this in my formal studies. I was surprised by her smile and general acquiescence, although not great enthusiasm for my wanting to deviate from more classical pursuits. She followed this with the revelation that she had been a student of Scharwenka and pointed to a signed photograph prominently displayed on her piano that I had not noticed before. There he was quite the distinguished and imposing figure in regal dress.

Scharwenka was born on January 6, 1850, in a region of mixed Prussian and Polish heritage. He rose to fame at the early age of nineteen with the publication of his third composition, a set of Polish Dances, of which the first, mentioned above, became very famous, ultimately selling over three million copies worldwide. He died on December 8, 1924, just short of his seventy-fifth birthday and just two years after publication of his delightful autobiography *Klänge aus meinem Leben: Erinnerungen eines Musikers.*

Many articles written about Scharwenka since his death have relied on material found in his autobiography. It is with great pleasure, therefore, that we can offer this first English translation of his book, affording a much wider audience an opportunity to appreciate the life and times of this talented and interesting performer and composer. The details of his life are well spelled out in his book; however, they do not include much third-person perspective, which I hope to provide below.

Charles Suttoni, commenting on the implausibility of performing artists remembering all the details and critical events in their professional and personal lives, states, "An artist's memoirs is one of the most self-elevating forms of social history, and Scharwenka's book is no exception."[1] In his published thesis on Scharwenka, Schneider-Dominco[2] found discrepancies between some anecdotal accounts in the autobiography and material from other sources (letters and program material). So we must caution the reader that while Scharwenka appears to have had an exceptional memory and possessed many relevant notes and other materials to which he could refer, literary license, wishful thinking, and/or memory lapses may have led to a few inaccuracies. Nevertheless, it is a charming, amusing, and in some cases intimate look into the life of this famous personality.

Death was unkind to Scharwenka in several ways. For one, there was a precipitous drop in his popularity and in the performances of his music soon afterward. One might have expected a decline in performances and recordings, but complete extinction? That such a famous personality could become *persona obscura* so rapidly and for so long is a bit of a puzzle when one reads about the man and his music. Of course Scharwenka, as pianist and conductor, was the main proponent of his own musical compositions and with his skill, energy, and entrepreneurship gone, this became a serious handicap. Perhaps another factor was his limited concertizing and conducting in the decade before his death.

Scharwenka produced solidly written works, firmly based in late-nineteenth-century romanticism. While his music was enjoyable both to listen to and perform, it did not push musical thought into new realms, and some writers blame this for the general lack of interest in his music after his death. Legions of other composers from this era shared his fate—Paderewski and his close friend Moszkowski are two who come readily to mind. Certainly part of the reason was the emergence of impressionism and the startlingly original soundscapes created by Stravinsky and the Viennese School led by Arnold Schoenberg, but perhaps, like clothing and hair styles, their idiom just went out of fashion for a while. On the other hand, these revolutionary trends in music did not alter the continuing public affection for certain romantic composers, such as Tchaikovsky and Grieg, whose popularity remained unabated after their deaths.

Loesser, in his book *Men, Women and Pianos: A Social History*, discusses this very issue. He allows that the "late 19th century produced a small quantity of piano music that transcended the conventional formulas of its time and whose strength of conception gave it some staying power beyond its generation." Citing Brahms, Franck, Saint-Saëns, and Grieg in descending order as belonging to this class, he then lists, together with some other composers, Raff, Henselt, Rheinberger, Rubinstein, Adolf Jensen, and Xaver Scharwenka, who during their time were "far from contemptible in the estimation of the day and regarded as safely and nobly over the heads of the Philistine herd. Alas the repudiative rage of the 20th century has swept them away, they are all trash now, if they were not then."[3] Thomas Arnold Johnson, in his 1939 article titled "The Pianoforte Music of Xaver Scharwenka," writes about the B-flat Minor Piano Concerto, "I cannot understand the total neglect of this very charming and agreeable work. Why do players not seek these by-paths now and then, and enable us to hear these compositions which are in danger of being completely forgotten?"[4]

Additionally we should not minimize the influence of public taste on program planning. Drawing audiences into the concert halls is a practical reality—from the beginning to the present time. Have concert managers misjudged the audience response to Scharwenka's music? Was musical snobbery partly a factor? I suspect the answer to this question is rather complicated, and I am not convinced that one single factor can account for the decline in fortune of many talented composers from the beginning of the last century until their current revival. The latter may have as much to do with audio reproductive technology as the music itself, for which music lovers can be very grateful.

By the early 1950s the name Scharwenka was almost completely forgotten. Even his most popular Polish Dance, op. 3, no.1 in E-flat Minor, which had been of similar stature to Paderewski's Minuet in G and Rachmaninoff's Prelude in C-sharp Minor, was rarely heard or performed. There were no recordings of his music listed under his name in the Schwann Record Catalogs of this period. While a few of his piano roll performances of his own music and those of other composers were resurrected by a few companies during the dawn of the LP era, his name was still obscured because these works were included under "piano collections" and not under the individual composers.

Clearly the main purpose of this book is to give Scharwenka a chance to tell you, in his own inimitable way, the details of his professional career and personal life. I thought, however, it would be helpful to give the reader a brief overview of his life.

Scharwenka was born in Samter (now Szamotuly), a small town in the then Prussian Province of Posen (now Poznan). The province was originally part of Poland until the partitioning in 1793. The German colonization increased greatly after the partitioning. It was given back to Poland after World War I. Scharwenka's father was an architect whose family had migrated from Prague during the reign of Frederick the Great. His mother was Polish on her mother's side. He was very close to her family, who had a farm and mill not far away, and they provided a warm family environment filled with music and laughter. It seems most likely that he derived his interest and perhaps his musical talent (which showed itself at an early age) from this side of his family. It was from this heritage that a good deal of his music derives its Polish flavor.

A financial disaster forced his family to move to Posen in 1858. Like Gershwin, he became interested in the piano when his older brother started taking piano lessons. When not playing childish pranks in the neighborhood, he would play pieces on the family piano by ear. Somewhat later he received some rudimentary formal piano training. He started composing around the age of fourteen. He wrote a trio, a violin sonata, and some church music, but these were apparently put to the torch as childhood indiscretions and are no longer extant.

In 1865, when Scharwenka was fifteen years old, the family moved to Berlin, where he immediately enrolled in Theodor Kullak's (1818–1882) famous Neue Akademie der Tonskunst. Kullak, a teacher of the highest standards, was a piano student of Carl Czerny (as were Liszt and Leschetizky), and Scharwenka took lessons directly from him. He also attended composition classes given by Richard Wüerst (1824–1881), who had studied with Mendelssohn in Leipzig. He made his informal student debut in Berlin as the soloist in Mendelssohn's D Minor Piano Concerto during an 1867 Easter concert that Kullak organized. After three years of diligent, intensive study in Kullak's school, he had apparently learned most of what there was to know about performing, conducting, and composing, and as a mature artist at the tender age of eighteen, he was asked to join Kullak's piano teaching staff. He stayed in this position for five years (1868–1873). On November 26, 1869, he made his public debut as a composer and performer at Berlin's Sing-akademie. Wüerst conducted the Berlin Symphony Orchestra in Schar-wenka's first orchestral composition, an overture. Scharwenka then per-formed as soloist in Schumann's Piano Concerto and Liszt's E-flat Major Concerto. In between the two concertos he performed works by Mendelssohn, Chopin, and Kullak. These performances received critical ac-claim and helped launch his professional career.

For Scharwenka 1869 was an exciting year. Breitkopf & Härtel published his first three compositions; first the aforementioned Polish Dances, op. 3, and then, shortly after, the Piano Trio, op. 1, and the Violin Sonata, op. 2. A year of military service interrupted his career until 1874. Thereafter he began his life as a touring virtuoso. In 1877, the same year he married a young Russian lady named Zenaide Gousseff (one of his piano students), he premiered his just completed first Piano Concerto in B-flat Minor in Hannover. This music became, and still may be, his most popular composition. He played this con-certo on the first of many successful visits to England in 1879 at the Crystal Palace. In 1881, when the Kullak School began to decline, he founded his own music school in Berlin and thus embarked on a third parallel career—that of an educator and administrator. The school came to be known as the Scharwenka Conservatory, and over the years he demonstrated his talent for organization and training young pianists. His brother Philipp helped im-mensely in this enterprise. Philipp, a trustworthy and able partner, was a re-spected composer and taught music theory and composition at the school. For about a decade (1879–1891) Scharwenka gave chamber music concerts in Berlin together with the cellist Heinrich Grünfeld (1855–1931) and, for the first two years, the violinist Gustav Holländer (1855–1915). Emile Sauret (1852–1920), a very fine violinist, took Holländer's place. Also during this pe-riod he arranged subscription concerts in Berlin, where he conducted orches-tral works by a variety of composers, including Beethoven, Berlioz, and Liszt.

In 1890 Scharwenka made his first trip to the United States. His repu-tation preceded him, but not in the way one might suppose (and you will read about this in his own account). However, he won over many audi-ences there during his first visit and on all subsequent excursions to the "New World." He was particularly pleased with a concert held in January 1891 at the Metropolitan Opera House where he performed both

Beethoven's Fifth Piano Concerto and his own first concerto, with Anton Seidl conducting. Entranced by the vitality of this young country and an opportunity to enhance his career he moved with his family to New York City in 1891 and founded a very successful branch of his conservatory. After a year in New York his brother, Philipp, returned to Berlin to take charge of the school there. In 1893, twelve years after its founding, the Berlin Conservatory merged with Klindworth's, and the new Klindworth-Scharwenka Conservatory became one of the largest in the world, having at its peak forty-two soundproof studios, sixty-two teachers, and a thousand students. At one time Max Bruch (1838–1920) and Serge Bortkiewicz (1877–1952) taught at this conservatory. Scharwenka stayed in the United States for about seven years, returning to Germany regularly during the summer months. During this period he toured extensively throughout the United States and Canada. In 1898 he had had enough of the rigors of barnstorming and administrative duties and decided to close the New York branch of his music school and permanently move with his family back to Germany. The strong pull of the fatherland, where his roots were, was also a major factor. When he returned, he took over the role of director of the Klindworth-Scharwenka Conservatory and at the same time headed up the piano department.

In 1910 he and his wife spent another five months in the United States and again crossed the Atlantic in 1912. They returned to Germany early in 1913. In 1914 Xaver resigned from the Klindworth-Scharwenka Conservatory. Further such travel to the West was curtailed when World War I broke out. The war years were filled with arduous but rewarding benefit concerts and other charity work, in particular for musicians.

On November 29, 1919, exactly fifty years to the date of his debut as a performing artist, he was given a grand anniversary celebration at the Singakademie, where his first performance took place. During his career he toured all over Europe and Russia, and many honors were bestowed upon him. Among other notable distinctions, he was court pianist to the Emperor of Austria and given the title of professor by Emperor Wilhelm II, King of Prussia. He was also elected a senator of the Berlin Akademie der Künste. In a letter dated January 29, 1905, Charles T. Griffes, one of the most gifted composers in America at the time, wrote that he attended a celebration of the emperor's birthday at the Royal Academy of Arts and remarked that the senators, who sat up on the platform, wore "very gorgeous robes of wine-colored velvet, lined with the same color of satin and with flowing satin sleeves, and finally velvet caps. . . . Among them were Joachim, Humperdinck, Xaver

Scharwenka, and several others who everyone knows."[5] A color photograph of Lucie Scharwenka's painting of her father outfitted in this costume is reproduced on the front cover.

In the course of over twenty years, he crossed the Atlantic Ocean more than twenty-six times. According to Ellis Island records, his last trip to the United States was in June 1924, less than six months before his death. He arrived with his wife and daughter Lucie on the *Saxony* out of Hamburg. He died of complications related to an appendectomy several months after his return.

He edited a number of musical editions of Chopin and Mendelssohn and for some years was a correspondent for London's *The Monthly Musical Record*. Scharwenka's account of his activities in the twentieth century is rather sketchy. He states that his publisher imposed a page limit, but one gets the impression that he was either running out of enthusiasm at that point in the book and/or perhaps was pressed for time.

Scharwenka presented a dashing figure throughout Europe and the United States. Such was the opinion of both men and women, especially the young ladies, many of whom traveled far and wide to Berlin or New York to study piano under his tutelage. Steven Heliotes, in his informative liner notes for Hyperion Records, quotes the noted *Boston Herald* critic Phillip Hale (1884–1934), who states, "He was a singularly handsome man of gallant bearing, giving one the impression that he should conduct his lessons in full and gorgeous uniform."[6]

One of the most famous descriptions of Scharwenka is that written by the oft-quoted writer Amy Fay, a Kullak and Liszt student from Missouri who wrote home of her adventures in Europe in the 1870s. In her book of letters from abroad titled *Music-Study in Germany*, she writes (in a letter dated December 18, 1872) that Scharwenka (then age twenty-two) was very complimentary about her performance of Rubinstein's Piano Concerto in D Minor (at a concert for Kullak students the week before). She comments: "Scharwenka and Moszkowski are both finished artists and exquisite composers, and play a great deal in concerts this winter. Scharwenka is very handsome. He is a Pole, and is very proud of his nationality. And, indeed, there *is* something interesting and romantic about being a Pole. The very name conjures up thoughts of revolutions, conspiracies, bloody executions, masked balls and of course grace, wit and beauty! . . . Scharwenka has a clear olive complexion, oval face, hazel eyes (I think) and a mass of brown silky hair which he wears long, and which falls about his head in a most picturesque and attractive fashion. . . . When concertos are performed he accompanies. He has a delightful serenity of manner, and sits there with a quiet dignity, his back to the windows, and the light striking through his fluffy hair."[7] Scharwenka apparently did not like being called or thought of as a Pole. This is indicated in this autobiography (as part of a rebuttal to some comments made by von Bülow), and in which he often refers to Germany as the "Fatherland" with great affection.

In a later series of published letters, Fay mentions meeting Scharwenka again, this time in New York City in January 1913 (forty-one years later) at "a jolly musical reception given for Scharwenka and his wife. . . . I am very fond of Scharwenka and his wife, they are both so genial and good hearted. They entered heartily into the thing and made everybody feel at home."[8]

Scharwenka often held Sunday afternoon musical teas or evening soirées at his Berlin home. It was a meeting place for musical celebrities living in the city as well as visiting artists. A. M. Henderson, a piano student of Scharwenka's between 1900 and 1902, describes being a guest at Scharwenka's house on Sunday evenings. On these occasions he met many well-known Berlin musicians including Richard Strauss (1864–1949), Felix Weingartner (1863–1942), Eugen d'Albert (1864–1932), and Moritz Moszkowski (1854–1925). Like Amy Fay, Henderson found Scharwenka a "genial and kind host who had a happy way of making everyone feel at home."[9]

We learn from Scharwenka's autobiography that he was a prankster as a child, and this predilection for joking led to a witty adult who liked to party with friends and enjoy a good laugh. He was also very devoted to wordplay. Alan Walker recounts a time when Scharwenka was at Liszt's (not long before the master's death) where there were some difficult personal relationships between a group of his students and Lina Schmalhausen. Walker comments, "The witty Xaver Scharwenka, who also attended the class at this time condensed the clouds of gossip swirling around the affair and distilled them into some clever wordplay on her name Schmal zu hausen."[10] (The name, according to Walker, means "to rummage around," and Scharwenka also refers to her "notorious inability to keep time.") Walker's translation of Scharwenka's witticism reads as follows:

> To pilfer from others
> To rummage shallowly in Art
> Without an inkling of notes or rests
> Merely tinkling—oh, what horror![11]

Scharwenka was urbane and fluent in English and French. He had five children: four daughters, Lucie (1878–1972), Zenaide (Zini, m. Charmak, 1879–1954), Marie (1880–1888), and Isolde (m. Knauer, 1885–1973), and lastly a son, Philipp (1886–1976). Lucie, an artist, does not seem to have married. Philipp and his wife Hildegard immigrated to the United States where they lived out the balance of their lives. Although Scharwenka does not give the reader much information about his family, we get the strong impression that he was devoted to his wife and children. Papa Scharwenka wrote to his family often when he was away. Many letters and other documents from his career have been preserved and escaped the ravages of the Allied bombings during World War II.[12]

Perhaps the term prodigy is a bit too strong to describe Scharwenka's early prowess with the piano, but he certainly must have had a good ear and a very large talent. In his era, talented virtuosos abounded (they were the pop stars of their day), and they, together with well-known composers such as Liszt, Richard Strauss, Mahler, Busoni, and Brahms, all appeared to hold his playing in very high regard. In fact, the complete lexicon of adjectives bestowed on his performances leaves little room for originality. The major impression is that his playing was refined, thoughtful, and could rise to dazzling heights of virtuosity. David Dubal starts his description of Scharwenka with "One of the most distinguished and brilliant personalities in the annals of pianism. . ."[13] Eduard Hanslick (1825–1904), a tough critic of contemporaneous musicians, comments that Scharwenka was "a totally outstanding pianist, dazzling and without charlatanry."[14] Thomas Arnold Johnson says, ". . . the beautiful quality of his tone being the most noteworthy of his qualifications as a player."[15] James Cooke thought he was a "pianist of great intellectual strength as well as strong poetical forces." He also was noted for "the power of his octave passages, the light sure swiftness of his passage-work, the transparent delicacy of his ornaments and the melodious effect of his trill sequences."[16] Harold Schonberg, in his book on famous pianists, comments that Scharwenka played with "charm, discipline and sensitivity."[17] Two examples of Scharwenka's playing are given on tracks 1 and 2 on the enclosed CD.

His highly esteemed playing helped bring him into many elite social circles in the United States and England. In a letter to his children he writes of his delight at performing Chopin on a gold piano in the White House. He also played at the Vanderbilts' estate in Newport at a party given in honor of Theodore Roosevelt. Over the years, various heads of state in Europe, including Germany, Prussia, Romania, Austria-Hungary, and Russia, bestowed honors on him.

The well-known Portuguese pianist Jose Vianna da Motta (1868–1948) was among many other aspiring students who studied piano with Scharwenka. A young Artur Rubinstein, looking for a piano teacher in Berlin, had an interview with the "methodical Scharwenka," as he was known in certain circles, but he ultimately went elsewhere for instruction. With regard to his teaching abilities, Henderson comments that Scharwenka had a "remarkable musical memory"[18] and could teach eight concertos within a month's time, remembering every bar of both the piano and orchestral parts. During lessons he would often play the second piano. Henderson describes him as "a fine artist, a fine teacher and a fine gentleman."[19]

While Scharwenka is linked to other instrumental virtuosos of this period who wrote music for the sole purpose of performing it themselves—as was apparently expected of them—it seems clear from his autobiography that he was interested in composing for its own sake. He liked to compose and had a need to express himself in this way. In the July 1, 1878, *Monthly Musical Record*, a rather enthusiastic writer discusses Scharwenka the composer: "This mention (of Scharwenka in this publication) is justified by the excellent, not to say extraordinary character of his musical mind, which places him so much above the general run of writers, only falling short by a small degree below the ranks of the highest genius."[20] Johnson, whose comments mirror those of most other writers, both past and present, states, "Scharwenka's music (strongly influenced by Chopin and Schumann) is well worth playing. . . . His compositions, mainly for the piano, are energetic, rhythmical, brilliant, always containing impeccable workmanship and sincerity."[21] David Dubal, in his notes for a Nimbus recording of Scharwenka performing a Chopin scherzo (see track 2 of the enclosed CD), concludes: "Scharwenka is a composer that one can spend many delightful hours with. His music is outgoing, crisp, finely crafted and sane, altogether the manifestation of a man and artist who was comfortable with himself and the world."[22]

In the enclosed CD I tried to give a representative cross-section of his works in a limited space. It is designed to let Scharwenka the virtuoso and composer both speak for themselves, just as Scharwenka the man speaks for himself in his autobiography. This will allow listeners to be their own judge on every aspect and, if so inclined, pursue further the pleasure that Scharwenka can provide on all accounts.

The Piano Concertos

Scharwenka wrote four piano concertos between 1876 and 1908. Although he wrote some very fine chamber and piano music (the latter forming the bulk of his output) these concertos make up the centerpiece of his compositional endeavors.

The First Concerto, op. 32 in B-flat Minor, started life as a piano fantasy and was finished a few years later with some advice from Liszt. It was by far his most popular large-scale work. The long-overdue Scharwenka revival began with this concerto. The concerto's first complete performance was held in Hannover in May 1877, with Scharwenka playing and Fischer (possibly Franz Fischer, 1849–1918) conducting, with an enthusiastic Liszt in attendance. Scharwenka reports that the concert was an outstanding success and helped launch his career. Liszt is said to have commented that it was "a remarkable addition to the pianoforte music."[23] It was performed shortly afterward in Berlin at a private gathering of friends and local artists. During this occasion Scharwenka played the soloist role while Liszt played the orchestral accompaniment. He does not mention a public orchestral concert with Liszt as the soloist. According to Henderson, "Liszt, to whom the concerto is dedicated, was particularly enthusiastic, and not only played it himself but recommended this work to all his friends."[24]

Hans von Bülow (1830–1894), who was very critical of contemporary piano concertos, was reportedly surprised by the new Scharwenka concerto. He called it "interesting and original, amiable throughout, perfect in form . . . admirable instrumentation."[25] Edward George Dannreuther (1844–1905) introduced the concerto to English audiences for the first time in 1877 at the Crystal Palace, and later Scharwenka performed it at the same venue on March 1, 1879. He performed it with Hans Richter conducting in Vienna in 1880.

Even Gustav Mahler, who was known to admire Scharwenka's music, performed the first movement in a student performance at his conservatory. It was perhaps his only public performance as a pianist. The concerto was thereafter played throughout Europe and America. On February 6, 1891, Scharwenka played it in Boston's Symphony Hall with the Boston Symphony Orchestra under Arthur Nikisch. On February 23, 1910, there was a celebration of Scharwenka's sixtieth birthday with a concert at the Blüthner-Saale, where he performed his B-flat-minor Concerto with the conservatory orchestra under the direction of Robert Robitschek. The concert also included a performance of his Symphony, op. 60. The concerto was also in the repertoire of Moritz Rosenthal (1862–1946) and Emil von Sauer (1862–1942).

This concerto was written when the composer was between twenty-five and twenty-seven years old and is a happy work containing lush harmonies and appealing melodies and featuring strong rhythmic elements. In fact, if you are walking while listening to this music, you might find it hard to keep your feet from dancing to the infectious rhythms. All of these elements are illustrated in the Scherzo selection offered on the enclosed CD (track 8).

In the late 1960's Earl Wild made a dazzling recording of it for RCA Records with the Boston Symphony Orchestra under the baton of Erich Leinsdorf. In an interview with George Bedell in 2002, Earl Wild mentions that his teacher at Carnegie Tech was a pupil of Scharwenka and gave him a copy of the concerto in B-flat minor. He learned it and many years later he received a call from Erich Leinsdorf, who asked if he knew the concerto. According to Wild, "I told him that I had been sitting by the phone for the last forty years hoping that someone would call me and ask me to play it!"[26] The recording was immensely popular, and thanks to Wild's brilliant playing and his advocacy, it stimulated further interest in the music of Scharwenka and perhaps other composers of this era. Not that everyone was pleased with this revival. On the other side of the ledger, Glenn Gould, in an article he wrote titled "Should We Dig Up the Old Romantics? . . . No, They're Only a Fad," comments that the late romantic piano concertos are "candelabra music" and continues, "The recent Schwann notes a release of Scharwenka's B-flat minor horror of 1877 from RCA."[27] He follows this with a denigration of the Henselt and Moszkowski concertos. Since Gould does not provide any erudite analysis of the Scharwenka concerto or mention whether he actually heard the music or saw the score, one has to wonder whether this rather curmudgeonly comment has any critical value. According to Wild, "Very few people know that it was one of Richard Strauss's favorite pieces."[28]

In addition to the Wild/Leinsdorf recording, which was reissued on CD by Elan Recordings in 1995, Scharwenka's First Concerto has received three other digital recordings, the latest of which—and a superb one at that—is performed by Marc Andre Hamelin on Hyperion Records.

Scharwenka wrote his Second Piano Concerto, op. 56 in C Minor, three years later. It was premiered in Vienna in December 1880 with Scharwenka as the soloist and then again in Magdeburg in June 1881. It was not as unanimously acclaimed. It was more conservative in style than the first, with a classical sonata format. It did, however, have its admirers. Raymond Lewenthal (whose lecture can be heard on track 3 of the enclosed CD) was very much taken by the finale (which he thought could stand alone) but personally was less enchanted by the first two movements. The finale contains a strong Eastern European flavor, perhaps even influenced by Jewish thematic elements. While there is no evidence that he had any Jewish ancestry, he certainly had many Jewish friends in the music community and also while he was growing up.

In his diaries, Edvard Grieg mentions attending a concert on November 17, 1906, in which Rolf Brandt-Rantzau (1883–1935) performed Scharwenka's Second Concerto. Grieg was disappointed by the performance but commented, "Scharwenka's concerto surprised me with its broad style and aspiring character. I would place it above his well-known concerto in B-flat minor."[29] Steven Haller comments in the *American Record Guide* that "the bustling introduction [of the second concerto] sets the stage in grand fashion; yet there is also a wealth of melodic richness."[30]

Perhaps influenced by the Wild/Leinsdorf recording of the B-flat Minor Concerto, Raymond Lewenthal was the first to record the Second for Columbia Records, albeit only the last movement (for the reasons stated above). This was followed two years later by a complete version by Michael Ponti on Vox Records. Elan and Vox reissued these recordings on CD.

Opposing views of this and the Third Concerto below are recorded in Peter Burwasser's review for *Fanfare Magazine*. Compared with the Brahms, Liszt, and Chopin concertos, he thinks these two concertos are largely missing the "soul of the creator," and "emotional strength and intellectual rigor." He goes on to say they are "expertly assembled, yet curiously hollow."[31] Of the two, he thought the third had greater structural integrity.

The Third Piano Concerto, op. 80 in C-sharp Minor, was written in 1898 during the time when Scharwenka was returning from the United States to reestablish permanent residence in Germany. In fact, part of it was written, as related in his autobiography, on the ship home. It was premiered in Berlin in January 1899, again with the composer as the soloist. It is the least well known of his concertos and is a more sober piece of music, with the orchestra playing a more prominent role. According to Martin Eastick,[32] the concerto is symphonically much stronger than the second. While the second follows more the model of Chopin and Hummel, the third has a cyclic pattern more reminiscent of Liszt. There has been only one recording of this Third Concerto, a fine digital performance for which we are indebted to Seta Tanyel and Collins Records.

The Fourth Piano Concerto, op. 82, in F Minor, was written ten years later (1908). It was premiered in Berlin in October 1908 with his student and later assistant, Martha Siebold, at the piano and the composer conducting. It was a great success. In 1910 Gustav Mahler conducted the New York Philharmonic with Scharwenka as the soloist. Again it was a great success. In the audience was none other than Amy Fay. She was very impressed by Scharwenka's masterly playing and commented that the piece was "awfully difficult to play" and that "he had such a perfect technique."[33] Leonardo De Lorenzo (1875–1962), one of the orchestra's flutists, points out that there was apparently "no love lost" between Mahler and Scharwenka, as evidenced by the fact that "neither during rehearsals or the performance of the concerti did the two men shake hands, as is usually the custom, nor did they look at each other."[34] In Scharwenka's discussion of this concert, he notes that Mahler was very sick at the time and, at a concert shortly before when he played Beethoven's *Emperor* Concerto, Mahler's tempos were so fast that Scharwenka had difficulty keeping up. Scharwenka, however, does not mention or even suggest any enmity between them. Mahler is reported to have conducted forty-seven concerts between November 1, 1910, and February 21, 1911, and died a few months later on May 18, 1911. Scharwenka at this time was sixty years old, and De Lorenzo comments, "In spite of the fact that he was quite old and far from handsome, he was extremely elegant and his appearance was that of a grand seigneur."[35] Shortly after the Mahler performance (February 17 and 18, 1911) Scharwenka performed his Fourth Concerto in Cincinnati, Ohio, under the direction of Leopold Stokowski.

Although written ten years apart, it should be noted that only two opus numbers separate the two last concertos. Scharwenka's attention was obviously diverted from composing during this period. The *Penguin Guide to Compact Discs* describes the Fourth Piano Concerto as follows: "It is ambitiously flamboyant and on the largest scale. Its invention, which manages a potent mix of bravura and lyricism, readily holds the attention, with plenty of interest in the bold orchestral tuttis. The second movement, allegretto, has much charm and is very deftly scored; a full flood of romanticism blossoms in the lento slow movement. The stormy con fuoco finale combines a touch of wit and more robust geniality with glittering brilliance and power."[36] The piece is known for its great technical and interpretive demands, and this may account for the lack of performances by other artists during Scharwenka's remaining years (they were probably happy to let the composer deal with the difficulties) as well as after the composer's death.

Emil von Sauer (1862–1942) was one virtuoso who performed this concerto and proved an able interpreter. There is only one recording of this concerto, but fortunately it is an excellent one by Stephen Hough and the City of Birmingham Symphony Orchestra on Hyperion Records. It also has made its appearance in the concert halls both by Stephen Hough and the National Symphony Orchestra with Osmo Vänskä conducting, and more recently (October–November 2004) with Alexander Markovich at the piano and Neemi Järvi conducting the Philharmonie Cologne. Writing in the *Washington Post* of the National Symphony performance, Joseph McLellan states, "The people who gave it a standing ovation may wonder why such compelling music has been so neglected, but it is not hard to imagine the answer. . . . I suspect that the real reason we don't hear him more often is that most pianists find him too formidable: too much work and too many possibilities of going badly wrong. It is a flamboyantly virtuosic work in a late romantic style that makes up in color, energy and breathtaking acrobatics what it may lack in introspective depth and subtlety."[37]

Chamber Music

Scharwenka wrote a small quantity of chamber music, all with piano. His most important and best works in this genre are probably the Piano Quartet in F, op. 37, written around 1876 during a very happy time in his life, which is described in his autobiography, and the Piano Trio no. 2 in A Minor, op. 45, from 1878. This mood is clearly reflected in the music. Bryce Morrison, writing for *The Gramophone*, comments that "these are two sadly neglected works. . . . Scharwenka's music is full of surprises and often real breadth and vibrancy. . . . The Quartet's Adagio is notably rich, and who can resist the Trio's second movement"[38] (see track 11). Of all the music recorded by Seta Tanyel, the piano quartet was her favorite.[39] Martin Eastick comments that like other music by Scharwenka, the Quartet and Piano Trio, no. 2, "possess energy, a rich source of melody and strong rhythm-qualities for which Scharwenka was renowned as a composer."[40] *The Monthly Music Record* from May 1, 1878, describes the op. 37 Quartet, saying the first movement starts with a "bold, yet quaint and altogether novel subject, with an equally striking rhythm." The second movement is "beautifully conceived and thoroughly carried out." While modeled on Schumann, it could not be by anyone but Scharwenka. The third movement, an Allegro vivace (see track 12), has "freedom, dash and interesting, almost humorous effects." The last movement "dashes off with a fire and spirit at once remarkable and daring."[41]

As mentioned before, Scharwenka wrote a number of musical compositions at age fourteen, including a piano trio and a violin sonata that he later destroyed. However, he must have felt comfortable with this medium and perhaps wanted to save some of the ideas from them for his first published chamber works, which were also the Piano Trio (no. 1) in F-sharp Minor, op. 1, and the early Violin Sonata in D Minor, op. 2 (selections on tracks 4 and 5, respectively). This curious coincidence, however, has not been confirmed. The violin sonata shows the influence of Schumann and Mendelssohn, but the final presto illustrates his strong individuality. Morrison found much to enjoy in these two early chamber pieces, including the "fire-spitting finale"[42] of the Violin Sonata.

Shortly after the Second Trio, he wrote the Cello Sonata in E Minor, op. 46, the second movement of which was later orchestrated. Selections from both pieces are given in the enclosed CD for comparison purposes (tracks 9 and 10). According to a review in the December 1, 1879, *Monthly Musical Record*, it "is at once a thoughtful, expressive, and remarkable specimen of his quality." With regard to the second movement, clearly the jewel in the crown of this work, the reviewer states that it "is marked by charm of melody and piquancy of thought . . . the modulations are cleverly and felicitously introduced."[43] Wilhelm Altmann, writing in *Corbett's Encyclopedic Survey of Chamber Music*, thought the themes in the first movement uninspiring but well treated, the second movement, with a Bach-like introduction, struck "a note of warmth and dignity which lifts it far above the commonplace," and the finale lively with cleverly handled, pretty themes.[44]

The last piece of chamber music Scharwenka wrote was the Serenade for Violin and Piano, op. 70.

Piano Music

Not surprisingly, the bulk of Scharwenka's compositions, around ninety works in all, are for piano. He wrote two substantial piano sonatas, over two dozen Polish Dances, and numerous other pieces and sets of pieces, some for piano duets or two pianos.

Three of the Polish Dances are given on the enclosed CD. Track 1 contains the famous Polish National Dance, op. 3, no. 1, in a performance by Scharwenka himself (from a piano roll recording). The discography lists numerous other recordings of this piece, including a variety of transcriptions for numerous instruments, combinations of instruments, and orchestra. Even Liberace performed this piece and included it in his very first recording. Akin to Scharwenka, Liberace's mother was also of Polish origin and this was reflected in his full name, Wladziu Valentino Liberace. It was Paderewski (at the time premier of Poland), during a visit to the Liberace family, who convinced young Wladziu's parents to encourage him to pursue a musical career and also to use only a single name. The Polish Dance under discussion was so popular that it was even mentioned in Ella Leffland's novel titled *Breath and Shadows*. The relevant passage reads, "Scharwenka's 'Polish Dance' was ringing out from the mandolin, the gayest of all melodies."[45]

Scharwenka commented that he would "deeply regret" if his work as a composer be judged by Americans solely on the basis of his Polish Dance. He hoped that they would become familiar with both his Fourth Piano Concerto, which he believed, along with some other critics, to be his best work, and the Theme and Variations, op. 48, one of his personal favorites.

At the suggestion of Evelinde Trenkner,[46] I have also included the Polish Dance, op. 3, no. 2 (track 6), which she preferred and performs here; and for contrast, a mature example of this genre, the op. 58, no. 3, as performed by Seta Tanyel (track 7).

Scharwenka wrote two substantial piano sonatas. The First Sonata, op. 6, in C-sharp Minor, was written in 1871 and dedicated to his teacher Kullak.

It is a youthful work described by Eastick as "full of ambition, sustaining a constant driving energy, within a fairly formal sonata framework." The second movement is a Scherzo and the third a slow movement "serving as an introduction to the furious and impassioned finale."[47] The Second Sonata, op. 36, in E-flat, was written in 1878. It is one of his most substantial works for solo piano. It is melodious and, as is typical of such a fine pianist, is well written for his instrument. Johnson considered both sonatas "first class works containing some fine, noble melodies treated in a Chopinesque and highly brilliant manner." However, he also suggests that they are somewhat shallow and that "pianists will enjoy playing these even if many do not feel that they rise to great heights." His own favorite was the First Sonata, in which he found "the Finale, an exciting and exhilarating conclusion."[48] Some critics preferred the second as a more imposing work. Scharwenka also wrote two piano sonatinas, op. 52. Christopher Headington,[49] reviewing the Tanyel recording of the First Piano Sonata, compares it with a rejected very early sonata in C minor by Chopin that was published against the famous composer's wishes. He thought the third movement the best, but lacking a memorable tune and personality. No faint praise here!

Probably Scharwenka's most important piano work is his Theme and Variations, op. 48. Scharwenka played it often in concert. It is a serious and thoughtful work, and aside from the Polish dances, Scharwenka's most popular piano piece. Claudio Arrau performed it in Berlin at the fiftieth anniversary celebration of Scharwenka's performing career. It was originally written with a theme and nineteen variations, but later revised and condensed by Scharwenka to twelve variations, including some rearrangement. Trenkner's recording on Orion Records was of the original version while Seta Tanyel recorded the revised version, although unaccountably fourteen variations are given. On the enclosed CD (tracks 15–24), a selection of the variations is given from the Trenkner performance of the original version. Eastick notes that in 1880, the German critic Karl Schelle, after hearing Scharwenka perform this work in Vienna, found that the Theme and Variations was a "fine work of great creative power."[50] Thomas Arnold Johnson[51] thought it was a powerful work modeled after Brahms in every detail. However, a different perspective is given in the August 1, 1879, issue of *The Monthly Musical Record*: "The theme in itself is most striking for its novelty and unconventionality, and in the manner in which Herr Scharwenka has treated it in the nineteen variations which follow is as clever as anything which as yet has been issued from his pen and brain. . . . The utter absence of conventionality and all-pervading warmth of expression and passionate power speak of the gifts of no common order."[52] The same writer in the

January 1, 1880, issue of the same journal gives a detailed, variation-by-vari-
ation analysis of the work that I recommend to those interested. His discussion starts with: "This masterpiece of musical constructive skill . . ."[53] This is
a case that the listener must judge for himself.

From among his other piano music the Polish Dances stand out. Johnson
thought the Polonaise and Mazurka, op. 16, "first class Scharwenka" and to
be strongly recommended. He also liked the "Two Tales (op. 5): fine concert
works especially No. 2." He also thought the Studies and Preludes, op. 27,
were splendid works and "The Staccato Study is a fine concert solo, far superior to the much hackneyed Rubinstein."[54] The Romanzero, op. 33, a four-
movement piece written in 1877, was dedicated to Brahms, who received it
gratefully along with the news of Scharwenka's engagement to Zenaide.
While quite a few of the piano works have been recorded, as listed in the
discography, still many remain unperformed and unrecorded. While not
overly effusive, Christopher Headington found the Polonaise, op. 42, as having "some grandeur" and the Valse-Caprice, op. 31, as having "a distinct
charm."[55] The Eglantine Waltz was also well regarded.

A number of piano pieces were transcribed for other instruments, including the Andante, op. 62, no. 11, arranged for band by Leopold Liegl for the
Alberta Band Association; a Scherzino for flute, oboe, and two clarinets
(Marquette University Libraries); and the Suite of Dances, op. 41, transcribed for piano duet, to name a few.

Some of Scharwenka's piano and chamber music was the subject of analysis in the thesis of Michael Mihalyo Jr.[56] and Timothy Saeed.[57]

The Orchestral Music

Scharwenka wrote only four compositions without piano. These include an
early overture (1869), his opera *Mataswintha*, a Symphony in C Minor, op.
60 (1882), and the previously mentioned orchestration of the second movement of his cello sonata, the Andante religioso, op. 46a (1881). Samples of
the latter two are included on the enclosed CD (tracks 9 and 10). The symphony, written when he was thirty-two, is dedicated to Constantine, Prince
Hohenlohe-Schillingsfürst. It was first performed in Copenhagen in December 1883, with Scharwenka conducting. After some promotion on his
part, it finally received a performance in Berlin in March 1884 with Franz
Wüllner conducting. On the same program von Bülow was performing
Raff's Piano Concerto, and Scharwenka relates an amusing incident with
regard to the needs and intent of the pianist and the composer's hapless part.
I will leave it to the reader to discover this for himself. According to the in-

formative liner notes by Christopher Fifield[58] for the Sterling recording, the symphony was later conducted by Scharwenka in Elberfeld (1886) and Moscow (1896) and thereafter by Carl Theil (Danzig, 1900), Theodore Thomas (New York, 1885), Robert Kajanus (Helsinki, 1899) and Dan Godfrey (Bournemouth, 1911 and 1912). Steven Haller, in a review of the Sterling recording for the *American Record Guide*, thinks the C minor key is a "clear link" to Beethoven's Fifth Symphony: "Not thematically, but its great surging energy, its almost relentless thrust and turmoil."[59] The four-movement symphony is not in the ebullient style characteristic of many of Scharwenka's other major compositions, but of a more somber, passionate mood. Critics reviewing this premiere recording were quite enthusiastic about this symphony and were happy to be able to hear it in a commendable performance.

The overture from 1869 is from the same period as the Polish Dances, op. 3, the first piano trio and the violin sonata. Unlike these exuberant pieces, however, this first surviving attempt at orchestration is much more like the symphony (written thirteen years later) in its somber mood.

Opera

Scharwenka wrote only one opera, *Mataswintha*, a medieval tale based on the historical novel by Felix Dahn titled *Ein Kampf um Rom*. It premiered in Weimar in 1906, with Bernard Stavenhagen conducting. It was reported to be a very successful debut. Seven months later, Walter Damrosch was enlisted by the Metropolitan Opera House management in New York to organize a four-week "German Season." According to the well-known New York music critic Henry Edward Krehbiel (1854–1923), Scharwenka "borrowed the company from Mr. Damrosch and on his own responsibility gave a performance of his Opera." Krehbiel was in attendance at the performance on April 1 and commented on the near disaster. First off, the chosen singer, tenor Ernst Kraus, became ill, delaying the performance. To make matters worse, a baritone, Gerhard Stehmann, had to replace Kraus in the role of King Witchis. There were other issues to confront Scharwenka as well, including a cast that had an "erratic quality" and had to learn their parts under rushed conditions. In addition, the nature of the story led to demanding scenery and costume requirements. Summing up, Krehbiel took a rather diplomatic tack: "Under the circumstances it may be the course of wisdom to avoid an estimation of the opera's merits and defects and to record merely that it proved to be an extremely interesting work and well worth the trouble spent upon its production. Under different circumstances it might have lived the allotted time upon the stage, which, as the knowing know, is very brief in the majority of cases."[60] Scharwenka comments in his book that he was pleased with this performance. Irving Kolodin also briefly discusses the debacle. He empathized with the composer, "the unfortunate man"[61] who in spite of these problems conducted with authority. While the opera has not been recorded or performed in the concert hall for almost a hundred years, Karl Krueger and the Detroit Symphony Orchestra did perform the overture to *Mataswintha*, and an underground tape of that concert has been available to collectors for decades.

According to Schneider-Dominco,[62] there is evidence that Scharwenka started a second opera but that project did not get very far. Scharwenka also wrote some songs, none of which, to my knowledge, have been recorded, a situation that I hope will soon be rectified.

Like most human endeavors, critical reviews are rarely unanimous and one has to appreciate that reviewers come from different backgrounds, expertise, and emotional makeup. While some think highly of Scharwenka's music, others have reservations and criticisms. There is little argument about his formidable talent as a pianist and the seriousness of purpose in his performance. As to the man himself, he was unprejudiced, funny, kind, and someone most of us would have enjoyed knowing. Finally, he was an effective and beloved teacher and a very skilled administrator.

Earl Wild, Raymond Lewenthal, and Michael Ponti were pioneers in the late-romantic piano concerto revival, and their recordings strongly stimulated the interest in Scharwenka's music. It was Seta Tanyel and Collins Records, however, who really put Scharwenka and his music into the limelight with a series of excellent recordings of all his chamber music and a large fraction of his piano music, a legacy that is being continued today by Hyperion Records. Finally, I must mention the Scharwenka Society, founded in 1988 by Professor Evelinde Trenkner, its current president. The reader can find information on this society at the following website: members.aol.com/etrenkner/.

Notes

1. Charles Suttoni, "Preface," in *Scharwenka: Piano Concerto No. 1 in B-flat Minor, Op. 32, 2-Piano Score* (New York: Music Treasure Publications, 1971), I.
2. Matthias Schneider-Dominco, *Xaver Scharwenka (1850–1924), Werkverzeichnis (ScharWV)* Bd. 6 (Göttingen: Hainholz Musikwissenschaft, 2003).
3. Arthur Loesser, *Men, Women and Pianos: A Social History* (New York: Simon & Schuster, 1954), 427–428.
4. Thomas Arnold Johnson, "The Pianoforte Music of Xaver Scharwenka," *Musical Opinion* 42 (August 1939): 945–946.

5. Edward Maisel, *Charles T. Griffes: The Life of an American Composer* (New York: Alfred A. Knopf, 1984), 70.

6. Steven Heliotes, liner notes for Hyperion recording CDA 66790 (1995), 3.

7. Fay Peirce, ed., *Music-Study in Germany, From the Home Correspondence of Amy Fay* (New York: Macmillan Co., 1903), 185–186.

8. S. Margaret William McCarthy, ed., *More Letters of Amy Fay: The American Years; 1879–1916* (Detroit: Information Coordinators, 1986), 138–139.

9. A. M. Henderson, "Xaver Scharwenka: A Great Artist and Teacher," *Etude* (April 1955): 11.

10. Alan Walker, ed., Prologue to *The Death of Franz Liszt: Based on the Unpublished Diary of His Pupil Lina Schmalhausen* (Ithaca, NY: Cornell University Press, 2002), 7.

11. Walker, Prologue to *The Death of Franz Liszt*, 7.

12. Schneider-Dominco, *Xaver Scharwenka (1850–1924)*.

13. David Dubal, *The Art of the Piano: Its Performers, Literature and Recordings*, rev. and expanded 3rd ed. (Pompton Plains, NJ: Amadeus Press, 2005), 317–319.

14. Suttoni, "Preface," III.

15. Johnson, "The Pianoforte Music of Xaver Scharwenka," 945–946.

16. Xaver Scharwenka, "Economy in Music Study," in *Great Pianists on Piano Playing: Godowsky, Hofmann, Paderewski, and 24 Other Legendary Performers*, ed. James Francis Cooke (Mineola, NY: Dover Publications, 1999; T. Presser, 1917), 252. Citations are to the Dover edition.

17. Harold C. Schonberg, *The Great Pianists from Mozart to the Present* (New York: Simon & Schuster, 1963), 323–324.

18. Henderson, "Xaver Scharwenka: A Great Artist and Teacher," 47.

19. Ibid.

20. Anonymous, "Concert (B moll) für das Pianoforte, mit Begleitung des Orchesters, componirt von Xaver Scharwenka, Op. 32," *The Monthly Musical Record* (July 1, 1878): 106.

21. Johnson, "The Pianoforte Music of Xaver Scharwenka," 945–946.

22. David Dubal, liner notes from Nimbus CD 8801 (1998).

23. Frank Cooper, liner notes from RCA LP, LSC 3080 (1969).

24. Henderson, "Xaver Scharwenka: A Great Artist and Teacher," 47.

25. Anonymous, "Xaver Scharwenka, Pianist and Composer," *The Musical Courier* (1911): 9.

26. George Bedell, "Calmer Passions: An Interview with the Pianist Earl Wild," *Shumei Magazine* 241 (September/October 2002).

27. Tim Price, ed., *The Glenn Gould Reader* (New York: Alfred A. Knopf, 1984), 72–74.

28. Bedell, "Calmer Passions: An Interview with the Pianist Earl Wild."

29. Finn Bedestad and William H. Halverson, eds., *Edvard Grieg: Diaries, Articles, Speeches* (*Edvard Griegs Briefwechsel*, herausgegeben von Klaus Henning) (Columbus, OH: Peer Gynt Press, 2001), 152.

30. Steven Haller, *American Record Guide* (May/June 1997): 193.

31. Peter Burwasser, "Scharwenka Piano Concertos: No. 2, No. 3," *Fanfare* 27, no. 3 (January/February 2004).

32. Martin Eastick, liner notes for Hyperion recording CDA 67365 (2003).

33. McCarthy, ed., *More Letters of Amy Fay: The American Years; 1879–1916*, 95.

34. Leonardo De Lorenzo, *My Complete Story of the Flute: The Instrument, the Performer, the Music* (Lubbock: Texas Tech University Press, 1996), 467–468.

35. Ibid.

36. Edward Greenfield, Ivan March, Robert Layton, and Paul Czaikowski, eds., *The Penguin Guide to Compact Discs and DVDs 2003/4: The Guide to Excellence in Recorded Classical Music* (London: Penguin Books, 2003), 1112–1113.

37. Joseph McLellan, "For the NSO Washington, at Long Last Scharwenka," Special to *The Washington Post*, April 11, 2003, C08.

38. Bryce Morrison, "Scharwenka," *The Gramophone* (March 1995): 66.

39. Seta Tanyel, e-mail, May 26, 2005.

40. Martin Eastick, liner notes from Hyperion recording CDD 22046 (2002), 7.

41. Anonymous, "Quartett für Pianoforte, Violine, Viola, und Violoncell (F dur) Componirt von X. Scharwenka, Op. 46," *The Monthly Musical Record* (May 1, 1878).

42. Bryce Morrison, "Scharwenka," *The Gramophone* (March 1995): 66.

43. Anonymous, "Sonate in E moll, für Pianoforte und Violincell von X. Scharwenka, Op. 46," *The Monthly Musical Record* (December 1, 1879): 191.

44. Wilhelm Altmann, "Scharwenka, Xaver (Franz X.), 1850–1924," *Corbett's Encyclopedic Survey of Chamber Music* (London: Oxford University Press, 1930), 332.

45. Ella Leffland, *Breath and Shadows* (New York: William Morrow, 1999), 137.

46. Evelinde Trenkner, e-mail, May 30, 2005.

47. Martin Eastick, liner notes for Collins Classics CD 13252 (1992).

48. Johnson, "The Pianoforte Music of Xaver Scharwenka," 945–946.

49. Christopher Headington, "Review of Collins Classics CD 13252 'Xaver Scharwenka, The Piano Works Vol. 1,'" *The Gramophone* (September 1992): 136.

50. Martin Eastick, liner notes for Collins Classics CD 13652 (1993).

51. Johnson, "The Pianoforte Music of Xaver Scharwenka," 945–946.

52. Anonymous, "Thema und Variationen für das Pianoforte, Componirt von X. Scharwenka, Op. 48," *The Monthly Musical Record* (August 1, 1879): 123.

53. Anonymous, "Xaver Scharwenka's Thema und Variationen, Op. 48," *The Monthly Musical Record* (January 1, 1860): 3.

54. Johnson, "The Pianoforte Music of Xaver Scharwenka," 945–946.

55. Headington, "Review of Collins Classics CD 13252."

56. Michael P. Mihalyo, *The Life and Keyboard Works of (Franz) Xaver Scharwenka (1850–1924)* (doctoral thesis, West Virginia University, 2004).

57. Timothy D. Saeed, *The Chamber Works and Piano Sonatas of (Franz) Xaver Scharwenka (1850–1924): An Analysis of the Sonata-Allegro Movements* (master's thesis, Boston University, 2004).

58. Christopher Fifield, liner notes for Sterling recording CDS 1060 (2004), 5 (Ger.), 10 (Eng.).

59. Steven Haller, "Scharwenka: Symphony in C minor, Overture; Andante Religioso," *American Record Guide* (September/October 2004): 181–182.

60. Henry Edward Krehbiel, *More Chapters of Opera: Being Historical and Critical Observations and Records Concerning the Lyric Drama in New York from Its Earliest Days down to the Present Time*, rev. 2nd ed. (New York: Henry Holt and Co., 1909), 263–264.

61. Irving Kolodin, *The Metropolitan Opera 1883–1966* (New York: Alfred A. Knopf, 1966), 129.

62. Schneider-Dominco, *Xaver Scharwenka (1850–1924)*.

Translator's Foreword

William E. Petig

Throughout this translation of Xaver Scharwenka's autobiography, *Sounds from My Life: Reminiscences of a Musician*,[1] I have maintained the author's paragraph organization and altered the sentence structure only when required for an idiomatic rendering in English or when complicated, multi-clause sentences in German would have hampered the ease of reading. Whenever possible, I have tried to preserve both the author's style as well as the unique German atmosphere that he creates when relating the experiences of his life. My goal has been to let Scharwenka speak for himself and to translate his words accurately into English, even if it makes him sound anachronistic at times. Scharwenka was an extremely witty person who loved humor and frequently used irony, wordplays, and puns to make a point. Although a challenge, I have tried to capture his humor and wordplays, and where these may not be readily accessible to the nonspeaker of German, I have explained the wordplay or pun in a footnote.

Although Scharwenka admits that he was often less than enthusiastic about school, he clearly received an excellent education in the Wilhelm Gymnasium in Posen, with its traditional emphasis on classical languages and literature. Even as an adult, he was still able to read and quote from the authors of classical antiquity in the original languages, and the numerous literary quotations or allusions that he weaves into his autobiography attest to the fact that he was very well read. Since Scharwenka neither identifies many of these literary citations nor elaborates on his many historical and cultural references, I have provided annotations that indicate the source or that explain the reference.

Scharwenka interacted with many composers, conductors, and performers of his time, especially those with ties to the German-speaking world. Annotations identify or provide background information for many of the interesting people with whom he worked or became acquainted during his concert tours as well as for the orchestras with which he performed or the places he visited. It is my hope that these annotations will provide a backdrop against which the rich historical and cultural tapestry of his life can be viewed and understood.

In conclusion, I would like to express my appreciation to my colleague Robert S. Feigelson, who first proposed this project and who generously read several drafts of my translation and suggested stylistic changes to improve the readability. I am also indebted to William Byron Webster of Stanford, who assisted me with the translation of some of the musical terminology and references and suggested stylistic improvements.

Note

1. Xaver Scharwenka, *Klänge aus meinem Leben: Erinnerungen eines Musikers* (Leipzig: K. F. Koehler, 1922).

~

Scharwenka's Dedication

To
Your Royal Highness, Princess of Albania,
Princess Sophie of Wied

Most Serene Princess

On the tenth anniversary of our meeting in person, when Your Highness kindly granted me such a beautiful, festive honor, the publisher K. F. Koehler approached me to write an account of my life for his firm. It took all of the not inconsiderable power of persuasion of the head of the firm—my dear friend, Dr. Hermann von Hase—to get me to agree, because I really did not believe that the general public could be interested in the portrayal of my simple life. I began with hesitation and apprehension; but from the beginning my intention of placing the following pages at your feet, Your Highness, gave my creative powers wings and momentum.

   With a thankful heart I recall the many inspiring and happy hours, brightened through the noble enjoyment of art and our common performance of our dear Musica. I remember the evenings dedicated to the muses in Your Highness's cozy home and the sunny summer days in Waldenburg's wonderful castle and grounds and the unforgettable days in the "cabin of the muses" on Lake Achen and in my own retreat on Lake Scharmützel in Brandenburg; I remember the trio rehearsals and performances in which Your Highness participated with such artistic enthusiasm and time and again came up with new ideas for our artistic endeavor.

This all lingers in my soul like a pure chord from those bright, immense heights, where "The sun contends in age-old fashion with brother spheres in hymnic sound."[1]

While the memory of these lovely days causes my intent to become deed, I ask Your Highness to accept the dedication of this modest work as a sign of my great respect and gratitude.

Note

1. The first lines from the "Prologue in Heaven" in *Faust* by Johann Wolfgang von Goethe (1749–1832); translation taken from *Faust: A Tragedy*, trans. Walter Arndt, ed. Cyrus Hamlin (New York: W.W. Norton, 2001), 9.cx

CHAPTER ONE

~

Samter, 1850–1858

The City and Something about My Family

On the railroad that goes from Stettin to Breslau, in the heart of our former province of Posen, lies the city of Samter, seat of the district court and of other institutions that are features of a district capital.[1] A small river, the Sama, that at high water levels offers the opportunity to swim and to do laundry, delivers its lazily flowing stream to the Warta, the main river of the province.

The most noteworthy building, towering over everything in this small, crooked city (which was unbelievably dirty in my childhood and at that time had four thousand inhabitants) is the large venerable Catholic Church that stands in the middle of a long-unused cemetery. A unique gate forms the entrance to the courtyard of this edifice, which reaches massively to the sky. In the open niches of this gateway hang large bells, which are rung by devout farmers in the area. In contrast to this imposing church building, an incredibly austere structure in a very plain style serves the religious needs of the Protestants. It dates from the sixties of the previous century and, with its stark ugliness, ruins the largest open square in the town. For the members of the faith of Moses there is a simple, unadorned temple, standing modestly in a side street.

Also among the noteworthy buildings is the monastery on the edge of the city on the way to the train station. It has not served its original purpose for a long time; only the chapel was still used for services on special occasions.

Except for a few rooms, in which the elementary school classes of the Klipp School were housed, the rest of the rooms were vacant and deserted. The coffins of deceased priests, monks, and other inhabitants of the monastery were in the vaults in the cellar. Some of the coffins were missing covers, and through the cellar windows one could clearly see the well-preserved corpses—like in the cellar of the Bremen cathedral. For some years the monastery served as the barracks for an infantry unit posted there. Soon, however, the military acquired a different garrison, and the monastery again fell into its lethargic sleep.

On the opposite side of the city is the old castle with its farm buildings and its badly neglected grounds, which border the extensive lands that make up the Samter estate. From these "lands"—today we would call it a nobleman's estate—the city gradually developed into its present form. In the twelfth century the noblemen of Ostrorog (Scharfenort) were the owners of these lands; then in the thirteenth century came the Szamotulski, from whom the city took its name. Before the division of Poland, Samter was called Szamotuly and currently bears this name again (1921). Raised to the status of a city in the fourteenth century, Szamotuly was completely destroyed by fire, but soon rebuilt again. Among the following holders of these lands must be mentioned Andreas Górka, who granted the Bohemian Brethren[2] a home and protection. He, to whom half the city had to pay tribute, handed the Catholic church over to the Brethren and gave them considerable privileges. But this did not last long; soon after Górka's death these rights were taken away from the Bohemian Brethren.

Hard times fell on the few Protestants in the following century. Pan Gostynski, the lord of Szamotuly, persecuted with a blind hatred all who did not take an oath to the "only true" church. The "heathen" could only hold their services in the closest family circle. Protestants did not get a church until the eighteenth century, but they were not able to afford their own pastor. The pastors from the neighboring cities of Wronke and Obersitzko conducted services for them. In modern times the owners of the Samter manor changed frequently; to be mentioned are Counts Kostka, Lonski, and Mycielski. Finally the Duke of Coburg-Gotha acquired the fertile property.

In the park stands a very old watchtower, the landmark of the city. An underground passage connects it with the parish church, and many gruesome stories of murder and killing are associated with this eerie structure with ravens cawing above it. The local people call it "the tower of the black princess." In his *Local History of the District of Samter*, the teacher Rudolf writes the following about the origin of this folktale:

A rich, proud nobleman had an extremely beautiful daughter, whom he loved very much and whom he wanted to give as bride to the most distinguished nobleman in the entire area. She, however, loved a lowly servant of her father's and only wanted to marry him. The father was very upset about this. She fled her father's wrath, and, forsaken by all, she wandered around in the area. But she was soon captured, and her father imprisoned her for life in the tower. She had to wear a black mask all the time, because he did not want to see her face anymore. *Wandering around alone* in Polish is *sam tulic sie*, from which the name Szamotuly (Samter) is said to have come. The name of the princess was Halszka von Ostrorog, and she died in 1582.

Although the alleged derivation of the name of the city seems somewhat dubious, the purported year of death of the princess (1582) causes even more unease, since, as was mentioned above, already in the thirteenth century the Szamotulski nobles could be authenticated as the rulers of Szamotuly.

The picturesque tower is reflected in a small lake, surrounded by bulrushes, and on whose bush-lined shores Mrs. Nightingale inspires her beloved to the most enthralling love songs. In the wintertime the youth have fun there with snowballs and skates. So it was at the time I attended the Klipp School; today the pond has long since become marshy and full of silt.

At the time of my childhood—around the middle of the nineteenth century—the population of the city, half Catholics, the other half Protestants and Jews, lived in complete social, political, and religious peace, disturbed neither by any class hatred nor by tensions of national or political origins. The inhabitants did not consider themselves to be Poles, Germans, Jews, Catholics, Protestants, and so on, but rather as "citizens of Samter." But this soon changed. With the Polish uprising at the beginning of the 1860s, the paradisiacal state of affairs ended, and the serpent of national and confessional strife raised its poison-swollen head. And now—1921? May God have mercy.

The small city lies on a fertile plain. In all directions of the compass one can enjoy the horizon unhindered by even a slight elevation of the ground. It's a completely level, round slice with the firmament above it. A few stands of pine near the city served the prominent citizens as welcome sites for summer outings, where things became very jovial. Playing and dancing alternated in random succession with coffee and cake, singing along with a guitar, and humorous speeches. The romantic guitar unfortunately was soon replaced by the terrible harmonica, and instead of the soft plucking instrument one heard the dreadful moaning sounds of the horrible melody of the only two tonic and dominant chord sequences that the player himself invented.

Art was not cultivated much. If one felt the need for theater or concerts, one went to Posen three miles away. The attempt to enjoy theater without traveling by wagon or train remained without further disastrous consequences. An amateur theater was founded. My father, an architect by profession, built a stage in the large hall of the Gilda Hotel; it held fifty-three people. My father not only constructed the stage, but also designed and painted with his own hands the decorations, the backdrops, the overhangs, as well as the curtain. The latter represented the starry heaven: blue background with golden stars. The art community was enthralled when viewing this marvel of colors. The theatrical piece was a harmless two-act play with vocal music inserted, whose name and author I have forgotten. I was only four years old at this performance. Except for a replay of this piece in the nearby city of Wronke, there were no further performances to my knowledge. The decorations were sold, and sorrowfully the muse Thalia covered her head.

Except for the Klipp School mentioned above—approximately equivalent to our local public school, but on a much lower level—there was a private grammar school, of which it was said that its pupils could be prepared for the fifth year (*Obertertia*) of the gymnasium.[3] Only ten students were admitted, because the school building was not spacious enough for a larger number. Headmaster Pfitzmann was a severe, strict man; he oversaw the instruction without any help and was director, teacher, janitor, and disciplinarian, all in one person. Regarding his pedagogical success, I can report that my brother Philipp, prepared for the fourth year (*Untertertia*), was placed into the second year (*Quinta*) of the Posen gymnasium. I was prepared for the second year, but was barely found ready for the seventh class (*Septima*). At the death of headmaster Pfitzmann, eleven people were liberated from their suffering at the same time—one sick old man and ten young human beings.

Near the city, about a mile away, were the farm and the mill of my uncle Ludwig Golisch, one of my mother's brothers. Washed by the waves of the broad Warta River and surrounded by extensive forests, it provided us children with a wonderful playground for all kinds of youthful, playful vacation sports, for which we—my brother and I—found very willing accomplices among our cousins of the same age. Oh, what happy pranks we devised and carried out there. Until an advanced age I spent a part of every summer each year at Ruxmühle—so the farm was named. This was my mother's birthplace. My grandfather, Anton Golisch, an able farmer and a master miller, was a Pole in his personality and disposition, although he was not of pure Polish ancestry. The family name points to Cassubia[4] or to some other region with mixed ethnic groups. Devoutly Catholic, he felt himself to be Polish and raised his children accordingly, fifteen in all, of whom thirteen reached an advanced age. My grandmother, born Anna von Zakulewska, was a true Polish woman of a good family, kind, friendly, and very generous to her grandchildren. After her father's early death, her son, my uncle Ludwig, mentioned above, took over the farm, gradually paid his siblings their inheritance, and the property, with its two merrily clanking water mills, flourished, in spite of a large fire, which destroyed all the buildings, house, farm buildings, and the mills.

In their free hours the children, who were raised to work diligently in the fields and forest and in the barn and mill, pursued music with a passion. Since no one could read notes, playing music on the violin and piano was limited to what had been heard or to traditional music. It was mostly dances, mazurkas, krakowiaks, and obertas, and similar dance forms of a national character. They were performed with a strict rhythm and with an intonation that was as pure as gold; and in every free minute the good old men would play their fiddles; so it was in the past and still is today. My mother loved music passionately, but did not play an instrument. Yet she saw to it that at her marriage a piano was purchased, which at first served as "a prominent room decoration," since my father was completely unmusical. As far as I know, none of his brothers nor anyone among his ancestors had been even loosely associated with music. Thus my brother's fondness for music and my own undoubtedly stems from the natural, richly flowing well that had its origin in the family of my mother.

In the vicinity of Ruxmühle, separated only by the Warta and a large, grand forest, was the Bomblin estate. In 1842 the owner, Herr von Dobrzycki, commissioned my father, who just shortly before had settled in Samter, to construct a castle and its farm buildings. The road from Samter to the site of his long-term work led my father via Ruxmühle, where the young builder by chance sought and found hospitable lodging. Here he soon gained the affection of the charming Apollonia Emilia, the fourth daughter of the family. The romantic union was consecrated in 1844 in the old Protestant church in Samter. In spite of the difference between the two faiths of the two parties, the marriage was an extraordinarily happy one. Both parents were free of any religious fanaticism, and so we two children—my brother and I—were raised in the Protestant faith, the faith of my forebear, Wenzeslaus Scharwenck, who emigrated from Bohemia to Frankfurt on the Oder in 1696. With the help of church records in Frankfurt on the Oder and Letschin (in the bogs of the Oder River), I was able to put together the following family tree (figure 1.1).

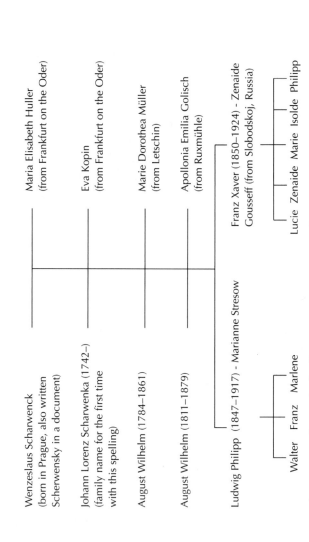

Figure 1.1 Scharwenka family tree

My research in Prague for older branches of the family tree unfortunately was not successful. I was told the documents were lost in the confusion that resulted from the Thirty Years' War. A few traces, which I was able to follow up, point to the family name Czerwenka of Leddetz. In any case, some of my ancestors in Prague already belonged to the Protestant faith; others were primarily in clerical or military jobs.

As can be seen from the family tree, mixed blood flows in my veins, however, predominantly of a Slavic hue. Only through my paternal grandmother—Dorothea Müller—did the black, white, and red corpuscles get into the blood stream of her descendants.[5] Since I was born in the Prussian province of Posen and come from a family that cultivated German ways of acting and thinking and German culture from time immemorial, I consider myself to be totally a German Protestant Christian. All of my immediate male ancestors were architects and—according to Jean Paul's clever joke— enjoyed music only in its frozen state.[6] In any case, it only became ice-free and melted through the two great-grandsons Philipp and Xaver.

Childhood and My First Foolish Pranks.
Grandmother's Wedding Celebration.
Der Freischütz and *Robert der Teufel* in Samter

And here I begin with the goal of writing down what life has given me in wonderful abundance and what it has denied me in its wise judgment.

I was born in Samter on January 6, 1850, a Sunday that is also a high Catholic feast day: Epiphany. At baptism I received the names Theophil Franz Xaver, the first from one of my godparents and the second and third from my mother's favorite siblings: Franz and Xaveria. My parents were loving and kind to their two children, and in their marital relationship they had the most tender feelings and loving regard for each other. My father, a handsome man with regular, strong facial features, from which dark eyes shone forth with eloquent expression, was considered a highly gifted, artistically trained architect. His architectural drawings were small works of art; the designs and plans for his structures as well as the buildings themselves found the unanimous acclaim of his professional associates far and wide. He was a patient, loving, and caring father and husband and a highly regarded member of society.

My mother, slender and lithe and in her appearance revealing her Slavic ancestry, ran the household in an exemplary manner; she was primarily involved in raising the children, which was not always easy, at least with regard to my own small person. My impetuous temperament very often led me to abuse my parents' patience—in contrast to my little brother Philipp, who was a quiet boy, lost in his own thoughts, and patiently endured his brother's bad behavior. He shed many a tear over me, and he covered up a good many of my dumb pranks with the cloak of brotherly love. Rarely did my brother blow up at me (I was three years younger), and even more rarely did he beat me up, unless I had been extremely rude.

My memories go back to the age of three. I remember exactly the house where I was born; it stood on the edge of the market place of the little town and was called by the local people the "Katerbau" after the name of the woman who owned it. It was a small one-story house with a shabby attic, in which the grim landlady resided. The architect's family occupied the few rooms on the first floor. When we left this home, I was three and a half years old; however, I vividly remember two shameful things I did shortly before our move from the house. Frau Katerbau had incurred my anger, and I plotted my revenge, which I soon was able to put into action. One fine day I noticed that the key to the old lady's only room was sticking in the lock outside. Without hesitation, I silently locked the door, put the key in my pocket, and carefully left as I had come. Hanging out near the house because of my bad conscience, I soon heard screams for help, which, as I suspected, emanated from the attic window of our house. A large crowd assembled at the site of the misadventure, and soon the perpetrator was caught and thoroughly whipped by his father, who had rushed to the scene. Oh, that really pleased the old woman. Since that stunt, I was the subject of much conversation, and the indignation at the architect's son increased even more after his second prank. Our neighbor, that is, the honorable Pan Hubinsky, had had the front of his stately house painted a pale pink. My sense of beauty was very much disturbed by this lack of good taste, because in my opinion the pink paint totally ruined the facade of the houses facing the market place, with their venerable patina of several centuries, which the locals called dirt. So following my burning sense of beauty, I decided to show Pan Hubinsky how in my opinion to deal artistically with the facade of his house. I took a large piece of charcoal from our fireplace and drew an enormous locomotive across the entire length of the house; even the engineer was outlined, and I supplied him with a wonderful coal-black top hat, as I had seen on our chimney sweep. That I just had happened to choose a locomotive was probably due to the fact that my father had to build a few station buildings on the rail line, and I got to see my first locomotives, which impressed me greatly. The overpowering impression that machines made on me made its surprise appearance on Pan Hubinsky's house front. For expressing this genuine artistic feeling, this disciple of art, intoxicated with beauty, received only a mild punishment, which my father only carried out pro forma; inwardly he agreed with me. Our maid Nastusia, armed with a bucket of warm water, soap, and scrubbing brush, first had to try to wash off my beautiful picture; but it did not quite help. The painter had to come again and destroy the samples of my talent.

Soon after this heroic deed, my parents moved to another apartment. In the house of headmaster Pfitzmann, who has already been mentioned, the upper floor became available; the rooms were freshly painted a soft light blue, green, and chocolate color. It was splendid, and in these rooms the old grand piano became an object of use and not just a piece of furniture. I gave up painting and turned to music. My brother Philipp, three years older than I, then took piano lessons from choirmaster Schlange, which I as a four-year-old little fellow listened to secretly and with greatest interest from the adjoining room. At that time, as already mentioned, the amateur theater was established. In the play a song occurred, whose music and text still stick in my memory. To the amazement of my parents, I played the melody, which I had heard in the theater, without a mistake and picked out the right harmonies for it. Also the pieces that my brother was studying under the guidance of choirmaster Schlange I played by memory without effort, because I could not read notes yet.

My parents did not tolerate it long in these newly painted rooms. Headmaster Pfitzmann was a terrible tyrant of a landlord, and he often stuck his inquisitive nose into our apartment to see if the splendor of the painted walls had suffered, also whether an unnecessary nail had been pounded in the wall, whether the fireplace was being misused, and so on. At that time my father was building a beautiful apartment house on the edge of the so-called New City, the large square with the church, and there he set up comfortable and spacious quarters for his family. However, headmaster Pfitzmann was to receive a remembrance from me. After the apartment had been turned over to him in perfect condition, and we had moved out, I sneaked into the empty rooms at dusk and armed with a sturdy nail, inflicted some serious scratches on the delicately colored walls. I escaped unnoticed; the perpetrator of this boyish prank was never found out. I did not commit the foolish boyish pranks with which I was charged out of a simple desire to destroy or to satisfy a general desire for revenge. There were always "more noble" motives that were the source of my naughtiness. "There must be a punishment," I said to myself and locked up the evil Frau Katerbau. So I committed the misdeed on the clean walls of the bad Pfitzmann, and only because of my offended sense of beauty did Pan Hubinsky get his locomotive. I even cruelly punished my brother Philipp once. As the result of a nasty prank, in which I had been badly wronged, I took his Sunday coat and threw it into the fire of the cook stove. Gloating and without fear I reported this heroic deed to my mother with the joyful sounding words: "The coat is burning." Immediate rescue attempts unfortunately remained unsuccessful; only three brass buttons of the garment were found. All hell rained down on my head, while the opposite end of my body incurred the punishment of my father's hand. I thought of revenge for this affront; soon I satisfied it. In addition to many other beautiful birthday gifts, my mother had received a magnificent small case, covered with blue satin, in which she kept small scissors, thimble, and similar small articles. In addition to a cake with a dedication in frosting, there were flowers, soap, books, and a small, cute jar of hair cream on her birthday table. After we had been put to bed and I could assume that my parents were also asleep, I got up very quietly, sneaked to the birthday table, and smeared the nice smelling hair cream in the small case with shameless delight. Then I closed the cover, and returned to my small bed, where I slept like a righteous person—or rather like one who has been avenged. Of course, all hell broke loose again after this dirty trick; the resulting spanking turned out to be so unpleasant that it dampened my desire to destroy things or seek revenge for some time.

More and more the piano exerted its irresistible attraction on me. I now not only played back what I had already heard, but looked for new melodic forms, and thus started to play improvisations, a form of playing that I indulged in with impassioned delight. It was a real treat for me to be able to watch the organist at the Sunday worship service in the choir loft of the church, and I was happy to be allowed to pull the rope sometimes that activated the bellows. Oh, if I had only been allowed to play some chords on the organ! In the meantime I had turned six, and my parents decided to have me take piano lessons. However, when cantor Schlange pulled the small hairs on the back of my head in a most cruel way when I made a mistake while learning notes, I jumped up from my chair and ran straight out of the lesson, out into the street, across the marketplace. I stayed away for two hours and barely ventured back into the house. Thank goodness, the lessons came to an end.

If I had made a lot of enemies through my boyish pranks, which were known throughout the town, I nevertheless had some good friends, among whom I could count dear old Mottje predki (in German the nimble Motteck). This most eccentric character of Samter was a Jewish tailor, who as a sideline took care of all kinds of small jobs for his clients. If one wanted to buy a dog, Motteck would provide it. If one needed something that was not so easily found, Motteck would find a way. I was happy when I had to deliver a message to the shop of the dear old man, who was stooped over and spoke with a stutter. He had me sit down next to him, told me beautiful strange stories, gave me apples and nuts, and finally brought me some small old boxes filled with wonderful buttons made of metal and horn, of which I was permitted to choose the most beautiful specimens. What a joy that was! But once the kindhearted, peaceful old gentleman became angry, and it came about so: My uncle Adolf, the brother of my father, came to visit us for a few days. He suffered from jaundice, and someone had recommended to him that he eat a louse with his vegetables. It's terrible to say this—but superstition indeed did exist.

Our uncle then asked our maid Marynka to find a louse. Since she herself had no supply of this medication, she innocently made her way immediately to Motteck and asked "for a penny's worth of lice." Marynka came back crying; the old gentleman went after her with his cutting shears and had roughly led the impertinent, but to be sure quite innocent, customer to the steps.

During the summer we usually spent a few weeks in Ruxmühle, which we could reach by wagon in an hour. That was always a holiday for us children. There we could pick fruit in rich abundance and boat on the mill pond surrounded with bulrushes, fishing and crabbing by torchlight, playing Indians, freely roaming about in the fields and forests. Oh, what a wonderful childhood; even if we sometimes received a spanking, we did not take it amiss.

In the evening there was usually a cozy chat at the home of our aged grandmother, who had made her widow's home in Ruxmühle. Although well over eighty, the old lady was still so alert and vigorous that she tended her small household all by herself and even found time to knit stockings for herself and her grandchildren and to make baby clothing that became necessary almost every year. The stork never flew over Ruxmühle without leaving behind a visible sign of the fruitful activity ascribed to him.

Our grandmother was an excellent storyteller. Captivated, we listened to her lively descriptions from the times of the Napoleonic reign of terror, the wars of liberation, the Polish revolutions, and other important events. We also heard a lot of interesting things of our immediate family circle. However, no story made a greater impression on me than the story of my grandmother's wedding night. My grandfather, Anton Golisch, was in the service of the Count of Mycielski as a supervisor on the Samter manor. In order to show the young energetic employee his goodwill and his satisfaction with his performance, the duke arranged the young couple's wedding celebration in the staterooms of the Samter castle. After the wedding dinner, the young couple had to sit in front of the fireplace, in which a cheerful fire burned, while the wedding guests filed past and presented their wedding gifts with graceful bows and humorous speeches. Suddenly there was a noise in the chimney, a crackling in the scattering pile of logs in the fireplace, mixed with a hundred screams of terror. In the flames lay a coal black human body, and the flames licked greedily at its clothing. The young husband plunged into the fireplace and pulled the burning corpse out of the flames. Water was quickly brought, and the fire extinguished. As it turned out later, it was the body of a chimney sweep who had disappeared several years before that caused this terrible incident. The poor fellow had probably lost his footing, had gotten stuck, had wretchedly starved to death, had gradually dried up, and finally as a result of the intensifying heat of the fireplace had slid down.

From Ruxmühle we always brought home plenty of booty: butterflies, bugs, and similar objects of youthful collecting zeal; but also objects of real value were loaded up for the trip home: potatoes, products of the mill, fruit, a slab of bacon, and several meters of Polish sausage. Then a tearful good-bye, and away we went back to the guardian spirits of our home.

On our return new joys and surprises always awaited us. Once our father had built for us children a charming miniature theater for puppet shows; he had painted the decorations, the curtain, and the figures; and he had also written the plays. For the first performance the *Freischütz* was performed in a loosely abridged version and of course without any annoying music.[7] The main attraction of the play was the special crack of gunshots, simulated by firing exploding caps. The appearance of Samiel, the wild hunter, was deeply moving. His entrance was always accompanied by an enormous flame, which was produced by pulverized resin blown through a thin tube through a burning candle. As a result of the terrible stench and smoke that developed, future performances of the *Freischütz* could only be given with open windows and several pails of water in readiness.

In the same way *Robert der Teufel*[8] experienced its first performance in Samter. The graveyard scene was always requested da capo, which caused the stage manager a lot of trouble, because the two nuns could only be induced with a great deal of persuasion to retreat again to their underground chambers. I do not recall much anymore about the course of the plot, which diverged significantly from Meyerbeer's original, but I remember that the characters in particularly complicated situations emitted a muffled "hm, hm, hm." The conclusion of the opera enjoyed great applause. Robert was hauled off by the devil. The bright red Beelzebub floated from above through the air, hooked the unsuspecting Robert, and disappeared with him in the same way amid thunder and resin. The curtain fell, and the audience—people of my own age—went home elated and fortified with chocolate.

Another time my father had painted transparent pictures, which were placed in the open door of a dark room and were illuminated from behind. A high mountain landscape with an alpenglow, a sunset on the sea, a large fire in Constantinople, the fire-spewing Vesuvius, and a caravan in the desert in moonlight were particularly spectacular portrayals. For these evenings, which for a while were the talk of the town, the prominent people of the town were invited.

In the Klipp School. The Spanish Cane and Other Educational Aids. Orchestral Studies in Salzbrunn

Meanwhile my school time approached. I had turned seven, a strapping, healthy, but spoiled young fellow, as was however the general opinion, yet a wily rascal, who besides his music had all kinds of pranks in his head and aggravated many in public and in private. My father took me to the Klipp School in the monastery, where Herr Redern, the strict professor, wielded the schoolmaster's cane. Boys and girls—however only of Christian faith—were taught at the same time. We were not acquainted yet with steel pens. At first slates were used; then came goose quills, which were prepared in the hot ashes of the family cook stove. As soon as a pen became blunt, we went to the teacher, who with his penknife—hence the name—made it usable again. I was properly enrolled and received the last place in the class. My brother at that time already had outgrown the Klipp School and attended the private school of the dreadful headmaster Pfitzmann.

My brother was supposed to accompany me on my first walk to school; it turned into a catastrophe. Together we began to walk to the monastery and leisurely strolled along the long path, furnished with a school bag and breakfast sack. But gradually I became restless and slowed my steps. I stopped near the monastery and did not want to go any farther. "It stinks," I said to Philipp. Was it my dislike of attending school or was it the moldy odor that came out of the windows of the cellar, in which the dead bodies were kept? In any case, I was stubborn and would not go farther. My brother pleaded to heaven with me, finally on bended knee, to follow him, but I took off, dashed back down the street to our home shouting, "It stinks, it stinks," while frightened Philipp ran after me and shouted just as loud, "It doesn't stink, it doesn't stink." All out of breath we made it home, where our good father took the cane, plain but terrible in its consequences, dusted the seat of my pants, and thoroughly cured me a posteriori of the "stink." Then he kindly took my hand, which he did not let go of all the way to the monastery, and delivered me to the schoolhouse, where I took my usual seat on the last bench. I asked the teacher to allow me to stand a while from time to time; he graciously allowed it without suspecting that sitting caused me pain.

I readily admit that attending school never made me happy. I was an inattentive, lazy student. It was due in part to the fact that music was constantly in my head, and second, to a great extent due to the teaching methods of that time, which (also later in my gymnasium days) were able to achieve more terror and fear in students than joy and enthusiasm. There were cruel and painful punishments in the Klipp School: kneeling on dried peas, slapping the ears so that one literally lost one's hearing, beating the palms of the hand with a cane, and similar barbaric punishments. Also later in the Posen gymnasium beatings and whippings with the cane were meted out as desired. If a cane by chance was not available, the poor delinquent had to go to the classroom next door in order to receive with his own hands the instrument for attaining higher cultural improvement. In the second year (*Quinta*) of the gymnasium Professor Dr. Schäfer, who by the way was well liked, had organized a regular committee to perform discipline. If punishment was about to be carried out, the Herr Doctor commanded: "Discipline unit forward!" Then the four strongest classmates would grab the victim, place him over a school bench, and by pulling his pants tight they made it easier for the Herr Doctor to mete out the punishment with the Spanish cane. It was also horrible to hear the crying and whimpering from the classrooms next door. Thus passed the years of our Lord 1858 to 1865 in the Wilhelm Gymnasium in Posen.

In the summer of 1856 my mother, who had come down with a painful sore throat, had to go to Bad Salzbrunn, and I was permitted to accompany her. We could take the train as far as Posen, but from there to Breslau there were only connections by coach. That was not such a bad way of traveling as some might imagine. From time to time there was a change of horses; at the stops there was sufficient time for meals and refreshments; and at last one got there. In Salzbrunn I was fascinated most of all by the orchestra of the resort. I stood captivated in front of the music pavilion during the entire time music was being played and never left the string or wind instrument players out of my sight. Soon I attracted the attention of the conductor, who at my request during the intermission took me into the orchestra and at my imploring showed me a clarinet and a bassoon. He also let me blow on them—without success of course. The following day I was allowed to become acquainted with a flute and a horn, and so I gradually learned to know the instruments of the orchestra while my knowledge of the literature of overtures and dances was enriched significantly. Those were blissful hours.

The following year I was allowed to accompany my mother once more to Salzbrunn; this time Philipp was also taken along, and proudly I was able to play the travel guide for him. The trip turned out to be more comfortable and less troublesome—the railroad tracks from Posen to Salzbrunn were finished.

In Breslau, where we stayed for a day on the return trip, my mother took us to the opera house; *Fra Diavolo* was being performed.[9]

Notes

1. Posen is the German for Poznan, the province and its capital in west central Poland.

2. The Bohemian Brethen or Brüdergemeinde (Moravians), the oldest Protestant denomination, was founded in 1457 by the followers of John Hus. Expelled from their native Bohemia, they were invited to settle on Zinzendorf's estate in Germany in 1722.

3. The gymnasium is the German secondary school that prepares students for the university. Since there is no direct equivalent in the American school system, the term *gymnasium* will be used here to refer to these schools.

4. Cassubia (Kassubei) is the area from the Baltic to the Notec and Warta rivers and from the Vistula to the lower Oder settled by the Kaszuby, a remnant of the old Baltic Slavs that make up the native population of Pomerania; they constitute the most distinct ethnocultural groups in present-day Poland.

5. This is a reference to the flag of the German Empire (1871–1918), which consisted of three bands of black, white, and red.

6. Scharwenka here refers to the metaphor of "architecture as frozen music," which has often been attributed to Goethe, Friedrich Schlegel, and Jean Paul, among others. However, it was first used by the German philosopher Friedrich Wilhelm Schelling (1775–1854) in a lecture at the University of Jena in 1803, according to K. S. Pascha, "Gefrorene Musik: Das Verhältnis von Architektur und Musik in der ästhetischen Theorie" (dissertation, Technical University of Berlin, 2004), 37–43. Jean Paul was the pseudonym used by the German novelist Johann Paul Friedrich Richter (1763–1825), whose idealistic and sentimental novels enjoyed great popularity during his lifetime.

7. Carl Maria von Weber (1786–1826) composed the three-act opera *Der Freischütz* (*The Marksman*) in 1821.

8. Giacomo Meyerbeer (1791–1864), the most frequently performed opera composer during the nineteenth century, was born as Jakob Liebmann Beer to a wealthy Jewish family in Vogelsdorf, Germany. In 1810 he combined his maternal and paternal family names into Meyerbeer. After spending nine years in Italy, he settled in Paris, where he spent the rest of his life. His grand opera *Robert le Diable* (*Robert the Devil*), with libretto by Eugène Scribe, was performed in 1831 to tremendous acclaim.

9. Daniel François Esprit Auber (1782–1871), a popular French opera composer, based his opera *Fra Diavolo* (*Brother Devil*) of 1830 on the Italian bandit and soldier Michele Pezza, who fought the French.

CHAPTER TWO

~

Posen, 1858–1865

In the Gymnasium

My father, who wanted to provide us with a higher school education than Samter was able to offer, decided a year later to move to Posen, where we were to attend the gymnasium. My father's resolve in this matter was strengthened through several business failures that almost ruined him financially. Through the carelessness of a foreman, the almost completed complex of buildings—the house, all the farm buildings, a distillery, and building for workers and servants—burned down completely. My father, who was commissioned with the construction, had to pay for the entire loss. In addition, a timber venture failed totally as the result of the extremely low water level of the Warta River. Those were serious reverses for my poor father, who now was really poor; yet he faced the future courageously without giving up.

In Posen there were no immediate opportunities to prosper. Hard times entered our home, little was saved from the disaster, and heavy cares weighed on my poor parents. Fortunately and to my indescribable joy the old piano survived the disaster; it still served me for many years, and then it made its way, when it seemed ready for the crematorium, to a schoolmaster in the village.

The street on which the small house stood that now sheltered us was called Am Graben and had acquired a certain fame through Gustav Hoffmann, the composer of the popular song "500,000 Devils."[1] In order not to be confused with other Hoffmanns, the artist called himself "Graben-Hoffmann" after the street, on which he lived for many years.

Behind our small house there was a small garden, which adjoined a truly ideal playground; it ran down to the Warta and was bordered by stacks of wood piled high. These provided us with the most wonderful material for all kinds of structures, with which our good father helped us in every possible way. At first two simple little "villas" were built, which were spacious enough so that Philipp and I could have our afternoon coffee and do our schoolwork there. Often playmates from the neighborhood came, with whom we fought many a hard battle. "Knights and robbers," scenes from the *Leather Stocking Tales*,[2] and similar adventures were performed with enthusiasm and often bloodied heads.

My father hoped to be able to find a fertile field in Posen for his real profession, but that did not materialize so soon. Out of necessity he went into a different line of business; he found employment as a surveyor. In the free time that school and music left me, I helped with the calculations and with operating the surveyor's level, an instrument newly introduced at the time, with which the surface area of a section of land could be calculated accurately. That gave me a lot of pleasure, and I acquired great skill in this interesting work.

Soon after our arrival in Posen, I was enrolled in the Polish Mariengymnasium and assigned to the sixth class (*Sexta*). However, my stay there was not long. After attending the school for only two days, I left the institution, first of all because the instruction was in Polish, of which I did not have sufficient command, and second, as the result of being forced to attend the half-hour Catholic service in the nearby St. Bernhard's Church every morning. I was then enrolled in the Wilhelm Gymnasium, where I was placed into the seventh class (*Septima*). I completed the lower grades rather easily. Latin, history, and geography were my favorite subjects, followed later by Greek, and even today I read the ancient authors without difficulty. I particularly enjoyed the choral singing classes, which were conducted by Headmaster Ritschl, who was a well-trained musician. He once managed to have the gymnasium choir perform all of Mendelssohn's *Paul*, and students even sang the solos. Ritschl, my professor in the lower fourth class, was gruff in class, but we revered him nevertheless because of his learnedness, his zeal for teaching singing, and because he could play the piano so well. He never gave into physical punishments, but scolded us from the fullness of his heart and deepest conviction. Unfortunately, this outstanding man was taken away by cholera in 1866. His students had pleasant memories of him.

Another prominent figure on the teaching staff was Professor Dr. Jacoby. As far as I can remember, this erudite teacher, who was loved and revered in spite of his immoderate sudden fits of anger, taught only Greek. Not until later did we learn that he was busy completing a Greek grammar book, which in the judgment of his expert colleagues was to surpass by far all the relevant books in this field in its pedagogical value, singular arrangement, and rational organization. Unfortunately, the work remained unfinished; the Grim Reaper snatched the productive pen from this small, unattractive gentleman, whom nature had provided with an expressive mind and a noticeable hunchback. Unpredictable and irritable to the point of senseless rage, the man did many things—let it be said in his honor—that he soon regretted. Thus he once slapped my brother on the ear that caused half of his face to swell and that resulted in the impairment of his hearing. The day after Dr. Jacoby appeared in our home, apologized to my parents with warm, sincere words, and showered his victim and me with friendliness and goodwill. Every week we were allowed—and how happy we were—to come to his bachelor apartment, where he helped us with our Greek; and while having coffee and cake, he read aloud heroic stories and showed us beautiful picture books. With the title of professor, which he soon received thereafter, the physical punishments ended. However, he did not enjoy the honorary title for long. Typhoid fever took him away, and the entire gymnasium paid him the last honors, which turned out to be very impressive. From the great hall of the gymnasium, where the body lay in state, the funeral procession set out for the parish cemetery accompanied by the tolling of the bells of St. Peter's Church. It was preceded by the band of the Sixth Infantry Regiment, which played first the funeral march of Chopin and then the heroic lament from Beethoven's Opus 26. It was a moving funeral service, in which the entire city took part. I never neglected the opportunity, when staying in Posen on the way from Berlin, to visit the grave of this unforgettable man.

Next to Ritschl and Jacoby, the other schoolteachers faded away completely, even the director, a busybody of unpleasant memory. At that time Mühler was the minister of education and had totally infected the region assigned to him with the poison of his hypocritical ambition and his reactionary molelike work. Every stirring of independent thinking in the student, every attempt at intellectual freedom was at times openly and brutally suppressed by underhanded, insidious means. It is not surprising that this system, especially in the upper classes of the gymnasium, aroused indignation, anger, and opposition. Like-minded schoolmates joined forces and formed a club with a liberal tendency, modeled after the student fraternities. A paper appeared weekly, produced in ink, for which members wrote articles, the content of which was partly about school politics and partly harmless stories. My brother supplied amusing drawings.

The director had gotten wind of it and charged one of the teachers with *Videant consules.*[3] In the headmaster's office they probably heard something about it, but could not figure it out. So all kinds of traps and snares were set for us. Naively the spy concerned asked if he could support us, to "bring more life" into the gang, to instruct us in real student customs, to provide student song books, and so on. The "kind" offer was declined with the "most heart-felt" thanks and "sincere" regret; also the location of our meetings was not betrayed. The club still existed when we moved to Berlin in 1865.

During our last years at the gymnasium in Posen, the peace of our school refuge was unpleasantly interrupted. The three largest educational institutions—the German Wilhelm Gymnasium, the Polish Mariengymnasium, and the nonclassical secondary school (*Realschule*) were located close to each other, separated only by a small area, the "green zone." On this spot, when the Polish revolution began—I remember the Polish leaders Mieroslawski and Langiewicz with his adjutant Fräulein Pustowojtow—bitter battles at the time developed between the German and Polish students. There were regular sieges and savage brawls, during which the German teachers were attacked, insulted, and pelted with stones. Without exception, the Poles were responsible for the attacks, and very often the police had to intervene to stop the fighting.

Bucolic and Musical Pleasures. The Black Sheep in the Family

Into the dreary darkness of my Posen school days sweet music came as bright sunshine. Without instruction I got so far that I was able to interpret flawlessly, for example, Mendelssohn's B Minor Capriccio and pieces of a similar level of difficulty. I also played with the oboists of the Sixth Infantry Regiment, under whose collaboration I experienced hours of the purest pleasure.

The first chamber music that I was allowed to play with my uniformed comrades was the C Minor Trio, op. 1, no. 3, of Beethoven. Oh, you divine fellow, you who have given us this music! Then came the wind quintet and many, many other pearls of our musical literature. The cellist and the violinist long since are under the sod. The first one, whose name was Pohl, a small, emaciated fellow, played first clarinet in the military band—he soon died of consumption; the other one, Drangosch, died in the war in 1866 at Königgrätz.

We also looked forward with greatest eagerness to our visits to Ruxmühle from Posen. As soon as the vacation homework was completed, we moved to the fields of blessed tranquility and refreshing youthful playfulness. Foolishly and regrettably, we were given an enormous amount of vacation homework to take along: to write the conjugation of twelve Greek verbs and of just as many Latin verbs. Abbreviations were not permitted. In addition, translations from the ancient authors, a German essay, written work in history and geography, shorter French and Polish essays, learning by heart large sections of Homer, Ovid, and Tacitus, and so on. Also one had to recite a new church hymn after vacation—*ad majorem Dei gloriam*. Our hands would become lame from all the writing, which we completed as fast as possible during the first week of vacation. During the other three weeks no one gave a damn about the homework. The intention of the school administration to keep pupils busy with useful homework during vacation failed completely as far as I know; only a few model boys followed the siren call of this shortsighted book learning.

On the occasion of one such vacation my uncle Ludwig performed for neighborhood guests invited to a harvest festival a cute comedy, in which I had to assume the main role. After one of the guests had plunked out a meaningless little piece on the piano—I as a little fellow was not part of the party—my uncle stated in passing that he had a twelve-year-old helper in the oil mill who could also play the piano quite well. At first they smiled at this, but then the pastor from Pinne, who was one of the guests, wanted to hear the boy wonder. Then my uncle secretly gave the necessary order: I was dressed in an oily suit, my face given the necessary color to go with the suit, my hair messed up—and after he had removed his socks and boots, the oil boy was ready. Timidly I came into the room and played my role extremely well according to my uncle's statement. I performed a few piano pieces with my usual bravado and garnered admiring recognition from the listeners. One of the brave souls said to me, "My boy, you are born to something better"—and in so doing pressed half a Polish florin (twenty-five pfennig) into my hand. This was the first honorarium that I received from my musical achievements.

At times things were very entertaining and amusing on the spacious top floor of the mill. There my good uncle, who was always in the mood for all kinds of fun and amusement, prepared many a merry evening for his servants and mill workers. He took up his violin, played tirelessly for the dancing, and let the young people have a good time. A quart of schnapps—half ninety percent alcohol, half *aqua pura*—heightened the general merriment. How the eyes of Josef, Woyciech, and Bartek glistened; how gracefully Tereska, Kasia, and Marynka twirled! There was a natural grace in these small, Polish, fiery-eyed sprites. And when my uncle wanted to rest his arms, which were tired from playing the violin, he grasped one of the barefoot dancers around the hips and swung her around in a circle with youthful vigor, while I played the fiddle.

Later I often retreated from Berlin to the solitude of the Polish forests when I was working on a large composition or when I wanted to prepare for a new program. For this purpose, dear old Duysen always sent a piano to Ruxmühle, and I moved into my grandmother's backroom, where I remained undisturbed. Only sometimes a pair of surprised eyes stared at me through the window and reminded me that I was not completely alone in the world. Also in the wintertime I arrived there with my wife and children and indulged fully my passion for hunting.

Once in the practice of this sport, which I pursued passionately all my life, I almost lost my life. With the cocked weapon on my arm, I was following the tracks of a hare on the high and steep banks of the Warta. A thick layer of snow covered the ground, and a fierce storm had swept the snow together on the high bank in such a way that the contour of the firm subsoil could no longer be discerned. In my eagerness and walking fast I slipped and tumbled down the incline into the Warta, which was flowing high with drift ice. Fortunately, I was forced against some bundled brushwood, where I was able to get a hold of a root and swing myself onto land. I had not let go of my weapon. Dripping wet, I ran, as fast as my legs could go, to the house that was about three thousand footsteps away, where at first I was properly dried and then packed into bed. A few glasses of grog got me pretty much back to normal; however, for a few weeks a full-blown head cold settled in my system and did not leave until I put an end to it with a proper sweating cure.

Not long after this incident the Grim Reaper knocked on the door of Ruxmühle. My kind, dear uncle Ludwig passed away. With his death, the spark was extinguished that ignited the invigorating fire in the hearts of his neighborhood and kept it full of life. I rushed from Berlin to his deathbed and closed his eyes. His farewell from me was touching and moving. He loved me like his own son.

Ruxmühle belongs now (1921) to the Polish Republic; communication is very difficult, but nevertheless many a small crate of desired country gifts found its way to Berlin, especially at the time of the "Yellow Peril,"[4] when the dreadful yellow carrot was served as a delicacy.

However, back to the year 1864, back to my old grand piano, to my wind- and string-instrument friends in Posen, back to the stuffy air of my schoolroom. The time of my confirmation neared, and the preparations for this moved me spiritually. Pastor Klette of the Church of the Cross, a clergyman with a heart full of true godliness, conducted the confirmation instruction and sowed the seeds of divine love into the hearts of the children of the congregation so that it might take root and bear beautiful fruit. At that time I wrote some religious verses and composed choral melodies for them. The church celebration on the day of my confirmation was impressive and very moving. I promised to get rid of my foolish ways and to become a hard-working, upright student. During the rest of my gymnasium time in Posen I made good headway and at graduation received a very good report card.

My piano playing never suffered as a result of my increased dedication to my homework, and I was able to devote myself with newly awakened desire and unimpaired powers to my composing. I had not enjoyed music instruction; whatever I composed was based on famous examples. So as a fourteen-year-old I wrote a trio in C minor, of course, several dances, and a violin sonata in D minor. The pieces have long since been forgotten and lost, and only the melodies have remained in my memory. But stop—no; I remembered the andante of the violin sonata; I used the main theme about thirty years later for a nocturne that was included in an album published by Peters.

My father's financial circumstances had not improved during our time in Posen. The only plus connected with the economic reverses that caused our departure from Samter was that my father was able to count as a success the fact that his two sons could get a secondary school education. However, there was also an unfortunate minus.

Uncle Ludwig provided considerable support for our family household—the picture of the dear man hangs over my bed—by boarding his three apprentices with us and by filling the family larder and cellar with many a wagonload of potatoes and similar produce from his farm and mill. He made me happy by asking me to give his three sons piano lessons for half a Polish florin for the hour. That was excellent pocket money at that time for a fourteen-year-old boy!

Friendly relationships were maintained with the other siblings of my mother in Posen. The children of these families worked their way up from quite lowly circumstances to high positions; but there were also black sheep in the flock. The one son, a very talented boy, was possessed by an inextinguishable desire to travel. All the good positions, which he got through his influential brothers, he left after a short time and, without saying good-bye, he took off on his travels on foot. At first he stayed away for only a few days, roaming around in field and forest. Then it became weeks, and finally he disappeared for several years. His wanderlust led him through almost all of Europe—he was even in Algiers, earning his livelihood through honest labor at each step of the way. I mention him because as my cousin on my mother's side and before running away, he was my inseparable and best playmate, but he was an incomprehensible enigma for us all. We could not understand that this tender, good-hearted, and intelligent boy, the favorite of his mother, whom he idolized, could cause his parents this unspeakable sorrow. Weeping and deeply contrite each time after his return, he fell at the feet of his deeply moved and forgiving mother, he promised by all the saints to improve, returned to work in the office, and then disappeared without saying a word after a few days. The last news of him came from Prenzlau, where typhoid fever had taken him away. At the request of his mother—I lived in Berlin at the time—I sent her a small amount of ground from his gravesite.

With the relatives of my father we were never able to maintain pleasant contact. My grandfather in Letschin, whom I got to see yet shortly before his death, was an old man of few words, gruff, and uninterested in his grandchildren; my grandmother, a little more quick witted and communicative, showed no real joy at our only visit to their home. We were badly disappointed by these stiff, joyless people. It made a big impression on me when my grandmother told us that her great-grandfather had been involved in the contemplated flight to England of Crown Prince Friedrich; wagons and horses had been requisitioned at night, and he had been asked to bring the fugitives over the border.

As children we also did not feel drawn to my father's siblings, although they turned out to be pleasant and friendly toward us and pretended to be good uncles and aunts. But the warm feeling of harmony among relatives was missing. Young hearts have a real sensitive feeling for this. How different it was among the relatives in Ruxmühle.

Notes

1. Gustav Graben-Hoffmann (1820–1900) was a vocal teacher in Posen before moving to Berlin. He composed piano and choral pieces and many popular songs, the most popular of which was "500,000 Devils" ("Fünfmal hunderttausend Teufel").

2. The five novels by James Fenimore Cooper (1789–1851) are known collectively as *The Leather Stocking Tales*; they include *The Deerslayer*, *The Last of the Mohicans*, *The Pathfinder*, *The Pioneers*, and *The Prairie*.

3. "Let the consuls be on the lookout."

4. Although some attribute the German term, "gelbe Gefahr" ("Yellow Danger") to Kaiser Wilhelm II in 1895, the English term can be traced to the title of a very successful series of short stories by M. P. Shiel (1865–1947), a prolific British author of fiction. These stories of anti-Chinese feelings, which appeared in 1898 in weekly installments in newspapers under the title "The Yellow Danger" and in later editions under "The Yellow Peril," expressed the supposed threat to Western living standards posed by the immigration of Chinese and Japanese workers, who were willing to work for low wages.

CHAPTER THREE

~

Berlin, 1865–1891

Rude Reception. Apprenticeship Years.
Kullak, Wüerst, and Dear Old Theodor Stöcker

The outlook for any improvement in my father's business situation with time had reached a low point. Building activity was slow, surveying was not profitable enough, and so my father decided with the reassuring encouragement of his brother Adolf, who carried on a thriving lumber business in Berlin, once more to break camp and move to the Athens on the Spree River. The move took place in the fall of 1865, and only the most necessary things were moved along. A small apartment had been rented in the Wassertorstraße in advance and had been furnished only very sparsely; we moved in on an inclement October evening. It was a sad evening and an even sadder time that then ensued. Right away on the day after our arrival an incident occurred, the consequences of which my mother had to suffer for quite a long time. Early in the morning my father left with me to buy some furniture. While we were gone, as we learned, a great noise arose in the vicinity of our home, which caused my mother to rush to the window. There to her alarm she saw a crowd of people approach carrying mutilated bodies and corpses on quickly improvised stretchers—probably fifty in number. If this spectacle was enough to terrify my mother, then the news that a furniture store in the neighborhood had collapsed alarmed her most frightfully. Horror-struck, the poor woman spent agonizing hours looking at the badly mutilated bodies, always thinking that she recognized her husband or her son. Fortunately, my father had made his purchases at a different place. The news of the collapse proved to be true. A four-story rear building in our neighborhood, in which a furniture factory operated, had collapsed completely as the result of the weight of the lumber and had buried all the occupants under its rubble. When I returned with my father, we found the doctor attending my mother; she recovered very slowly from the scare she had endured.

After our new home was comfortably furnished, and we had had a look at the sights in the big city and had satisfied our initial burning curiosity, I was supposed to continue or complete my gymnasium education with the aim of studying medicine. With my elementary school certificate in the pocket, I was enrolled in the gymnasium; I entered in the middle of the class. New textbooks, new teachers, and new classmates. Everything was so strange, so terribly bleak, and so hopelessly dreary; it was impossible for me to feel at home there. That simply was not possible. I came home with very mixed feelings. It was on a Wednesday, the afternoon was free, and so I used the favorable opportunity to assail my father's good heart. With eloquent words I described the awful impressions of the forenoon, but probably exaggerated a bit. I was able, however, to convince him that in view of the hopeless situation regarding my ability, it was very doubtful, if not impossible, for me to finish the gymnasium under current circumstances and to be able to study medicine. Rather I wanted to become a musician, a profession to which I felt myself strongly drawn. First of all, it offered the possibility of an income more quickly, and secondly, it would not require nearly as much money to prepare for as university studies would. To my great joy my father consented, and the medical profession became one person poorer. I left the gymnasium, whose benches I occupied for one entire forenoon. I rented a square piano[1] for nine marks a month—the old piano from Posen was not able to make the strenuous trip to Berlin because of its venerable age—and with a joyful heart I went to Theodor Kullak.[2]

The New Academy of Music, which was founded and directed by Theodor Kullak, was located in an old, run-down house in the Dorotheenstraße, where the Charlottenstraße runs into it. Through a dilapidated front door and up worn wooden steps one reached the second floor, whose rooms served partly for instruction and partly as the apartment of the director. The institute at that time (1865) may have had three hundred students. However, with time, especially after the French war, the number of students grew significantly, so that Kullak felt compelled to find more respectable accommodations for the flourishing institute and the increased number of students. He found rooms in the house at Number 93 on Friedrichstraße. Although there was now sufficient space available, the new rooms definitely did not meet the needs posed by a music school. It was unpleasant to be able to hear clearly through the thin walls singing, scraping on the violin, and pounding on the piano in the rooms next door, and from the hallway it sounded like the dress rehearsal for a new insane asylum. That was especially disturbing during music theory instruction. At the time of my admission—October 1865—the institute was still in the Dorotheenstraße, and with a pounding heart I knocked at the door.

Soon thereafter I was standing before the famous teacher. Kullak, whose name at that time already had an international reputation—students from all countries of our planet streamed to him—was a striking, extremely imposing figure. On the thin but seemingly sinewy body of scarcely medium height was an interesting head with not exactly beautiful facial features. Through the sharp lenses of his glasses flashed intelligent eyes shaded by heavy eyebrows. The face was thin and bony; on the upper lip was a closely trimmed, bristly moustache; the lower lip protruded somewhat. His hair was combed in an old-fashioned way over his ears, about the same way that Robert Schumann wore his hair. The most unusual thing, however, was his hands; never have I seen—not even in the case of Liszt and Rubinstein—hands and fingers so matched to the keyboard. Shaped by practice, of course, the fingertips had become small pads, and the placement of the hand on the keyboard had to arouse the envy of all piano teachers.

The famous teacher received me in a friendly and dignified manner and asked me to perform something. Shaking with fear, I ventured to play the B Minor Capriccio by Mendelssohn; then I had to play some scales and finally sight-read something. To my great joy I could report to my father that Kullak accepted me among his personal students. Instruction began immediately, and I was assigned as my first pieces the Impromptu in A-flat Major by Chopin and the D Major Etude from Czerny's *Kunst der Fingerfertigkeit* (*The Art of Finger Dexterity*).

In the piano class, which took place twice a week, there were six to eight music students, of whom, however, only three or four got to play each time. But one nevertheless learned a considerable amount in the class, even if one did not get to play, first of all through the mistakes of the others, second, through Kullak's excellent critical comments, and third, one became acquainted with a lot of new musical literature. The newest of the new was placed before us. In addition to Bach and Beethoven, we studied most meticulously the larger and less well-known works of Chopin and Schumann, similarly those of Raff and Brahms, and the most substantive and musically most valuable works of Liszt. The instruction was not tailored just for the inferior showy recital pieces. We also had to study chamber music and had the opportunity for ensemble playing at the institute. Of my classmates in the piano class, I remember well Moritz Moszkowski and Jean Louis Nicodé, Hans Bischoff, and Alfred Grünfeld. Also Agathe Bakker, a charming Norwegian woman, was studying with Kullak at that time; she distinguished herself also through her remarkable talent in composition.

Music theory was taught by Richard Wüerst,[3] who also directed the orchestra class, which was made up of students from the string instrument classes. The missing wind instruments were replaced by the piano, which meant that the designated student received very useful practice in playing scores. Wüerst was a very conscientious teacher, well disposed toward his students, and from the school of Mendelssohn. Clean harmonies, no cross relations, and for heaven's sake no sequences of fifths. In order not to disturb our revered teacher's nightly rest, we brought him carefully crafted compositions of flawless harmony. His instructions for the fugue and sonata form were brief and precise: "Take as an example Bach and Beethoven; they are the best masters!" Thus he concluded his explanations, and we proceeded accordingly.

In his capacity as a critic, he was the terror of the younger generation, who were influenced by what was modern. The triumvirate, consisting of Wüerst (*Fremdenblatt*), Engel (*Vossische Zeitung*), and Gumprecht (*Nationalzeitung*), formed the highest critical authority in the "Metropolis of the Intelligentsia."[4] When discussing Schumann's C Major Fantasia, I remember that one of them—I think it was Wüerst—made the remark, "This music gives the impression as if the pianist were working the keyboard with his feet and the pedals with his hands." This statement was not only supposed to describe the lack of ability of the performer, but this was also the impression the critical listener had of Schumann's work!

Outwardly the three members of the triumvirate were "marked." One was blind, and nature had outfitted the other two with noticeable hunchbacks. The wicked Berlin popular wit called the corner in the opera house where the three powerful men sat "Ebenezer."[5]

Music director Kriegar, the brother-in-law of Adolf Menzel,[6] taught us how to play scores. When Kriegar retired, he was replaced by Heinrich Dorn,[7] the conductor at the Royal Opera. Dorn was a fine, clever, witty fellow, who was one of the severest critics of his former student, Richard Wagner. People said that when "old Grimmbart"[8] set foot on Opera Square after the dress rehearsal of the *Meistersinger* and [he heard] the military guard marching by, he is rumored to have exclaimed: "Thank God, finally decent music again!"

Choral singing was also cultivated. With great love and energy Bernhard Scholz conducted the choral class, which was made up of the students from the choral and instrument classes. We were very serious in our studies; the chorus could give a very respectable performance of its conductor's requiem on a special occasion. During the large break between each practice session, advanced instrumental students performed pieces. Even outside artists did not disdain to be heard here. So occasionally Clara Schumann delighted us by performing the symphonic etudes of her Robert.

Kullak's New Academy of Music had come out of a music institute founded together with Julius Stern.[9] However, the founders separated again, and thus emerged the above-named New Academy with Kullak at the helm and the Stern Conservatory, named after its founder, which is still flourishing today and enjoys great esteem. After his death Kullak's creation passed to his son Franz, who for a while continued to lead it. But soon he lost interest in the once so flourishing but gradually deteriorating institute. Slowly the students scattered, and one day the New Academy of Music belonged to the past.

My training lasted three years; I rarely got to perform, because I was not able to practice much. The lender picked up my rental piano after two months of use, because I could not pay the rent. So I tried to appeal to the sense of comradeship of my fellow students and had the good luck that some of them from time to time permitted me to use their instruments. Gradually piano students also came to me for lessons at fifty pfennig an hour, and after several months I was able to rent a piano again. However, as the result of my increased teaching, I did not find sufficient time for my piano study on a continual and regular basis. The distance between the homes of my students took a lot of time and shoe soles, since it had to be covered by foot. It was a time of sadness and self-denial. In spite of his most zealous efforts to find suitable work, my father had become completely unemployed, and so I kept looking for ever new sources to provide the necessities. With a heavy heart and with great reluctance, I finally decided to increase my income by playing on dance floors and in pubs. At the end of this time of suffering—it lasted a full two years—came my first appearance in one of the performances, which Kullak organized annually and in which the best students of the institute were presented to the greater public. These performances took place with an orchestra in Arnim Hall, Unter den Linden No. 44, and later in the Singakademie.

In addition to the Bechstein instruments, preferred already at that time by the greatest virtuosos, such as Tausig,[10] Rubinstein,[11] and von Bülow,[12] the Stöcker grand pianos were also heard in concert halls. Very solidly built, with a flawless mechanism and with a soft, songlike tone, they were the right instruments for home use and for chamber music, since their tone accommodated the string instruments most favorably. We students used these pianos in the above-mentioned performances.

In one of these concerts—around Easter 1867—I played Mendelssohn's D Minor Concerto. When I had finished, the old court piano builder Stöcker asked me whether I liked the piano that I had just used. To my honest and cheerful "yes" I heard the magical sounding words from his mouth: "Well, then I'll send the piano to your home tomorrow; keep it as a remembrance of old Stöcker." And so it happened. The next day the splendid three-legged grand really and truly arrived in my modest home of the Muses. I was overjoyed, and now I seriously began to become acquainted with my new roommate. My dear, loyal friend, Stöcker, you probably scarcely suspected how happy you had made a young musician. I was able to register one more no less pleasant success with Schumann's concerto: Kullak hired me to teach at his institute. An improvement in my financial situation to be sure did not take place, since my wages—seventy-five pfennig an hour—were charged against my student fees. After a year my hourly remuneration rose to one mark. As a duly appointed instructor I now had calling cards prepared with no small pride with the rich sounding title: "Instructor at the New Academy of Music." But alas, the engraver had printed "gymnastics" (*Turnkunst*) instead of "music" (*Tonkunst*), and in order to save the costs of a new printing, I corrected the unfortunate mistake on each individual card by hand with penknife and eraser.

Breitkopf & Härtel. My First Opus. My First Public Appearance. Visit to the Home of Liszt. Composer Festival in Weimar. Princess of Carolath

The following year—1869—was abundantly eventful and interesting. Around Easter the annual performance of Kullak's institute took place in the Singakademie. On this occasion I directed an overture that I composed and played Liszt's E-flat Major Concerto. In addition to the regular assignments that required counterpoint and other studies, I wrote two larger compositions: a Trio for Piano, Violin, and Cello in F-Sharp Major, op. 1, and a Sonata for Piano and Violin in D major, op. 2. At this time the first book of Polish Dances, op. 3 originated, of which the first dance was to find a surprisingly wide distribution. After the five small works were finished, I sent the booklet to Breitkopf & Härtel and offered it for publication. I had only little hope of receiving a positive response; I had heard that young unknown authors usually had to assume the cost of publication themselves. So I was very happily surprised when I received an acceptance letter from this international company with the promise to take on the small work in their publishing house; however—as was stated later in the letter—I had not requested royalties. Good heavens—that was unexpected! I would have been overjoyed to see my first work actually in print, and now in print and with royalties! After I had recovered from my initial very happy shock, the last words of the idealist robber Karl Moor came to me, and I acted accordingly.[13] With well-chosen words I replied boldly and piously that a royalty in the amount of one Friedrichsdor[14] per piece ought not to seem to be too high. (Alas, at that time there were still real gold pieces.) With return mail I then received a very heavy letter (in a thick canvas envelope) with the label in bold letters: "Enclosed 5 Friedrichsdor in gold." The shiny gold pieces were expertly wedged with care into the slots in pieces of stiff paper. As I later learned from Carl Reinecke,[15] he had recommended as Breitkopf & Härtel's agent and advisor that they accept my small work.

In possession of such a large sum I now proposed to undertake something unusual. I decided to deepen and develop further my relationship with the publisher, took my Trio and Violin Sonata under my arm as luggage, purchased a third-class ticket to Leipzig—a fourth class did not yet exist at that time—and took off cheerfully into the beautiful spring morning. Without even tentatively giving the sights of "little Paris"[16] a single glance, I proceeded with my "luggage" directly from the train station—at that time still far outside of the city—to the office building of Breitkopf & Härtel on Nürnberg Street. There I announced myself, was led by an employee through a long, narrow hall, past a nearly endless row of occupied desks, and soon stood before two dignified older gentlemen. The two heads of the international firm, Dr. Hermann Härtel and city councilor Raymund Härtel, were very different in their outward appearance. The first one, a distinguished, interesting individual, the perfect German professorial figure, was very communicative, tall and thin, dignified in his movements, and serious, but not unfriendly. The other one was of smaller stature and somewhat portly, with a very friendly expression and a winsome naturalness. Both gentlemen received me in the most kindly manner; I was very happy with their words of approval of my opusculum, which sounded extremely pleasing in their familiar Saxon dialect, which both men controlled masterfully.

The two gentlemen told me many interesting things about Robert Schumann and Mendelssohn-Bartholdy. Thus I learned from them, among other things, that Schumann's Sketches had to lie unnoticed in the corner for years as dead stock and that the engraved printing plates were finally melted down, since his work found no buyers. As both an eye- and earwitness, councilor Härtel related the following amusing incident about an orchestral rehearsal in the Gewandhaus,[17] in which Schumann rehearsed his B Major Symphony. Schumann stood shyly and ill at ease at the conductor's podium and beside him was Robert Franz,[18] who was to assist him with the supervision of the orchestra. Soon after beginning the symphony, there was a terrible discordant note—an F sharp instead of an F emanated from the row of wind instruments. Since Schumann kept on conducting without complaining about the mistake, Franz nudged him, which resulted in Schumann calling out a timid "F" to the orchestra. Franz, however, vigorously prevailed on the director to stop the music and to have the section repeated. The same mistake and again Schumann's timid "F." He then conducted the movement to the end without paying attention to the entreaties and urgings of Robert Franz, then turned to his assistant and said with a sad expression: "He played F sharp anyway!"

In the course of our further conversation, I diplomatically steered the attention of the gentlemen to my "travel bag." Somewhat timidly, with the dagger under my robe, I now drew my sword, and to the question: "What did you want to do with that dagger, speak!"[19] I opened my bag and laid the contents on the firm's table. Without hesitation the gentlemen accepted my two works and requested that I perform for them some of their firm's very newest works. They led me into an adjoining room, in which the firm had a grand piano. Cheerfully I sat down at the instrument and played parts of individual sections of the two pieces and during the performance reaped such comments as, "Splendid; my God, how beautiful. Here we have a real musician for a change!"

After I had finished, the gentlemen led me through the firm's offices and workrooms. A huge business! In one of the workrooms I was able to watch an engraver, who was working on the production of the plates for my Polish Dances. A laborious job, much more complicated and time consuming than composing. The tour took a full hour.

The question of royalties then was quickly settled. One hundred shiny taler and six free copies. With warm, encouraging words and wishes for continued successful work, the fruits of which I was always first to offer to Breitkopf & Härtel, the dear old gentlemen took their leave, and I departed extremely happy. First I went to a clothier's shop, where I purchased some fine brown wool material for a dress for my mother; then to a cigar shop, where I bought one hundred genuine Leipzig cigars for my father. Thus loaded down I went to Ackerlein's Cellar and fortified my body, which was very tired from the trip and the exciting business, with a festive meal (dinner without wine was three marks!). The happy event—the success of my trip—I celebrated with a half bottle of Josephshöfer. After I had visited the hallowed site of Mendelssohn's and Schumann's successes—the old Gewandhaus—I wandered to the train station, and by evening I was home again, where I was received with jubilation. My parents had tears in their eyes, as did I. It did not take long, and I found six free copies of the splendidly printed dances in my hands, which trembled with joyful excitement. In the course of the year the trio and the violin sonata also appeared.

During the summer I was seriously busy with the piano, because I planned to give my own concert with orchestra in the Berlin Singakademie during the coming winter. But I also did not let my composition pen rest, as far as my teaching duties permitted me this luxury. I spent part of my long vacation (in July) in my dear Ruxmühle, where I energetically helped with the harvest and also made myself useful in the mill. Evenings there were games, dancing, and all kinds of other entertainment.

The last week of vacation I used for a trip to Rügen. Uncle Ludwig had generously dug into his old leather purse and provided the means for this extra trip; he placed the sum all in single so-called Polish half-florin pieces (at twenty-five pfennig) before me on the table of the house. Travel at that time was awfully cheap—if you still have an uncle!

On my return trip I stopped in Greifswald to visit my school friend Below, who was studying medicine there. He received me splendidly, and in his student lodgings he prepared afternoon coffee as well as a delicious goulash of horsemeat for the evening meal, the main ingredients and seasonings for which we had purchased together. The goulash was in no way an imitation, but rather an intentionally genuine equine dish. The taste was exquisite, and neither one of us had the need to neigh after the meal. Below was a connoisseur of horsemeat and a student of anatomy! Thus, with unerring expert knowledge and with the sharpened eye of the expert, he had gotten his hands on the juiciest piece in the butcher shop—a magnificent rump steak.

While smoking our pipes and drinking beer from Eldena, we discussed the plan for a concert that I was to give in Greifswald. The concert actually took place in the course of the winter; it was very successful, since Below had beaten the advertising drum masterfully, gotten his fellow students to come, and written a few terrific articles for the newspapers.

On November 26, the concert planned for the Singakademie took place with the Berlin Symphony Orchestra under the direction of Wüerst. It opened with an overture by me. Then I played the piano concerto by Schumann and the E-flat Major Concerto by Liszt. In the middle I played the Prelude and Fugue in E Minor (*Notre temps*, no. 7) by Mendelssohn, the B Minor Scherzo by Chopin, and an Octavo Etude by Kullak. With a few encores the outcome was magnificent—beyond all expectations. The reviews were encouraging, and Kullak, beaming and carried away by the success of his student, offered me a fifty-pfennig salary increase per hour. I accepted.

A concert with an orchestra was "an event" at that time. There were no concert managers, agencies, and the like, that is, no institutions dedicated to the true love of art. One went to Bote & Bock[20] (located at Unter den Linden), agreed on the necessary arrangements, and received a statement, which in comparison to one today is like comparing a mosquito to an elephant. Unknown were the luxury tax, business license, and such, and the organizations that so intensely promote art and those called to represent it.

I began the year 1870 playing the piano, composing, teaching, and with my heart full of joyful hope. It began auspiciously. Old Stöcker came to my birthday on January 6 and placed three one-hundred-taler bills on the birthday table, decorated by my loving parents, with the remark that my concert with the orchestra in Posen scheduled for January 12 might show a deficit. At any rate I should go to the piano there without any worries! I embraced the old gentleman and kissed him on both cheeks according to Polish custom.

Now well provided for and prepared, I moved shortly thereafter to the old, well-fortified, provincial city of Posen, of which I have many pleasant memories. Here I had experienced the happy hours of my first acquaintanceship with Beethoven, when the heart of this fourteen-year-old student for the first time glowed with passionate love for "this being from a higher realm," and where I could greet almost every house like an old, dear friend. Oh, it was indeed wonderful that, now after being separated for such a short period of time from the school bench in Posen, I could stand before my astonished relatives, before my old teachers and classmates as an artist. Indeed, when I sat down at the grand piano and caught sight of the provincial president, the commanding general, and the director of the gymnasium, my heart pounded audibly against my ribs. However, I courageously started playing; the excitement animated the wings of my musical soul to take flight. It was a delightful evening, and the newspapers reported good news the next day. A few shorter trips to Greifswald, Sommerfeld, Wismar, and the immediate vicinity of Berlin followed this concert.

The new year brought another significant event: my acquaintance with Liszt. My Polish Dance, op. 3, no. 1, which later was to attain such great popularity, was to become the innocent cause for this. And it came about thus: Moritz Moszkowski[21] and his friend Karl Wittkowski—the latter an excellent, although not professional, musician and pianist—had stopped on their trip to Weimar in Thuringia and on Kullak's recommendation had knocked on Liszt's door, which was readily opened to them. At the request of the illustrious master, Moszkowski played a Hungarian Rhapsody, the performance of which was favorably received by the composer. When Liszt asked whether the young travel companion also mastered the keyboard, Wittkowski sat down at the piano and played my Polish Dance, op. 3, no. 1. Liszt asked who the composer was and when told, he conveyed greetings to me and kindly added that he would be pleased to meet me. Thus Moszkowski and Witt-kowski informed me on their return. It is understandable that this news excited me greatly. I was to meet Liszt, the Liszt, whom I admired, idolized. And it was his wish to meet me, the greenhorn who had barely outgrown boyhood. That was almost too much luck! Without delay I rushed to Kullak, took two days vacation, and borrowed twenty taler from him for the trip to Weimar. The next day I traveled by train to Ilm-Athens.[22] After arriving there, I first got ready for the visit in the Erbprinzen (hotel) and, with great inner excitement, I set out for the Hofgärtnerei.[23] Pauline (pronounced Bauline), the faithful maid of the great man, showed me upstairs. There Spiridion, the master's Hungarian valet, welcomed me. He asked my name in pure Mikosz dialect, the nature of the visit, and for my calling card. Unfortunately, I did not have my calling card case with me; but wait—an ingenious idea came to me! In place of the usual monogram in my collapsible top hat, I had pasted the opening measures of my Polish Dance in order to avoid confusion with other, similar "silk hats." Without hesitation I collapsed the top hat with an audible snap and handed the hat that had become a tray with introduction to the rather maliciously smiling Spiridion with the request to deliver this unusual calling card to his lord and master. He did as I requested, and soon the door opened—Liszt stood before me with outstretched arms, laughing heartily; happily I rushed toward him. My strange calling card had caught his fancy. The remarkable man had not forgotten; at the sight of the few measures in my top hat he remembered my name exactly, asked me into his inner sanctum, and inquired with kind interest about everything concerning me. Finally he gently pushed me to the piano, and I played his Ricordanza and two of my Polish dances for him.

Now I came with a big request: I said I would very much like to study his C Major Polonaise and asked him to play the wonderful piece for me. Without hesitation, the kind man fulfilled my wish and played as only he could, as if lost in dreams, improvising the beginning, then the sweet love duet of the middle movement with charming, inimitable expression; then suddenly and loudly plunging into the monumental variation of the first theme. The elemental raging of the episode, which raced along like a storm, produced amazement, almost fear, and then led gradually with a dull, thunderlike rumbling to the blooming fields of the fantastic, glittering cadence of magnificent colors. Liszt did not play everything according to the music; many small variations slipped in, namely in the tender, delicate weaving of passages, whether conscious or unconscious—I do not know. In response to my enthusiastic thank-you, the dear master offered me one of his Havana cigars and a very good cognac—the first in recognition of my performance of the

Ricordanza and the Polish Dances, the cognac, however, for listening so well. In the afternoon I attended a piano lesson, in which a boy and girl produced some good and a lot of mediocre playing. I then said good-bye to the great, kind master and had the joy of receiving an invitation for the soon-approaching celebration of Beethoven's one-hundredth birthday, which I also complied with at the end of May.

For this celebration, which was combined with the annual musicians meeting of the Allgemeiner Deutscher Musikverein—it took place from May 25–29—Liszt had written a Beethoven Cantata; a stirring, nobly shaped piece that made a deep impression. In the town church an excellent performance of Beethoven's *Missa Solemnis* was presented by the Riedel Society of Leipzig under Riedel's direction. In the Hoftheater Liszt conducted the Ninth Symphony; in the choral movement there were some deviations, but the total impression was a powerful one. Here Saint-Saëns could also be heard; he used the sheet music to play Beethoven's C Minor Variations! Carl Tausig, with whom I had made the trip from Berlin to Weimar, gave a delightful performance of Beethoven's E-flat Major Concerto; Liszt directed. As with the variations, the grand piano sounded harsh and rough, probably due to the acoustics in the theater being unfavorable to the tone of the piano. In between there was new chamber and choral music. Even Saint-Saëns offered a new piece: the *Marriage of Prometheus*.

The celebration was favored with wonderful May weather; the city of the Muses showed itself in its most delicate spring dress. These were beautiful, memorable days almost overflowing with music making; but there was also room for social gatherings. We met after the concerts in the hotels Erbprinzen, Elefanten, the Russischer Hof, and in many others, as well as in cafés serving bodily refreshment to carry on either relaxed or lively conversations while consuming the blood of grapes or the juice of barley. Often we saw Liszt with his loyal followers at these Ilm-Athenian symposia. There was always enthusiastic applause for the master, who accepted it in his modest, inimitable chivalrous manner and had a friendly word for everyone.

The place was overrun with celebrities and those who wanted to become such. At the home of Liszt I became acquainted with Frau Pauline Viardot-Garcia and her inseparable friend Turgenieff; and then the Baroness Schleinitz, who fought with lion-hearted courage for the master of Bayreuth; then Ernst Dohm, Joachim Raff, Hellmesberger, and the dear friend of Felix Mendelssohn, Ferdinand David of Leipzig; in addition to those named also *dii minorum gentium* (lesser known luminaries).

Count Kalckreuth, the director of the art school, as well as many of his fellow citizens, had made available part of his spacious residence to the participants of the celebration, and I had the privilege of receiving hospitable accommodations in his home; I lived right next to George Henschel and Ernst Rudorff.

Not long after the Weimar celebration, threatening storm clouds on the political horizon appeared; they solidified within a short time into a violent storm, which swept the French emperor from the throne and created a single Germany. The war also called me to the military. I reported immediately to the district command in the Niederwallstraße, where in the courtyard of the grounds temporary offices were set up. There I received a card and a number with the notation to report at the brigade command. I received an affirmative answer to my question, if I could join the Franz Regiment, the barracks of which were near my home. My card, which had the number 743, was taken from me, and I was advised that I had to wait for written instructions. In spite of my second registration, I did not receive the awaited answer, and so I had to forgo military service.

After the war, when the blessings of a billion dollars poured into Germany[24] and when entire new city districts arose through feverish construction activity; when the peasant daughters from Schönberg[25] were sent off to Dresden or Geneva "to become educated"; when the old Berlin disappeared and new grand buildings of stucco sprouted out of the ground like inedible mushrooms,[26] my father finally succeeded in grasping the tail of good fortune. He was now able to support his family appropriately. Therefore, I no longer had to perform menial labor, but was able to follow my own inclinations— playing the piano and composing.

In the period that followed, as in the previous two years, I was frequently engaged with charity concerts and other events serving artistic and social purposes. My complete program collection gives the following information about organizations and societies, in which I was active as a pianist or frequently as an author. There was the Berlin Tonkünstlerverein, over which Professor Dr. Alsleben, a musician of great knowledge and rich experience, presided with dignity and collegiality. In addition, there were the Akademische Liedertafel (Academic Choral Society), with Professor Richard Schmidt as the choral conductor at the helm; the Gesellschaft der Freunde (Society of Friends), where Professor Rehfeld, the first concert master at the Royal Opera, did the musical honors; the Artistisch-literarische Gesellschaft (Artistic-Literary Society), founded and directed by Frau Gayette-Georgens; the Assemblee (the Assembly), an organization made up of young civil servants whose members danced merrily after the musical part of the soiree and, at the coffee break at midnight with mocha and pancakes, offered up all kinds of humorous performances; and the Frauenverein für die

Gustav-Adolf-Stiftung (Women's Organization for the Gustav-Adolf Foundation), and others. It was a very impressive number of organizations for the rather small Berlin of that time, and it was very active in its obsession with clubs. In addition, there were a large number of events for all kinds of charitable purposes: for the needy in East Prussia; for the survivors of soldiers who had fallen in war; for the blind, the poor, the widows of firemen killed in service, and so on. From this time comes a relief that the young sculptor Steinmann made of me (see figure 3.1).

Figure 3.1   Relief of Scharwenka by F. Steinmann (1870)

One of the private welfare organizations made a very strong impression on me; it was a musical evening at the home of Frau Eva Krause, the wife of the son of the well-known banking firm. A large group of happy and elegant members of society had accepted the invitation of the charming young hostess and listened attentively to the musical performances. Among the performers were Fräulein Lilli Lehmann, the shining rising star of our Royal Opera, and Frau Harriers-Wippern, at the height of her ability at that time. In addition, the cello virtuoso Jules de Swert and the young violinist Felix Meyer were there. The beautiful concert culminated with a well-spread banquet table at which pink champagne was served in wonderful crystal glasses. It was the first champagne in my life—consequently the deep impression of that evening on me.

Being very active on the concert podium and in the classroom, I had very limited time to compose. The composing demon possessed me firmly and would not let go. In rapid succession I wrote the Scherzo, op. 4, and the Erzählungen am Klavier, op. 5. Then came the Piano Sonata, op. 6; Polonaise, op. 7; Ballade, op. 8; a collection of Polish Dances, op. 9; and the Lieder, op. 10. All were published by Breitkopf & Härtel according to our agreement. Also for my fellow student Hermann Heiser, who asked me for some easier piano pieces and who wanted to found a publishing house in case I agreed, I wrote a few short pieces in the requested style: Tarantella, Grande valse brillante, and Polonaise (French titles were very popular at that time). Breitkopf & Härtel seem to have taken note of this disloyalty, because they rejected in the most polite manner a larger work that I had offered them, but not without certain justification. It was an extensive Fantasy for Piano in B minor. As it turned out later, the rejection was very fortunate for me. I shaped, filed, scraped, and planed around on the piece and finally came to the inspired thought of adding the orchestra. Thus the Piano Concerto, op. 32 in B Minor, which later achieved such success, came into being. It is dedicated to Liszt.

Breitkopf & Härtel were soon again placated; they published the Lieder, op. 15; Polonaise and Mazurka, op. 16; the Impromptu, op. 17; and later still a long series of very extensive works.

In 1871 I gave my second concert in the Berlin Singakademie. The unforgettable Heinrich de Ahna,[27] a true artist who was in no way inferior to his fellow quartet member Joachim,[28] supported me in the performance of my Violin Sonata, op. 2. In this concert I played, among other pieces, Liszt's Spanish Rhapsody and the Variations sérieuses of Mendelssohn. On the morning of the concert I woke up with a terrible headache. Antipyrine and similar painkillers were not known at that time, and so my solicitous mother prescribed a hot footbath, which was to draw the blood from my head. Since

I had to use every minute to prepare for the evening—piano lessons and the rehearsal with de Ahna awaited me—a basin full of hot water was placed in front of the practice piano; I began the treatment, during which the piano pedal of course stopped working, and I soon felt relief. My brother Philipp captured this moment of the footbath in a pencil drawing (see figure 3.2).

Figure 3.2   Variations sérieuses (Mendelssohn) by Philipp Scharwenka

The tomcat, an attentive witness to this unusual circumstance, was a real living creature, not just a symbol of the cause of my condition.[29]

A short time thereafter I received a request from the Russian Court via Professor Grünwald, the chief instructor of violin classes at the Neue Akademie der Tonkunst, as to whether I would be willing to move to St. Petersburg to teach the sons of Grand Duke Konstantin Konstantinowitsch. It was a splendid offer; Kullak tried hard to persuade me, although he was reluctant to see me leave. But the appointment never came about. St. Petersburg requested my photograph, curriculum vitae, and other credentials. The result was that I was deemed too young! With time I overcame this shortcoming. Although the failure of this promising appointment disappointed me very much, it turned out in the end, however, to be to my benefit.

In 1872 I undertook a concert trip together with Frau Franziska Wüerst, the wife of my revered teacher Richard Wüerst, which took us to Bromberg, Thorn, Marienburg, Danzig, and Königsberg. I was a frequent and welcome guest in the Wüerst family. To the children, Franz and Beate, I was "Uncle Schari." I performed a lot with Frau Franziska, a sensitive Lieder singer, and profited substantially by accompanying her, while in the next room the master of the house, in his profession as critic, thrashed the poor victims of the previous day so that the fur flew. Visibly relieved, the heartless fellow joined us at the family tea table and read aloud to us the death warrant that he had written and signed. From time to time, I was able to soften one or more of his caustic judgments on behalf of my fellow sufferers when—unnoticed by the sharp-sighted lady of the house—I poured a small glass of rum into his teacup, which never failed to accomplish its intended purpose.

Through Frau Wüerst's connections, I got to know a lot of interesting people on the trip. In Thorn we stayed at the home of the well-known, eloquent Reichstag representative, Dr. Meyer-Thorn, who was an enthusiastic performer of music and outstanding authority on music literature and who superbly accompanied his wife, an accomplished Lieder singer, on the piano. Our friendship was later renewed in Berlin and carefully cultivated.

In Königsberg we stayed with the just elected Lord Mayor Szczepanski, who on the morning of the day of the concert was memorizing his inaugural address out loud in the room next door. In between he came to the breakfast table for a glass of port wine to moisten his throat, which was dry from speaking.

In Königsberg I also met Louis Köhler, the chief music authority of the old [Prussian] coronation city. Author, composer, educator, critic—all in one person, he had a quiet, contemplative temperament, was more scholar than musician, and left his standing desk only when absolutely necessary. A few things from his instructive piano pieces, above all his *Systematic Method of Piano*

Instruction, a well thought-out, exhaustive work, can still be recommended today.[30]

I also became acquainted with the doyen of Königsberg musicians, the honorable Professor Zander. He was at our concert and after my lectures looked me up in the performer's room, where he complimented me on my *Erzählungen am Klavier* that I had just performed and analyzed the pieces in a sensitive manner according to their poetic content. It was very gratifying to know that I was understood.

In connection with the Danzig concert is the vivid recollection of the book and music dealer, who had made such good arrangements for the concert that we were able to arrange a second evening. The kind and hospitable gentleman invited us to dinner, and at this occasion I noted that he had two thumbs on each hand, which did not hinder him, thank goodness, when counting the gold pieces from the concert proceeds.

In December I gave my third concert in the Berlin Singakademie with a completely new program: Chopin's F Minor Fantasy; the great A Minor Etude, op. 25, no. 11; and the Andante spianato und Polonaise, op. 22; and in addition Schumann's *Carneval,* some of my own pieces, and at the conclusion the *Tell Overture* by Liszt-Rossini.

During the summer in Ruxmühle I had thoroughly prepared myself; one could tell it from the Duysen piano[31] as well as from me: I broke three piano hammers, seven strings, and a thumbnail.

There is not much that is noteworthy about music to report from the year 1873. In January I performed a successful concert with Conrad Behrens, the powerful bass singer, in Kiel, where I had the opportunity to become acquainted with Swedish punch. Ignorant of the intoxicating effect of this sweet poison I probably overdid it after the concert at the home of the Swedish consul Schneekloth. We had to go directly from the dinner table to the train station, because Behrens had a rehearsal in Berlin the next day. I do not remember how I reached the train station; however, I suddenly found myself opposite Behrens in a train compartment, who with a kind smile informed me that we had just passed Spandau. I was ashamed—but I had slept without dreaming and felt very well; a footbath was not necessary.

During the course of the summer I accepted an invitation from Princess Elisabeth von Carolath-Beuthen to visit the Carolath Castle in Silesia. The court conductor Carl Eckert had introduced me to the princess, and I found in that kind, charming, and gifted woman an enthusiastic admirer of our art. My "job" obligated me to do nothing other than to offer sacrifices before the altars of the household deities, Beethoven and Wagner. Often guests came from the surrounding area, mainly officers from nearby Beuthen. Also Princess Alma, the previous owner of the Carolath estate, who as a widow then made her home in a small castle nearby, appeared from time to time. I had the pleasure of enjoying the special favor of this noblewoman, who was so fascinated with art. The friendly connection that began there later became a very pleasant association for my wife and me once I had established my own home in Berlin. During the day, in my beautiful, spacious study from which I had a wonderful view of the park and the Oder River into the distance, I composed or was busy with the revision and the instrumentation of my B Minor Concerto. If I needed a change, I took a gun from the plentiful gun case of the prince—which I was permitted to do—and walked "through the fields and meadows."[32] Wild rabbits, squirrels, wild dogs, and cats fell victim to my bloodthirstiness.

From time to time Princess Elisabeth traveled to Berlin to Gustav Richter, who had been given the pleasant task of painting a life-size portrait of the lovely woman. The splendid portrait was exhibited in Berlin and won favorable recognition. Some years later in Venice I met the celebrated princess, who was revered by young and old alike. A veil, woven of melancholy and resignation, lay over the lovely figure; a happiness had died—the Iron Chancellor had destroyed it.[33]

Standing in Formation. *Anton Notenquetscher.* An Unlucky Tour. Carlotta Patti. Camillo Sivori. Bote & Bock as Matchmaker

After a six-week stay in Carolath, I went to Rügen to strengthen myself by swimming in the sea for the approaching difficult time—my year of military service. The first of October found me with forty-three other young future sons of Mars—among them Alexander Moszkowski—on the parade grounds of the barracks of the Kaiser Franz Regiment. It was first made clear to me by the officer, who was supposed to train the recruits, that I would immediately have to get rid of my ample adornment of hair. Captain Freiherr von der Horst, who arrived soon thereafter decreed, after seeing my smooth, unwrinkled face, that I was to report the following day "with a mustache." I stood at attention and allowed myself to smile a little, which was against all military discipline; however, the captain, a humane and liberal superior who several times during the course of the year made things easier for me, overlooked my offense and also smiled—however somewhat grimly as it seemed to me.

My military service began: At first *piano e teneramente*, then *crescendo poco a poco, accelerando, più crescendo, con fuoco, furioso fortissimo al Fine*—until my poor bones and tortured joints failed to function, and my desire to live disappeared. My officer had taken part in the war of 1870–1871, which did not contribute exactly to the improvement in the way in which he dealt with his subordinates. We learned new affectionate names for the term "recruit" from the rich treasury of expressions used in the military. First came silent indignation on our part, then indifference, and finally laughter until we were sick inside. Thus I remember vividly a reprimand from one of my officers for not standing straight, an expression for which the archbishop of Posen, Herr von Ledochowski, who was often named during the cultural battle and later was arrested, had to lend his name. The officer—he was substituting for one of ours who had reported sick in quarters—probably thought I was a typical stubborn Polack or an arch-Catholic. Angry and completely beside himself on account of my improper posture, he snorted the words to me: "Just you wait, you damn Ledochowski, I'll bend your bones straight yet."

As I already indicated, Captain von der Horst proved to be a lenient superior, who was well disposed to me, as far as the military possibly allowed. As he said to me, he would have been glad if the people in his company would sing well while marching. Would I perhaps be able to contribute to this? I volunteered with pleasure. The company had to perform in the gym, and first I selected the most usable voices. Soon regular practice sessions began under my direction. On a blackboard I explained the notes to these rough warriors; a piano was brought in, and within a short time the best-loved marching songs resounded in two-part harmony and in quite passable performance. From the top group of troops, I formed a small elite choir for four voices, which devoted itself with joy and love to this peaceful occupation. My chorus sessions enjoyed general popularity, because on the days of chorus practice the singers were excused from drills and bayonet practice.

I thanked my revered superior for his decent attitude by taking the job very seriously, by conducting myself perfectly, and at the end of my year of military service, by being the best in the review before the brigade commander. I was promoted to officer and received the qualifying certificate of lieutenant of the reserve.

The strict, strenuous military service, especially during basic training, took nine to ten hours a day. Later in the company, it became more bearable, that is, I had become accustomed to the hardship. My muscles turned into steel, and my nerves with regard to strength could be compared with strong anchor chains. Since I did not have to live in the barracks, I could devote the evenings to my liking. I completed the instrumentation of my Piano Concerto—it appeared later as op. 32—and wrote some piano pieces for the publisher Carl Simon in Berlin: Menuett, op. 18; Scherzo con duo Intermezzi, op. 19; three piano pieces, op. 20; Nordisches, op. 21 (for four hands); and six preludes and etudes, op. 27.

However, there were some duty-free hours for socializing and for the harmless joys produced in the company of pleasant, intellectually stimulating people of your own age, who are blessed with humor and wit. A small circle of friends came together, among them Moritz and Alexander Moszkowski, as well as Karl Wittkowski, who were joined later by Alfred Pringsheim, the mathematician and enthusiastic friend of music. It was like an association without bylaws and with the unexpressed purpose of joviality, cracking jokes, and harmless, young-blooded fun. The get-togethers, not bound to any certain day, took place alternating in our homes, at the Moszkowskis' and later, long after the completion of our military service, in the Palazzo Pringsheim, Wilhelmstraße 67. It caused enormous merriment every time when Alexander Moszkowski read a just-completed chapter of his *Anton Notenquetscher*.[34] The camaraderie reached its high point when the author for the first time read "Das Lied von der Glocke"—an interlude from *Notenquetscher*—to his listeners who were writhing with fits of laughter. We learned this parodistic work by heart, which was not difficult in view of the fact that we were all familiar with Schiller's original,[35] and yet even after almost a half century, quotes from this masterpiece of humorous poetry automatically slip out of my lips:

> Kind are the hands then,
> As long the person cannot play,
> If he leaves them rest quietly in his lap,
> They will never harm anything.
> However terrible fate afflicts us,
> When technology gets involved here,
> Enters on the trail,
> The daughter of the keyboard!
> Woe, if she is let loose,
> She begins to pound,
> And with lots of powerful blows,
> Cripples a piano!
> > Because reasonable people hate
> > The one who pounds like that.

Here in these few lines are an entire series of suitable quotes that we can use all too often when we have the opportunity to visit our concert halls. My brother Philipp had adorned the work with extremely humorous illustrations and therewith proved that his gift for drawing was not inferior to that for music.

We brothers frequently visited young Franz Skarbina, who lived right next door. He was a quiet, introverted disciple of art, who was amazingly industrious and who knew no other joys in this world than his brush and paints and a quiet, cozy chat over a small beer and cigarettes. We remained close friends until the end of his life.

After my discharge from the military at the end of September 1874, I had to try to make my hands and fingers, strained by military work, usable again. The thumb on my right hand had a large bony swelling on the joint—it has not receded to this day—and from the last field exercise in pouring rain I brought along a bout of fever, from which I did not immediately recover.

However, all things considered, the year of military service had strengthened my body enormously. On the loss of the adornment on my head, which I had previously thought absolutely necessary, I soon consoled myself. As compensation and on the orders of my captain, the sign of true manhood sprouting on my upper lip now decorated my face, and in memory of the carefree, happy, but not always so pious time in the military, I resolved to give it sanctuary until the end of my life. However, the year of military service also did a lot of good for my inner person: I gained increased energy, courage, the ability to make quick decisions, ambition, the spirit of adventure, and a sense of comradeship that remained steadfastly with me in all the situations of my constantly changing life and steered me safely through many reefs, on which the small ship of fate of many others probably would have been wrecked. The characteristics mentioned above bore good fruit and contributed especially to the success of the greater undertakings, which I launched or which I helped to bring to good standing and reputation: the music conservatories in Berlin and New York, the orchestral concerts in the Konzerthaus, the three performances of Berlioz's *Requiem*, the subscription concerts in the Singakademie, the founding of the Music Teachers' Federation (Musikpädagogischer Verband) and the Federation of German Performing Artists (Verband der konzertierenden Künstler Deutschlands), and others.

I now sat down again in front of the keyboard, which during the first days proved very uncontrollable and unyielding, and practiced scales, thirds, sixths, octaves, chords, and runs until the neighbors revolted and the landlord threatened me with eviction. In order to avoid that, I devoted myself by necessity to composing, and at the encouragement of the publisher Praeger & Meyer in Bremen the following piano pieces came about: Anecdote and Melody (Novellette und Melodie), op. 22; Travel Pictures (Wanderbilder), op. 23; From New and Old Times (Aus alter und neuer Zeit), op. 24 (for four hands); two Romances, op. 25; Pictures from Hungary, op. 26; and in addition for Breitkopf & Härtel, six waltzes, op. 28; two Polish Dances, op. 29; and an Impromptu, op. 30.

In December I was sufficiently adjusted again to civilian life that I could commit to a concert tour on a grand scale; however, it had a premature and embarrassing ending.

The businessmen for this tour, Messrs. Becker and von Piwnicki, using the model of concerts arranged by Ullmann, had engaged a series of local and foreign artists, among whom the name of my future sister-in-law Marianne Stresow as well as my own name appeared quite modest. Donna Silvia Montoja from Spain! Signor Augusto Parboni from Naples! Signor Ernesto Palmeri from Milan! Herr de Worobieff from St. Petersburg! Mlle. F. Bontemps from Paris! What an illustrious group! Herr Becker had gone to Paris by express train first class, of course, and he had the incredible good fortune there to engage these first-rate stars for the proposed tour with enormous fees. An unusually extended trip was planned; it was supposed to last six weeks.

The first concert in the Berlin Singakademie—we opened with a trio of mine—had attracted a large audience. Already during the afternoon rehearsal, I became concerned when Palmeri, the tenor, started to bleat like a goat, and then Parboni let loose with his completely unrefined basso profundo. I placed my hopes on the "star" of the group, Signora Silvia Montoja, who was distorted by atrocious advertisements to the point of being unrecognizable. My God, I thought, how will this turn out tonight? A small voice as thin as a thread with a conservatory coloratura. What will the Berliners say to that? Mlle. Bontemps from Paris made the best impression; her first name was Frieda. There you have it! Even Worobieff, the cellist, did his job quite well.

The concert evening came. I harbored the quiet hope that the foreign vocal trio had only put on an act during the rehearsal and perhaps due to the unfamiliar acoustics of the hall had been overly cautious in using their vocal instruments. But no—Palmeri bleated like a goat on a green meadow, Parboni roared like a Polish bear in front of a nest of bees, and the beautiful Silvia similarly was an unequivocal and complete failure. This took place on December 15.

A second concert was scheduled for the 18th. I thought that because of the unfavorable review it would not take place, but the two managers insisted on their agreement, and we had to comply with our contract. There was gaping emptiness in the hall and in the cash box.

On December 26 the disaster was repeated in the Leipzig Gewandhaus. The end of the story was that the two managers, after depositing their watches and valuables in the hotel, which, however, did not completely cover the entire bill, took off and left it up to the sad people left behind to settle the shortfall. The foreigners had been taken care of, but for us poor

Germans there were no funds available. We had not come prepared with large sums of cash, since our contract guaranteed our hotel and travel expenses. Fräulein Stresow had nothing; Herr von Worobieff had thirty-five marks and seventy pfennig at his disposal. Herr Sternberg, our accompanist, had already borrowed money from me, and Mlle. Frieda Bontemps—see Stresow.

The following day I marshaled the rest of the group together and explained to the people that I wanted to try to help them out of this predicament. I asked Breitkopf & Härtel to lend me five hundred marks, for which I promised to deliver compositions. My request was very readily granted without this provision, the owner of the hotel was satisfied, and we returned with utmost speed from the shores of the Pleiße River (in Leipzig) to the snow-covered Spree River (in Berlin).

The eventful year—1875—began very auspiciously. In the large vocal and instrumental concerts conducted by Professor Julius Stern in the Reichs-hallen on Dönhoffsplatz in Berlin on January 20 I played the piano part of Beethoven's Choral Fantasy and on April 14 my B Minor Concerto for the first time with orchestra. That was "des Lebens ungemischte Freude" (life's pure joy).[36] Here this joy was granted to a mortal. The joy of a young mother cannot be greater, nor more sublime, than when that which forces itself into the open from the mysterious recesses of one's own soul now appears in sound. I was completely satisfied with the instrumentation; however, I was not satisfied with the form of the Concerto. I again fiddled around on the piece and finally gave it the form in which it soon appeared in print.

Later I performed concerts in Bremen, where I played my Violin Sonata, op. 2, and shortly thereafter completed a large program for solo piano in the Künstlerverein; in addition, I played for the Music Society in Görlitz with the charming singer Hedwig Müller, whom Martin Blumner later brought home as his bride to his comfortable apartment at the Singakademie, and finally in Quedlinburg and a few other cities.

During the summer I paid a visit to Liszt in Weimar and played my Piano Concerto for him, which he received along with the dedication in the friend-liest manner. The day after he invited me to afternoon music, at which also the grand duke appeared in the Hofgärtnerei. At the master's request, I played my Piano Concerto again, which he accompanied from the score on a second piano, an upright. At the conclusion of the performances, the kind host gathered his guests around the large table of the dining room, on which a huge punch bowl stood resplendently. We partook freely. Playing music as well as listening—especially at 20° C in the shade—as is well known, makes the throat dry—even of the nonmusician.

Part of the summer I spent in Reichenhall, where I wanted to put an end to the lingering head cold, an unpleasant souvenir of my last army field exercise. Here I met Princess Alma von Carolath, to whose kindness I owed many pleasant hours of my convalescence, which was modestly enhanced by warm milk from a cow and by baths in warm springs. The princess had a piano in her rooms, which I, of course, did not ignore, and often in the late afternoons there were small excursions by wagon into the surrounding area and a few times to Mauthhäusel, where the trout tasted so wonderful. Once the charming Princess of Mecklenburg, the future grand duchess of Wladimir of Russia, came for a visit on her way through; on that evening she sang two of my songs from op. 10: "Es muß was Wundersames sein" ("It Must Be Something Wonderful") and "Sonnenlicht, Sonnenschein" ("Sunlight, Sunshine") with a small but well-trained voice and a moving and unpretentious manner of expression.

Having returned to Berlin, I took up my teaching job again. Among my most interesting female students was Fräulein Zenaide Gousseff—but more about that in a separate section.

In January of 1876 I set out on an extended concert tour, for which I had signed up with the impresario Weiser; planned in the manner of Ullmann and advertised as "Patti" concerts, the undertaking was a brilliant success. Besides me, others taking part were Signora Carlotta Patti, the three-year-older sister of Divina Adelina Patti;[37] Camillo Sivori,[38] who proudly called himself "the Paganini student"; and conductor Richard Metzdorff, a sensitive accompanist on the piano. The trip began with a concert on January 10 in Stuttgart and led to Karlsruhe, Frankfurt am Main, Wiesbaden, Darmstadt, Heidelberg, Neustadt a.H., Würzburg, Chemnitz, Dresden, Prague, Görlitz, and Breslau, where it ended on the 24th—a respectable achievement within a short two weeks! Everything was superbly prepared—just like a Stangen tour to the Orient.[39] The program had to be completed on the minute so that—heaven forbid—we would not miss the night train. In the hotels we found our rooms nicely prepared, easily found according to numbers for the individuals, and most of the time free of bugs; the assistant, who hurried on ahead, had performed excellently. Impresario Weiser looked pleased when he checked the cash receipts and even splurged and had us served a champagne dinner. I retained very pleasant memories of this trip.

In the long run, however, the monotony of the ever-recurring aria and the "Laughter Song" of La Traviata and the repetition twelve times of the rest of the pieces on the program was tiresome; poor Metzdorff! At least I heard the music only muffled from my backstage room, but the poor guy had to suffer through the rich blessing of the music coram publico. I myself had insisted on three different programs for my performances, because I seriously feared for my better self if I had had to play the *Appassionata* twelve times in rapid succession.

As was well known, Carlotta Patti was slightly crippled; for that reason a folding screen usually had to be set up for her on stage, behind which she passed the time when she did not sing. In this way she was spared the difficult trips from her room to the stage.

The appealing appearance of the singer, her beautiful, pliable voice, and her extraordinary virtuosity in the coloratura range assured her unqualified success. In our contact with each other she was always extremely reserved, because she hated the Germans with an open passion since 1870. The diva was also annoyed by an article from a south German newspaper, in which she had to read that the designation "Patti-Concerts" was an unfortunate choice, since Xaver Scharwenka was the only one who made really serious, good music, and so on. In spite of her antipathy to everything that was called German, the unapproachable woman pocketed with unfeigned joy the gold coins with the image of our venerable emperor on them. At the conclusion of our trip she voluntarily honored me with a signed photo of herself and asked me for mine. Thus we parted as reconciled enemies.

In Wiesbaden there was a tragicomic scene in the backstage room. During the long intermission August Wilhelmj came to us, and soon there was a lively exchange of views between him and Patti. The conversation became louder and louder and more and more heated, to such an extent that we were afraid of a brawl. Fortunately, the signal sounded that called Patti to the stage. With gestures of disgust toward Wilhelmj and eyes flashing with anger, she walked out onto the stage and sang the "Laughter Song." Definitely a sign of strong self-control; I would not have been capable of that.

Camillo Sivori was cast in a completely different mould. A small, older, wizened man, he made a very sad impression, yet he played his Stradivarius most adroitly and lively. Unfortunately he delivered his stupendous technique only for completely trivial virtuoso showpieces. His sound was not large, not noble; also his technique, particularly in the higher positions, was not always reliable—everywhere the dot over the i was missing. In his youth Sivori was a brilliant virtuoso—so to say, a homeopathically greatly slimmed down Sarasate.[40] Small in stature, taciturn, with a constantly changing expression on his face, and shivering and wrapped in his fur coat, he cowered in the corner of the compartment during the train trip. From time to time he took a nap, would suddenly jump up as if startled, scratch the back of his head, yawn, stretch, and mutter a few sentences in Italian to himself. It was a strange sight—like a small monkey on a hurdy-gurdy.

Of the rest of the trip only Görlitz stayed in my memory. There dear acquaintances of mine lived: the mayor Minzlaff, an enthusiastic friend of music, who did such extraordinary things for the musical life of Görlitz; the chamberlain von Keszycki, in whose family I was hospitably received, and the Countess Matuszka von Topolczyn, who as the result of an illness was unable to attend the concert, however, for whom I willingly devoted an hour at the piano the following free forenoon.

For some time I considered devoting myself again creatively to chamber music. With exception of the Trio, op. 1; the Violin Sonata, op. 2; and the Piano Sonata, op. 6; as well as the two Liederhefte, op. 10 and 15, I had written exclusively for piano. So I went to work and outlined the first movement of a quartet for piano, violin, viola, and cello. The work flowed from my hand, because the themes possessed that elasticity of melodic and harmonic structure, which is very favorable, indeed essential, for further development and contrapuntal use.

Now, however, I have to pause in my report on the progress of my work and make mention of an episode that was to influence profoundly my current bachelor's life.

One day in October a young man was announced, who wished to speak to me about a teaching matter. I had him come in. He introduced himself: "My name is Scharwenka." "So," I replied, "I thus have the pleasure of welcoming a relative." "Oh, excuse me," the young man apologized somewhat embarrassed, "I had your name on the tip of my tongue while coming here so that I expressed it involuntarily at my introduction. My name is Bernhard Kübler. I am the son of the director of the Wilhelms-Gymnasium and come on behalf of Frau Sophie Gousseff, who recently wrote to you to inquire whether you would be inclined to give her daughter piano lessons. Her son Sascha is my classmate and boards at the home of my parents. And so Frau Gousseff asked me to inquire personally with you, because she had not received an answer."

Now indeed I had received a letter from Frau Gousseff with the request referred to. Since, however, there was no address enclosed in the letter, and the address book also provided no information, the matter had to be left pending on my part. I asked the young gentleman—he is now a famous professor at the University of Erlangen, and I greet him heartily with these lines—to explain my innocent silence most sincerely at the relevant place, and I promised to visit Frau Gousseff at No. 5 Viktoriastraße the next day. The elegant lady from Russia had been traveling with her daughter Zenaide for some time—a serious, incurable illness confined her husband in St. Petersburg—and she intended to take up residence in Berlin for the next years. On her inquiry at Bote & Bock my name was mentioned as a piano teacher for her daughter. So I became acquainted with my wife. Marriages, as we all know, are made in heaven, however sometimes under very peculiar circumstances—in the present case through the mediation of the firm Bote & Bock.

The piano lessons began. The elegant young woman, graceful, vivacious, and perfectly chic, was talented and diligent and made commendable progress, so that by the beginning of the year she was able to perform the G Minor Concerto by Mendelssohn with correct technique and very musically.

There was a lively social life in the hospitable home, in which I was most kindly invited to take part. Soon a harmless and friendly relationship developed between teacher and pupil, which the gentle eyes of the mother watched with delighted interest. I was indulged by both sweet women, and I allowed this to take place without complaining.

The work on my quartet made gratifying progress, and I also did not neglect playing the piano, since there was the possibility of some concerts in spring.

Adventure on Rügen. Brahms as Prophet. Venice. Paris. The Two Priests. Composer Festival in Hannover. Visit in Weimar. Hans von Bülow

The summer approached, and with it the question, where to? Since Frau Gousseff had invited me to make a summer trip together with her family and asked for advice and specifics about the when and where, I suggested Sassnitz on Rügen,[41] which was cheerfully agreed to. The night before the departure two furniture wagons brought the thirty-six suitcases, the contents of which the ladies thought they needed in Sassnitz, to the Stettin train station. Sassnitz at that time was a small fishing village with thatched-roof houses. A piano was also taken along. The entire house of the fisherman Hahlbeck was already secured in advance, since our party was large in number: Frau Gousseff with daughter and son; the tutor of the latter, Herr Feiertag, a doctoral student of theology; the French lady companion, Mlle. Lenoir; the cook Mina and the maid Amanda; in addition to my worthy self—eight people in all. In Greifswald the luggage—remember thirty-six suitcases and a piano—had to be transported from the train station to the ship. It finally took place, but the ship's departure was delayed for an hour. It was the same catastrophe at the landing pier in Lauterbach. Then came the five-hour trip by carriage at a snail's pace. We arrived in Sassnitz around midnight; the circle of carriages (three handcarts and two landaus) was unloaded of its contents, and we got to bed around sunrise. A few hours of sleep put us back in order, and the fried flounder for breakfast allowed us to forget completely the strain we had undergone.

My first swim in the sea, at six o'clock in the morning, was to offer me an interesting acquaintanceship. I splashed around unaware in the gently rippling waves, when an apollonian-shaped figure approached me—I instinctively had to think of Böcklin's "Spiel der Wellen" ("Playing in the Waves")[42]—and said: "May I introduce myself? I am Ludwig Barnay."[43] I also said my name. We shook hands—still treading water—and I remarked to the tireless swimmer that today for the first time I had the chance to admire him in this role. In an invigorating manner we enjoyed the delightful, refreshing water for a little while, conversing while swimming on our backs.

After leaving the water, by chance I ran into George Henschel,[44] at that time at the zenith of his singing fame. His first question after we greeted each other was: "Have you seen Brahms already? No? Then come to the Hotel Fahrenberg tonight. You will find us both there on the veranda. Adios and good-bye." After a hearty morning meal and full of anticipation, I went for a morning stroll in the wonderful forest of beech trees, surrounded by the whispering forest and rushing of the distant sea. "On a lonely forest path,"[45] in the darkness of the pine forest, walking along, I noticed in the distance a person approaching me, of medium stature, stocky, without a beard, in a suit of a strange cut and indeterminate color, predominantly a dull reddish brown with small checks, with short baggy pants, and carrying his hat in his hand. The lonely hiker passed by silently. After a few steps I looked around, and the fellow in the brown plaid also turned around at the same time, and so for a moment we stared into each other's eyes. The meeting with this strange-looking man did not leave my thoughts all day.

In the evening I made my way to the Hotel Fahrenberg. Henschel met me and led me to the fellow in the brown plaid. My God, what a surprise! It was Johannes Brahms! We now conversed like old acquaintances, since he also remembered our meeting in the woods. To his question whether I was an early riser, which I could affirm, he asked me to go flounder fishing with him at three o'clock the next morning. Of course, I gladly agreed. In the course of the conversation Henschel, who was very skilled with a pen, drew all kinds of funny things on the backside of a menu—the term "Speisekarte" was still little known in Germany at that time—and caused great amusement, especially with the comical caricatures of well-known personalities, among whom the happily smiling master turned out particularly well. I asked for the menu with this pièce de résistance for my collection. On the way home we went with Brahms past my "wigwam," in which I occupied an attic room.

Brahms wanted to pick me up at 3:00 a.m. sharp; I was supposed to wait for him in front of the house door. Thus we parted; it was probably 11:00 p.m.

He disappeared into the dark of the night toward Krampas,[46] while Henschel returned to the hotel.

I soon fell asleep. Exhausted from the trip and lulled to sleep by a good many glasses of Pilsner beer, I must have been in a fairly deep and sound sleep. Suddenly there was a horrible noise, the terrible sound of broken window-panes. With a frightful scare I jumped up from my sweet dreams. A man's voice resounded from the street *ben marcato e con energia*: "Get up; the rooster has crowed for the third time." Right! I had overslept the agreed-upon time; it was three o'clock on the dot! What had happened? In order to wake me, Brahms broke the windowpanes with a pole. A real Brahms![47] I was out of bed quickly and into my clothes. Leisurely we strolled to the shore, where the good Hahlbeck was waiting for us with his boat. In the evening we ate our catch prepared with parsley sauce at the friendly table of my kind hostess.

The culinary skill of our Swedish cook must have impressed my illustrious fishing partner immensely, because he invited himself to have dinner with us the next day without hesitation, about which, of course, we were very happy. Brahms arrived—it was very hot that day—and after the greetings immediately asked permission to remove his shirt collar, and did so with universal approval, which he seemed to take for granted. We saw in his embrace of the spirit of informality an encouraging sign that Brahms felt completely at home in our company. At dinner our honored guest, now without collar and at that time without a beard, made personal and humorous comments with meaningful winks and gentle taunts to the daughter of the family and her teacher [Scharwenka]. Really and truly—at that time there was as yet no reason for these quite harmless suggestive remarks. But all the same—Brahms was a prophet!

Unfortunately my new, great, undying friend soon had to leave us. After a few weeks I could inform him of my engagement to Fräulein Zenaide and at the same time request that he accept the dedication of my Romanzero, op. 33, which originated in Sassnitz, as a token of my great respect and admiration. Brahms answered with the following lines:

My dear sir!

It's all right for you to laugh,
And make others happy!

You made the right decision; I can only be pleased and congratulate you heartily. However, I want to be satisfied with my choice, with my music paper, and indeed—but now it is difficult for me to say—how happy I am about it and how I look forward to it. When I think back to Sassnitz, I know what I can expect from your music—but that is also an art—and now I come back to your decision, and that since Sassnitz I would have found it contrary to all world order, had things not turned out this way.

Today I can only greet you heartily and send my kindest regards to the ladies. Once your music notebook is lying in front of me, there will be no listener who is more grateful or attentive. For the time being, my address is Karlsgasse 4, Vienna.

My apologies for these confusing lines.

Yours faithfully,
J. Brahms

The lovely days in Sassnitz passed all too quickly. Brahms, Barnay, and Henschel had departed, and of our close circle of acquaintances only Gustav Kadelburg remained, who turned out to be a fanatic entomologist. On calm evenings he would sit in front of the door of his cabin, which lay off to the side of the forest's edge, with a lamp in front of him on the table, and catch moths fluttering around the light with a skilled hand, trained to the highest degree of dexterity. When he had also left us, we packed our suitcases—excuse me, all thirty-six suitcases and an upright piano—and moved homeward.

On the evening before our departure, oh, it was such an enchantingly beautiful evening with a full moon, I walked down to the seashore once more with Fräulein Zenaide in order to take leave of all the splendors, which the all-bountiful mother of nature spread extravagantly on this small richly blessed spot of ground. Moved to silence, we looked from our favorite bench through the leaves of the beechnut trees to the silvery sparkling sea, lost in the dreamlike beautiful view. No one said a word; no leaf moved. There were only slight, glistening ripples on the silvery path, which the heavenly sleepwalker drew on the shimmering water in the dim glow. How did it happen that our hands with a light squeeze found each other, that we leaned toward each other and finally came to the conclusion that our lips were not created exclusively for making sounds and as the opening to our mouth—how did it happen? The old night watchman on the canopy of heaven knows exactly; ask him. He has no doubt observed something like that very often, but has remained silent. Even today he escorts two happy people into the house. Brahms is a prophet!

Not until Berlin did we inform her mother about the bonding of our hearts; the kind woman received her future son-in-law into the family with sincere, heartfelt joy. My parents were very surprised, but happy, and so our future appeared in the rosiest light.

During the next days I completed the Romanzero intended for Brahms and a Valse Caprice, op. 31, which I embellished with the name of my fiancée.

And then came a wonderful time. My future mother-in-law wanted to please me out of the goodness of her heart and asked what I might wish for. I said, "Bayreuth and then Italy." Said and done. Some suitcases were not unloaded yet and could be taken along on the engagement trip without being touched, just as they had remained in Sassnitz.

In Bayreuth we enjoyed the premier of *The Ring of the Nibelung*, and our engagement was announced there on the day *Siegfried* was performed.[48] Then the trip continued via Munich to Salzburg and into the mountains. We had rented a landau, which took us during the next six weeks to the most beautiful places in the Salzkammergut.[49] The weather was not favorable, mostly rain or overcast skies, but in the carriage there was nothing but sunshine. We got out of the vehicle in Wörgel and set out for Innsbruck, where we found our heavy luggage in the Tiroler Hof and where for a few days we rested up from the six-day carriage trip—thank goodness without rain. Our next goal was Riva, where we spent a heavenly evening on Lake Garda; it was vividly reminiscent of the moonlit farewell in Sassnitz. After a two-day stay the steamboat took us to Peschiera, from which we continued our trip to Venice. There we arrived just as it started to get dark and enjoyed the enchanting view of a serenata organized by the Venetians to celebrate the presence of their beloved Crown Princess Margherita. We joined a flotilla of hundreds of gondolas decorated with flowers that set out from the train station, ahead of a specially built bargelike boat, on which an orchestra and a large chorus were set up. In magical illumination the journey proceeded along the Grand Canal to the swelling sound of music, past the palazzi, magically lit up in a thousand shining colors and lavishly decorated with daisies, to the harbor, where the ships, decorated with colorful pennants, reflected this incredible parade in Bengal light. There the real celebration took place. Homage to the Crown Princess took the form of choral singing with orchestra, an official speech, fireworks, "Evvivas"[50] from a thousand voices, cannons firing, orchestral fanfare, the waving of small flags, and similar signs of southern enthusiasm.

During the course of the rest of the trip we visited Verona, Bologna, Florence, Pisa, La Spezia, Genoa, and Turin and spent several days in all of these cities, during which my two female companions, who knew Italy well, served as excellent travel guides. Through the Mt. Cenis tunnel we traveled to Lake Geneva, from which the trip home was planned. But the *promessi sposi* (the betrothed) received a very special surprise—in Ouchy (Switzerland)—which was that the return tickets were not stamped "Berlin," but "Paris." A tremendous, delightful surprise! The engaged couple shouted with happiness and danced in immense joy around the kind, motherly travel officer. The suitcases were quickly packed again, and the next morning we were in Paris.

Before I went to see the sights of the city, the churches, the statues, the museums, and other art collections, my curiosity drove me first to view the places mentioned in the war of 1870–1871. I studied Versailles with particular reverential interest. As far as it was permitted, I visited everything that was available to my eyes, which were interested in the glorious past. I saw the castle, the park, and the places where the dear old emperor, the crown prince, Bismarck, Moltke,[51] and the rest of our heroes had welded together the German Reich. Then I began expeditions throughout Paris in order to become acquainted with the character of the city—my ladies trustingly let me go; besides Paris was not unfamiliar to them. Together then we visited the art collections—in front of the beautiful Venus de Milo we had a particularly solemn hour—and then visited the great immortals of the Père Lachaise. After we satisfied our first curiosity and enjoyed the opera and the Théâtre Français with rather exhausted senses, the women got to the actual purpose of the changed itinerary, that is, the question of the dresses! We spent many an entire morning in the Grand Magasin du Louvre and Bon Marché department stores. I stood uninterestedly at the counter, but feigned incredible interest in the purchases. My God, what did I know about dresses, material, scarves, hats, and ribbons? Sometimes I was sent out. Items were to be selected, which I was not permitted to see yet. I blessed these oh-so-short moments and could smoke my Havana with pleasure *extra muros*. In the Hotel du Louvre, where we had taken lodging, I admired the Boulle furniture,[52] with which our sitting room was furnished. My admiration for these expensive pieces resulted in a carriage being ordered, which brought us to the Grand Magasin, where a set of furniture in the style of Louis XVI was ordered for our future home in Berlin.

Finally there was nothing left to see or do in Paris. I urged that we start for home, the bags were packed—two new ones were added in order to bring along the acquired treasures—and soon we were on the green shores of the Spree River again.

It had become October. After collecting my thoughts for a few days, I returned to work on my Piano Quartet, of which the first movement and the Adagio were finished at the end of November.

Into this early happiness came the sad news of the death of my future father-in-law, who succumbed to his serious illness in St. Petersburg. His wife and daughter rushed to see off the one who passed into the night of the spirit. As I learned from his wife and daughter, with him departed a generous, noble, good person, a loving husband and father. By profession a business man of the first guild, which corresponds approximately to our "Kommerzienrat,"[53] for the most part he devoted his life to the administration of his estates, which were situated in the Province of Wiatka and in whose capital Slobodskoj the family had their permanent residence.[54] Here my fiancée and her seven siblings came into the world. Since Slobodskoj did not offer the possibility of a complete education and the cultivation of a higher intellectual life, the children, as soon as they had reached the appropriate age, were sent to the Imperial Institute in Moscow. There my future wife enjoyed her further scholarly development.

We possess an artistic, very valuable painting, which shows the deceased in the company of his family and which allows one to get an idea of his kind-heartedness and friendliness from his finely and nobly shaped countenance. I had proof of his generous helpfulness in connection with the inheritance provision. Many promissory notes for large sums of money were found, which the receiver had never repaid and the lender had never called in. Also numerous thank-you notes for gifts to churches, hospitals, and other charitable institutions were found among the papers left behind; likewise letters, in which the writers expressed their thanks for a horse, a cow, or the like that was given to them. A fortune lay accumulated there before us. The promissory notes, whose amount totaled well over a hundred thousand rubles, were consigned to the flames. May their ashes rest in peace!

The surviving wife, my future mother-in-law, Finnish by birth, came from an old military family. Her father, Karl von Nymander, served as a general in the army; he was described to me as an energetic man, full of character and soldierly virtues. He afforded his children an excellent education. I met and became very good friends with the youngest of his sons, Peter von Nymander. He died as the president of the Higher Regional Court of Kalisch.

After the return of my loved ones from St. Petersburg, we had to proceed, our hearts full of sadness, with the preparation and decorating of our future home, which we had found at No. 1 Regentenstraße. The day and the hour were set at the marriage registry, and I accompanied my fiancée to the Russian priest, Herr von Seredinski, in order to discuss the church wedding. The consecration of our wedding according to the rites of the Greek Orthodox Church was necessary, because marriage between a Russian woman and a man of a different faith according to a different rite is not recognized in Russia; also in that case deeds to property are confiscated by the state. Herr von Seredinski was more papal than the pope. To be sure he was willing to consecrate out marriage, but with the condition that I sign a declaration that obligated me to have my future children baptized and brought up in the Greek Orthodox faith. There you have it.

It goes without saying that I vehemently refused this outrageous demand.

"Then I cannot marry you," said the man of God, who was so concerned about the spiritual welfare of my yet unborn children. I repeated that I would have to turn to a different priest, since it did not matter to me which priest performed the ceremony.

"You will not find a priest who will perform the vows without the declaration," the priest countered.

"That is my business," I concluded the conversation. We took our leave and considered what was to be done. The next thing was to try our luck with the priest of the church in Dresden. On the same day yet we went to "Florence on the Elbe"[55] and found the spiritual head of the Russian Church to be very accommodating. The pleasant, imposing man was surprised at the refusal of his Berlin colleague. As he informed us, for a long time already a decree of the Russian emperor was in force, which permitted the marriage between a Greek Orthodox Russian woman and a foreigner of a different faith without any restrictions.

"But I would be very thankful to you," the priest added to his explanation, "if you would make a small offering for the poor blind people of our city—by all means no requirement requested on my part, but as a freewill offering." I gladly expressed my willingness and placed an appropriate bill in the offering bag that was extended toward me. The way was now clear.

The boring formalities at the registry in Berlin were taken care of on January 20, 1877; the church wedding took place in the Russian church in Dresden on January 21 with very impressive, but extraordinarily complicated and tiring ceremonies. In the afternoon the wedding guests, relatives, and friends from Berlin, and both partners of the firm Breitkopf & Härtel, Dr. Oskar von Hase and city councilor Wilhelm Volkmann of Leipzig, attended a grand banquet in the Hotel de Saxe. Herr von Hase, who was very Germanic and virile in appearance, proposed the first toast. Impulsively and buoyantly he jumped up from his seat, slipped on the smooth parquet floor, and fell full length under the table. Immediately up on his feet again, he got himself and the guests over this scare by dealing with his fall with humor and spoke very warmly and impressively. I remember that he attributed the content of his speech to the Pied Piper of Hamelin.[56] At the end of the meal we and the guests from Berlin took the night train to Berlin, where our beautiful home, prepared down to the last detail, received us.

After the usual visits and return visits were attended to, I returned to my work. I wrote the Scherzo of my Piano Quartet, a Piano Sonata, op. 36, and several pieces for piano. In April I played my Piano Concerto in Bremen, there for the first time in the new three-part version. The score, which in the meantime had been published, I sent to Liszt, who had recommended the work for performance in the meeting of musicians of the

Allgemeiner Deutscher Musikverein. He sent me a card with the following words:

> F. Liszt is pleased to see Herr X. Scharwenka again at the meeting of composers in Hannover and to thank him sincerely for the dedication of his Concerto. Wishing this outstanding work the best success, with kindest greetings, F. Liszt.

The composers' festival in Hannover in the beautiful month of May opened in the Hoftheater with a performance of St. Elizabeth by Liszt. The orchestra and chorus were arranged in the style of an amphitheater—an imposing view. A very high podium was set up for the director of the festival. Tension among the festival participants was rising; Liszt was in the small manager's box on the right side of the stage. All eyes were riveted on him. With the audience in rapt silence, the orchestra began the introduction of the work. However, no lucky star was shining on this performance. Already during the first measure there was an alarming unevenness in the orchestra. The general unsteadiness of the entries increased from measure to measure, and the audience sighed with relief when the first part ended. The second part went even more poorly, and one saw clearly on Liszt's face how he was suffering. The catastrophe came shortly before the end of the work. The conductor, whose name I will not disclose, suddenly grasped the railing of the raised podium with his left hand, leaned backward, and the railing broke apart with a crash. The unfortunate fellow fell backward at least four meters at the feet of the members of the audience in the orchestra section. Screams of alarm from many hundred voices—general confusion, good-hearted expressions of sympathy—all without cause. Nothing had happened to the man; he had only become sober!

Before the performance he had already consumed too much alcohol and during the intermission between the two parts of the work—as eyewitnesses reported—he had drunk fourteen glasses of strong beer. The intemperate fellow maintained the opposite; it had been only thirteen. He was finished as the festival conductor; in his place for the rest of the concerts stepped conductor Fischer,[57] who on the following day conducted my Piano Concerto. The performance paved my way and that of the piece into the great concert halls of the world.

At first I played it in Kassel. On my return to Berlin I found a message from Liszt, informing me that he was staying for a short time in Berlin and would be happy to see me. I went to see him—he was living at the home of Count Schleinitz, the minister of the royal household and the husband of the patron of the Bayreuth Festivals. I had the pleasure of being asked by the master to perform my Piano Concerto for the friends gathered around him and his art-loving hosts, during which time he himself played the orchestral part on a second piano. It is not my fault that the next day some newspapers reported on this private event. I state this emphatically in view of a statement by Hans von Bülow, which I will refer to at an appropriate place.

At his special invitation, I visited Liszt in Weimar with my wife in the summer of the same year. The master had expressed the desire to become acquainted with my quartet; he personally invited the other members of the quartet, among them the excellent violinist Kömpel. After a thorough rehearsal, we played the completed three movements in the Hofgärtnerei. In place of the missing fourth movement of the quartet, as Liszt said, we had a very fine bowl of punch, which kept us entertained until nightfall.

We reciprocated for the punch. In the Hotel zum Erbprinzen, where we had taken lodging, we arranged for a splendid banquet the following day, to which we had invited the master and his friends, among them Sophie Menter, Anna and Helene Stahr, and organist Gottschalg, among others, as well as the most outstanding of his students. After the meal we amused ourselves with all kinds of entertainment: riddles, rebus, card tricks, and the like. Even Liszt contributed to the general amusement. So he asked me to draw a crowing rooster, and when I was finished with the work of art, he took the pencil out of my hand and wrote into the beak of the household prophet the little word *pianissimo*. No one found the solution to the riddle. After a suspenseful silence, the master explained: "That is a government secretary (he crows very softly)." At the end came a very special surprise. At my nod the serving genius appeared with a covered bowl, which he placed on the table in front of Liszt. I asked the master to raise the cover, which he also did. Our extremely small, silky haired spitz, Bello, who lay under flowers in the bowl, raised his little head toward him. Liszt took the cute little animal, caressed it very tenderly and carefully, and then passed it on. When we departed, Liszt asked us to come again, when the Piano Quartet was completed, which we of course gladly promised to do.

Having returned to Berlin, I threw myself into composing with renewed delight, completed the Quartet, wrote a Trio for Piano, Violin, and Cello, op. 45, and a Sonata for Piano and Cello, op. 46. Heinrich Grünfeld[58] came to our home at that time, and so I had an excellent interpreter of the cello part.

In October I was busy again at the piano. Hermann Ritter[59] had constructed his alto viola after laborious studies. As is generally known, this instrument was used in the Bayreuth Orchestra, and he intended now to present his invention to a greater public. He planned a concert tour, first to Bavaria, and asked me to go along with him. Others taking part in the tour were Philippine von Edelsberg, the celebrated singer at the Berlin Hofbühne; Heinrich Sontheim, the tenor; and Eduard Hermann, the violinist from St. Petersburg. The concerts began in Nürnberg on October 15; then followed Munich, Augsburg, Regensburg, Bamberg, and Würzburg. As ensemble numbers on the program we had Mozart's Viola Trio in E-flat Major and the "Fairytales" of Schumann. Hermann Ritter, whom I had gotten to know through Kullak, became a dear, trusted friend during the tour. Later he devoted himself to musicology and published some valuable writings, among which his *Repetitorium der Musikgeschichte* deserves special note. Today he lives as a professor at the Musikhochschule in Würzburg. The end of the year brought performances of my Piano Concerto and Quartet in Braunschweig, Bremen, and Hannover.

As far as I know, I was the only interpreter of my works up until then, and so I was filled even more with joy when I learned that my Piano Concerto was successfully performed in one of the famous Crystal Palace Concerts in London (Sydenham)[60] by the excellent pianist Edward Dannreuther.[61] This happy news I owed to one of the lively travel letters, which Hans von Bülow, who was performing in England at that time, addressed to Herr Bartholf Senff, the publisher of the *Signale für die musikalische Welt*, and in which he described his impressions of English musical life in his favorite colors: lively red and dark gray, pleasantly alternating with toxic green. Hans von Bülow writes (November 1877) the following about the performance:

The second piece was a recent composition: Herr Scharwenka's B Minor Piano Concerto played by Herr Edward Dannreuther. Recently I had the misfortune of being afflicted by various piano concertos, in part painful or causing pain, whose mastodontic size suggested to my unassuming sensibility that they were no longer at the peak of "modern times" and that caused me to reach for Mendelssohn's and Moscheles' G Minor opera to recover. I prematurely included Herr Scharwenka's B Minor Concerto among these monsters; also a quick reading of the two-piano arrangement had startled me because of the unmistakable borrowings, which the Pole chose to make from the Russian (that is from Tschaikowsky's Concerto in B Minor, op. 23, dedicated to me). Finally the all too American advertisements of the *Berliner Blätter* filled me with unfriendly distrust. The same ones had disturbed me last summer with their fortissimo fanfare that Herr Abbé Dr. Franz Liszt[62] had traveled by express train from Weimar to Berlin in order to arrange a celebration for Xaver with two Bechstein pianos in that very aristocratic hotel, where tea is not served with sandwiches (which of course the guests themselves have to make), but with tickets for the patrons. All the more refreshing was my surprise at the thoroughly charming, often interesting, and original musical work, distinguished by a natural flow and almost unintentionally elegant form. Like a work by Chopin, it has the advantage of naturally conforming to the piano, but with a superb orchestration, an advantage that Chopin's E Minor Concerto first received from Tausig and his F Minor Concerto only from Klindworth.

The composer may be proud of the local success of his opus with the public and the critics; however, he may also express his thanks to the interpreters for their excellent rendition of the principal parts. Herr Dannreuther played it in a fiery fashion, bright and clear, like the trousers that the pianist has to wear in English morning or afternoon concerts (frock coat and colorful tie complete the informality) if he does not want to make a fool of himself, which he can achieve, however, by putting on the Order of the Falcon[63] or ribbon pretending to be the legion d'honneur from afar.

I feel compelled to correct a few historical inaccuracies that are found in the lines cited above and to report *urbi et orbi* that, first of all, nothing could be read about an express trip by Herr Abbé Dr. Franz Liszt that was undertaken for the purpose mentioned. Second, when the outline of my Piano Concerto dawned on me, I was not acquainted with the work by Tschaikowsky. As I reported in a different place, I had the idea for my composition, which I had originally sketched out very early as a piano solo fantasia, at a time when Tschaikowsky's work was still completely unknown in Berlin and the surrounding area. What the "unmistakable borrowings" consist of, which the "Pole"—who I have neither the honor nor the ambition to be—is supposed to have made from the "Russian," never occurred to me or to one of my critics. Third, I would like emphatically to protest being praised as a successful rival of Tausig in instrumentation. Just look at his "reworking" of the Chopin E Minor Concerto. The edition can still be had, if it has not been reduced to pulp, as I hope.

Thus I have freed my heart from a heavy burden and now am able to sleep peacefully again. I was really sincerely happy about the travel letter; I expressed my great admiration for the letter writer by dedicating my Second Piano Trio, op. 45, to him. At that time Bülow was giving a concert at the Berlin Singakademie, in which he played the five last piano sonatas of Beethoven exquisitely. Full of admiration for this extraordinary feat, I wrote to him how delighted I had been with the "last Beethoven." Apparently Bülow connected this remark, which was meant for the entire cycle, only to the last sonata, op. 111, because he answered my letter, which at the same time contained my inquiry regarding the dedication, with the following lines:

Hannover, October 27, 1878

Dear Sir!

Herewith permit me to give you my sincerest thanks for your considerate opinion of my Berlin venture. The truly tropical heat of the area had crippled my strength in a manner even surprising to me at first. It is therefore doubly comforting to me when a competent brother in Apollo understands that I am capable of doing it better than I did. Looking forward with joy to becoming acquainted with your new piece and gratefully accepting from you the honor you intended,

with deepest respect,
yours faithfully,
Hans von Bülow

In Kassel in January 1878 I played Beethoven's E-flat Major Concerto under the direction of the old royal conductor Reiß as well as my Piano Quartet, the violin part of which the royal concert master Wipplinger, a student of Spohr's, performed. Then on February 8 in Berlin I performed my B Minor Concerto under the excellent direction of Franz Mannstädt. For February 14 Carl Reinecke had invited me for a performance of this work in one of the Gewandhaus Concerts, which followed a concert on the 15th in the same hall, in which, together with Reinecke, I played Schumann's Variations for two pianos. It was very interesting for me to hear from Reinecke something about the tempo and playing of this work, as he had heard it from the mouth of Schumann.

The concert, a benefit performance arranged for Reinecke, was poorly attended. He was very disappointed about the financial failure and became teary eyed by the apathy of the people in Leipzig.

With Our English Cousins. Family Opus I.
Death of My Father. Vienna and Budapest. Prince Konstantin
zu Hohenlohe. Brahms. Ferdinand Hiller. Liszt Blesses
His Godchild. Subscription Concerts in the Singakademie.
Hans Richter. Liszt and Frau Zenaide Play Four-handed Piano

A short time after this the firm of Augener & Co. in London inquired whether I was willing to publish some compositions in their publishing house. At the same time I received an invitation from Mr. George Augener, the head of the company, to visit London and during my stay there to be his guest. That excited me tremendously. In the beginning of March I traveled across the channel, became miserably seasick, cursed Augener, myself, everything, and whatever else was suited to being cursed. It was a dreadful crossing; it lasted six hours instead of the usual two hours. The small boat swayed so much that water ran into the smokestack. Finally I was in Dover and soon at Blackfriar Station, where Mr. Augener, who had waited for hours, met me and took me first of all to the Hotel de Kayser. On the following day I moved to his own home on Adelaide Road, where I soon felt at home. Out of our business transactions grew a friendly relationship, and I spent very happy days with the host's family, which was blessed with numerous children. The city impressed me immensely, and I did not hesitate to study it thoroughly. An acquaintance of the publisher, Mr. Hermann Franke, a violinist and concert impresario, provided me with the opportunity to be heard in some concerts; for the next year's season—1879—concerts on a grander scale were planned. After a three-week stay in London, I returned home, not without a certain dread of the channel trip; but wind and weather were merciful.

In April I accepted an invitation to perform my Piano Concerto in Posen. Then came a few weeks of rest, to which I was condemned as a result of a knee injury caused by an unfortunate fall.

In July there was again a longer concert tour. A well-known oratorio singer tried to arrange concerts after the loss of his magnificent voice and invited Marianne Brandt, the unforgettable alto of the Royal Opera, Heinrich Grünfeld, and me to a series of concerts in some of the most visited spas. Proposed were Soden, Homburg, Langenschwalbach, Neustadt a.H., Kreuznach, Kissingen, and Marienbad. In Soden, where we arrived in the afternoon and were supposed to appear in the evening, we noticed to our amazement that the concert was not announced in any way; there were neither posters in the spa garden nor announcements in the newspaper. We went to the concert organizer named by the impresario in order to ask for information about the concert's starting time, the hall, and so on. The man did not have the foggiest idea; he was issued no order, and a concert would not take place that evening. That was an auspicious beginning of our concert tour.

The rest of the concerts proceeded smoothly; only shortly before Neustadt a.H. did we have a small adventure. The concert there was to begin at three o'clock in the afternoon. This unusual time had been selected so that concert goers from far away would have a timely trip home. Our train, which was to bring us to Neustadt at two o'clock, had to remain at a station a short distance from our travel destination because of a mechanical problem. In any case, we wanted to get ready for the concert, came to an understanding with the stationmaster, had our luggage taken out of the baggage car and brought to the property barn, and got dressed for the concert—Marianne modestly behind a piano box! Soon after our metamorphosis, a freight train went to Neustadt, which made it possible for us to begin the concert with a half-hour delay. I gave a short apology to the restless audience, and the concert took its undisturbed course.

For the end of August I was invited for two concerts in Norderney,[64] which I completed together with my cousin Elizabeth, a very talented young singer. Then in November I played my concert in Braunschweig, at which old Franz Abt[65] waved his baton. A very good-natured old gentleman, who knew how to appreciate his liquor—as long as there was not too little. He talked a lot and very humorously about his trip to America and the successes that he had on the other side of the great pond with the singers and also with the public.

For this excursion I had invited my father. During the entire time of his stay in Braunschweig he strolled through the streets of the city and—as an architect by the grace of God—enjoyed with the eyes of an expert the beauties of the interesting cityscape.

December brought the most important event of the year: family opus 1, which appeared on December 12, published by the parents in their own publishing house. To be sure tiny in form, yet well developed in the formation of its individual parts and structurally perfectly formed, the new opus proved to be a thoroughly viable addition to my collected works; in a word: it was well made.[66] For the present this small female citizen of the world was a winner and dominated the situation with a very high, however still untrained, voice.

In the midst of the joy that this small creature brought us came to our great anguish the sad news about the alarming condition of my father's health. Already for some months he had been suffering from the aftereffects of a light stroke, which became worse around Christmas, so that he was constantly confined to his bed. His most ardent wish to hold his first grandchild in his arms could not be realized at the time. He was bedridden, and we could not risk exposing our small, delicate creature to the prevailing barbaric cold at the time, since it was a long way to the home of my parents.

In the upsetting days of January 1879 there was an evening performance in the Kaiserin-Augusta-Stift, for which my participation was requested. The Empress Augusta had said she would attend and had appeared punctually. After my performances, the noble woman requested an encore from me: the Andante and Finale of Beethoven's *Appassionata*. Fortunately I had the sonata well in my head and fingers. There followed a friendly thank-you on behalf of the empress and the following day a kind gift.

Then came weeks of worry and serious concern about the health of my father. I was with him daily, but to my great sadness I had to watch how the end gradually approached. I had received an invitation from Bernhard Scholz for March 18 in Breslau to play my Piano Concerto there. Deeply moved, I said good-bye to the sick man; however, I did not suspect that the end was so imminent. After the concert, without changing clothes I drove from the concert hall in Breslau directly to the train station, was in Berlin early, and rushed immediately to the bedside of the dear sick man. I came too late—he did not recognize me anymore, and so I could only close his eyes. The burial took place in the Jerusalem Cemetery; however, the body was transferred later, when I acquired a family burial plot at the Matthäi Cemetery.

With the passing of my father I lost a real friend and counselor. I owed it to his kindness and patience that I was permitted to choose my life's work at my own discretion. His kind, unassuming nature, his joy in innocent family fellowship, and above all the ability not to let his family sense anything of his business concerns helped spread sunshine over his family life. The beloved evenings in the most intimate family circle will remain for me a lasting memory; my mother fiddled with an almost impossible article of clothing, while the male trio performed a "Partie 66" with "drums and pipes" and at the same time smoked a mild tobacco (Eigenlob brand), and enjoyed a few glasses of alcohol-free drinks. Oh, what wonderful times! They had now disappeared, and in addition to the memory there remained only a fresh grave.

However, soon life demanded again its tribute from the survivors: a certain amount of work and energy. We had laid our dear departed one to his last rest on February 22; on the 25th my profession again called me away.

August Manns,[67] the conductor of the Crystal Palace Concerts in London, had invited me to play my Piano Concerto there on March 1, in the same place where a year and a half earlier, Dannreuther had performed it. Although with a heavy heart, I followed the call; and after the successful performance, I received a large number of engagements in London and in the larger cities of England. However, first I still had to complete some concerts on the continent. Already on March 4 I played my Piano Concerto in the Cologne Gürzenich[68] under the direction of Ferdinand Hiller.[69] Hiller had invited me personally and at the same time asked about the specifics of my fees. Jokingly I answered that the concerto consisted of three movements, and each of those was to be paid a hundred marks; however, none of the movements could be left out or shortened, since it was a "Kürzenich"[70] concert to which I was invited. Oh dear! I had met my match! At our meeting in Cologne sometimes even worse jokes hailed down from him, and even the orchestra rehearsals and the performance were not spared from mutual bombardment. I played at his home at noon, and before the meal he led me into his library. Maybe to give me an appetite? The one large cabinet contained only scores of oratorios from his own pen. On the leather spines of the well-bound and -preserved copies, as a result of their limited use, glistened in gold print a lot of famous Old Testament names. Hiller was a dear old gentleman, small and well nourished from his appearance, witty, entertaining, well meaning, and occasionally also sarcastic, yet never insulting. My meeting with him remains a pleasant memory, which I renew from time to time through the reading of his humorous letters and epigrammatic postcards. I returned to Cologne once more the beginning of April on my trip to London and performed a number of my chamber music pieces in the Cologne Music Association.

On March 8 I played a benefit concert in Berlin to fund an obelisk base. The obelisk was supposed to stand on Potsdamer Platz, of all places. The plan, however, was never carried out, whereby many an accident was certainly prevented. After a short trip during which I came to Danzig and some of the smaller cities in Pomerania, I returned to England, where I first appeared in one of the afternoon concerts that were arranged by old Ella[71] in St. James Hall, at that time the grandest concert hall in London. The hall provided a different view from the usual arrangement of seats. The grand piano stood in the middle of the hall on a raised platform that was specially built for these concerts; the audience sat all around in a circle. Ella, a small, dignified, old gentleman with an extraordinarily sharp profile formally welcomed his aristocratic audience, greeting the most prominent members personally. Then from his raised viewpoint, he gave a biographical sketch of the performing artist and analyzed in well-considered words the works to be heard. Then the music began. After the performances, which were not permitted to last longer than an hour—the five o'clock train was waiting—I was presented to some of the most notable people and received invitations and nice words from the ladies and gentlemen—among them the Earl of Aberdeen, the Count of N.N., the Prince of X, and many other celebrities. Ella obtained my promise that I would play with him again.

Immediately following this I was to have the opportunity for a daring act, which was highly praised by the press and the public. One Saturday my wife, who in the meantime had arrived in London, and I were among the members of the audience in the Crystal Palace Concert. We had seats near the orchestra. After the overture Mme. Montigny-Remaury from Paris was to play the E-flat Major Concerto by Beethoven. A rather long, expectant pause occurred; the audience began to become restless. Then I suddenly saw August Manns, the conductor of the concerts, step down from the podium and come toward me. Excitedly he informed me that Mme. Montigny-Remaury had not appeared for the morning rehearsal and was nowhere to be seen. Manns asked whether I would play the concerto; the orchestral parts lay on the stand, the orchestra was reliable, and my deed would undoubtedly find appreciation with the press and the public. I readily agreed and stepped up on the stage with Manns, from where he described briefly the situation to the audience. Tremendous applause sounded, which after my performance increased to an enormous ovation. I then played once more during this season at the same place, gave some of my own recitals in London, and took part in several concerts in the capital and out in the provinces.

We had very pleasant accommodations in Wigmore Street. Broadwoods, whose grand pianos I used in my concerts, had provided me with a very good instrument. Above us lived Ignaz Brüll; however, we did not disturb each other, and so I could be active creatively. Here my Variations, op. 48, originated, as well as some smaller piano compositions for two and four hands, which Augener & Co. published.

At the end of June we returned home, and I had the sense that I could return next year, which also happened.

I spent part of the summer in Ruxmühle, enjoying the joys of country solitude after the turbulent London weeks. In order not to be tempted to make an attack on the ailing table piano, I placed my suitcase on the four-legged case and so thought I was protected from the urge to play. Soon, however, I had to remove the suitcase from the piano at the irresistible urging of my composing demon, which outranked my playing demon. The work on my second trio and a new piano concerto (C minor) led me regretfully again to my old familiar instrument, which willingly accepted my caresses with pleading whimpers. With the works almost completed, I returned to Berlin, where the joys of a change of residence awaited me. To be sure the current accommodations met the present requirements; however, a conscientious head of the family also is concerned about the future!

Without difficulty I found a suitable apartment in the Gerson Haus, Bellevuestraße 10, on the corner of Lennéstraße. Specially fixed up for Gustav Richter, the painter, it offered us a beautiful, spacious concert room—the former studio of the painter—in which my two grand pianos, an American Steinway and a Bechstein, hardly gave the room the feeling of being cramped. Here I completed the trio and the Piano Concerto. In addition, I was gratified to learn that my concern for a more spacious apartment had not been totally unfounded, because on November 8 the family trio was expanded to a quartet, in which the newly joined bawler—the feminine form "Schreihälsin" is probably not permissible—assumed the soprano part, for the time being without regard for melodic lines or rhythmic precision. The new family member was baptized with the name of her mother "Zenaide," but unfortunately she had the habit of always raising her very clearly audible, but not always melodious, voice when it was least desired. This bad habit embarrassed us once in no small way. Franz Liszt, the illustrious godfather of this tiny citizen of the world, had come to Berlin in spring 1881 for the performance of his *Christus*. One morning the master honored us with his visit and asked solicitously about his godchild with the wish to see it. The eager mother hurried to get the child; however, to my dismay she brought the wrong opus. Before the situation could be cleared up, the kind Abbé placed his hands on the small creature and blessed it with devout words. As I learned later, the real godchild had screamed so incessantly and incredibly that it seemed impossible to the mother to present it to her dear godfather. At the solemn moment of the blessing and also afterward we lacked the courage to clear up the mistake, and so a "screaming" injustice was done to the absent screaming monster.

At a quickly improvised snack, our dear guest took only a small glass of port wine and a small serving of the beet salad; we knew from Weimar that he liked this side dish very much. With great interest the master asked about my pieces; I could present him with the completed score of my Second Piano Concerto, likewise the new trio. He also asked about Bello, the little silky haired spitz of Weimar memory, and he frowned comically when I had to inform him that the four-legged little dwarf had descended to the dark Hades for dogs. When he left, we could say "see you soon," since the music association in Magdeburg, where I was to play my Piano Concerto and which Liszt had promised to attend, was approaching soon.

I have to go back to the year 1879. In the fall of that year I led a true nomadic life; there was no end to concerts! Aachen, Krefeld, Halle, Posen, Stettin, Magdeburg, Brandenburg, among others. Tired of leading a vagabond life, I decided to settle down and made plans to establish a conservatory; however, it was to take until 1881 to accomplish, since suitable accommodations could not be found immediately—especially allowing for intense musical activity. To express my intention to settle down, however, I founded together with Gustav Holländer[72] and Heinrich Grünfeld the subscription concerts, of which three were to take place in the hall of the Singakademie. The venture was a splendid success, which has continued to be true up to the present. Holländer remained part of the association for only two years; in 1881 he followed a call to Cologne, where he found a job more to his liking as teacher and conductor. In his place stepped the worthy, distinguished Emile Sauret,[73] who assisted with the subscription concerts for ten years. In 1891 he was called to the Royal Music Academy in London as Sainton's successor. I left my position at the piano, which had become dear to me, a year before Sauret's departure and moved to the western hemisphere of our planet for a longer sojourn. To the vacant violin position came the excellent master of the violin, Florian Zajic, who faithfully stayed at his position for a quarter of a century.

The organizing, recruiting, and driving force of our association was and remained Heinrich Grünfeld. From the concert podium he impressed and charmed by means of his elegant and persuasive art of performance; and he was society's favorite darling through his social talents, which he spiced with his quick wit and delightful humor. One met Grünfeld everywhere, in the palaces of the millionaires, at premieres, at great balls, and at the homes of ministers and high officials.

For me Heinrich Grünfeld was and still is a dear, loyal friend and an always-obliging colleague. Whenever I called him, he was right there with his cello. Just recently I received the following card from him: "When and wherever you want, I will always gladly play with you, even if you want me to play on top of the Siegessäule,[74] as long as there is no draft. On November 20 I will play your sonata with great delight. Your old H.G."

Also there was a bond of true friendship between Sauret and me; I will say more about him later.

In my time, that is, from 1879 to 1890, programs always began or concluded with a piece of chamber music, in between which each of us performed a solo piece. Often we called in a singer or instrumentalist. The program of the first concert follows:

1. Trio for Piano, Violin, and Cello, op. 37, E Major Fr. Gernsheim
2. Three Lieder, sung by Frau Adelheid Holländer
3. a) Romanze for Violin   ⎫   G. Holländer
   b) Canzonetta   ⎭   B. Godard
4. Theme and Variations, op. 48   X. Scharwenka
5. Two Pieces for Cello
6. Three Lieder
7. Two Fairytales for Piano, Viola,
   and Clarinette, op. 136   R. Schumann
   (Clarinet: Herr Huth, Royal Chamber Musician)

From the programs of the first years, the following works are mentioned: the Trios for Piano, Violin, and Cello by Fr. Gernsheim, op. 37; Hans Huber, op. 20; Rob. Volkmann, op. 5; Carl Goldmark, op. 33; C. Saint-Saëns, op. 18; Beethoven, op. 11; Schubert, op. 100; Ph. Rüfer, op. 34; X. Scharwenka, op. 45;

and Hans v. Bronsart, G Minor; also mentioned were Joh. Brahms, Quintet for Piano and String Instruments, op. 34; Albert Becker, String Quartet; X. Scharwenka, Quartet for Piano, Violin, Viola, and Cello, op. 37; Mozart, Trio for Piano, Clarinet, and Viola, E-flat Major; Dvorak, Gade, E. Hartmann, Grieg, and Schumann, smaller ensemble pieces with various players.

On December 4 I played my Cello Sonata with Grünfeld for the first time publicly in a concert of the Seiffert Gesangverein in the Berlin Singakademie. Shortly thereafter I went to Vienna. Hans Richter,[75] whom I knew from London, had invited me to play my B-flat Major Concerto in the Philharmonic concert on December 14. I was very happy that I would have the opportunity of seeing Brahms again. My first outing after my arrival in Vienna was intended for him; unfortunately, I did not find him home, and so I walked to the Währing Cemetery, to the hallowed sites, which hold the mortal remains of Beethoven and Schubert. What musician, what civilized person in general, can stand before these simple graves without showing his silent tribute of amazing admiration and respectful feeling of gratitude to both of these immense giants, these wonders, who rest beneath these stones, for what they have left us with regard to the wonderful, sublime values of eternity. Deeply moved I left the place in order to go back to my own business, which now seemed so insignificant, first of all to the orchestra rehearsal with members of the Philharmonic. Hans Richter thoroughly rehearsed my piece with really loving attention to the intentions of the composer—a model for so many other conductors, who think they have done enough if they see to it that players and orchestra find each other again at the end of the movement. In this connection I have had sad experiences, mostly with famous conductors. The Vienna performance was splendid; the success with the audience and press was far beyond all expectations. Even from my fellow musicians and performers I earned sincere words of recognition. Thus I became acquainted there with Josef Hellmesberger,[76] at that time the director of the conservatory, then Julius Eppstein and Anton Door, both old masters in the teaching field. Even Alfred Grünfeld, my former classmate, had come to welcome me and shake my hand.

At the conclusion of the concert, Prince Konstantin zu Hohenlohe, the first steward of the emperor's household, honored me with a visit. The prince, a brother of our third chancellor, appreciated art and was genuinely devoted to our dear muse of music; several of his attractive, well-set compositions testified to his serious studies. I used one of his simple melodic ideas later for a larger piece of Variations, op. 57. The friendly, aristocratic author of this theme became my kind patron and friend and was favorably disposed toward me until the end of his life.

The great success of my concerto upset all my good intentions regarding my hoped-for, settled state of existence, and I gladly accepted engagements, which after this concert were offered to me in large number.

In January I undertook with Sauret a short concert tour, which took us to Schweidnitz, Görlitz, Lauban, and Brieg. In one of these cities there was a funny incident during the concert. While I was playing the tender Nacht-stück, no. 4, by Schumann, the blaring trumpet sounds of an outdoor military exercise were suddenly heard from the main guardhouse across the street. Of course, I interrupted my playing, which, however, as I learned later, caused immense displeasure with the audience. My behavior was found to be shocking, and I think that it would not have been possible for me to play again in this small town.

On January 13 I gave my own concert with orchestra in the large hall of the Musikverein, which was followed by an evening piano recital in the Bösendorfer Hall. The press treated me most kindly. Eduard Hanslick wrote in the *Neue freie Presse*: "On January 13 Herr Scharwenka repeated his Concerto in B-flat Minor, which was so enthusiastically received in the Philharmonic concert. Scharwenka is an excellent pianist, dazzling and without charlatanry. The power of his octave runs, the delicate, confident flight of his passages, the clear delicateness of his ornamentation, and the melodic roll of his chains of trills; those are all qualities—held together and enhanced by a sound musical performance—that can hardly be found more beautiful anywhere else."[77]

Eduard Schelle[78] wrote the following review: "Thus two outstanding artists, Sarasate and Scharwenka, closely passed by each other in the same room. However, Sarasate is a virtuoso in the first instance, even if a virtuoso in the noblest sense of the word; however in the case of Scharwenka, it is virtuosity, even if it is a towering virtuosity, as the means to a higher purpose. In him the virtuoso goes hand in hand with the composer, and the composer has something completely different in mind than to please only the virtuoso. There was a great improvement between the Monday evening and Tuesday evening concerts, which was reflected also in the program. Scharwenka first performed his Concerto for Piano and Orchestra and played Chopin, Schumann, and Liszt. Then he performed some of his own compositions, a very charming, but also very difficult Staccato Étude and a composition of a grander scale: Theme and Variations, a piece that has a serious, artistic imprint and bears witness to a creative force. Finally he crowned his performance by playing the powerful E-flat Major Concerto by Beethoven and to be sure a very magnificent crown. This evening Herr Scharwenka celebrated a true and well-deserved triumph."

My stay in Vienna this time was also not of a long duration, but I had the joy of being able to greet Brahms. Our reunion was celebrated in the Red Hedgehog Pub, with cauliflower soup, smoked pork with dumplings, and Linzer torte. The same evening we met at the home of Billroth, where Brahms asked me to perform my Variations, op. 48. About noon the following day he dropped by my hotel, asked for a copy of the Variations, looked it over carefully, and said that I should have exploited the conclusion of the theme more fully. I promised improvements at the very next opportunity, and we made our way to the Red Hedgehog Pub, where we met Carl Goldmark at the entrance. The two did not seem to have a close relationship, since Goldmark did not join us but after a short greeting went to the upper rooms of the restaurant. Later I met him a number of times, yet I could not acquire a liking for him.

From Vienna I went to Budapest, where on February 13 I played my Piano Concerto with the Philharmonic under the excellent direction of Alexander Erkel. Liszt, whom I had the joy of meeting again, had already arrived in Budapest from Rome in January in order to perform his duties for a time there as the president of the Hungarian National Music Academy. I found the master sick and out of sorts; as he said to me, he was suffering from being "away," and longed for his beloved Hofgärtnerei in Weimar. My joy at seeing the revered master again was only brief, since I was expected in England already on February 18.

Of the much-extolled beauties of the Hungarian capital I saw nothing more than what my eyes could see from the hotel window and could glimpse in passing on the way to the concert hall. The view from the Hotel Hungaria across the Danube over toward Ofen[79] is indeed enchantingly beautiful, and I could depart with the hope of being able to expand and deepen soon my hastily won impressions.

My next travel goal was London, which I reached early on February 18, thoroughly shaken up. A hansom cab took me directly from the train station to the orchestra rehearsal in St. James Hall. The orchestra was already assembled, and Mr. Cusins,[80] a perfect gentleman—the part-time orchestra conductor—was waiting for me impatiently, the sign of his office in his hand. The rehearsal began immediately and proceeded to everyone's satisfaction, which on the part of Mr. Cusins was so great that he hired me for a concert with the Old Philharmonic Society in June. I was able to accept, since I intended to spend the coming season in England.

Mr. Cusins had the pleasure of enjoying the special favor of the queen and the Prince of Wales. He was a professor at the Academy of Music, royal organist, and the queen's master of music, and finally was knighted, after which he could be addressed as "Sir William."

The evening concert was festive and sparkling; in the middle of the front row, close to the orchestra podium, the Prince and Princess of Wales sat inconspicuously in good bourgeois clothing. During the rather long intermission that followed my performance, the Prince of Wales appeared in my room backstage, introduced by Mr. Cusins. The prince offered us cigarettes and conversed freely with us. Then he said to me that his wife would be happy to meet me and asked me to follow him into the hall. There he led me to the princess and introduced me most gallantly. I was able to thank the lovely, charming woman with proper respect for the many kind and appreciative words with which she paid tribute to my performance.

Such an incident in a Berlin concert hall would have caused turned heads; there in London one found nothing unusual about it.

After I had completed an additional evening piano concert in London and a few concerts in the country, I was finally able to devote a few days to my family. On my arrival in Berlin I was received with very sad news. Just before my return, my mother-in-law had lost her eyesight as the result of a sudden attack of rheumatic fever. In spite of the most attentive care and consultations with the most prominent eye doctors in Germany, this insidious disease, which had come overnight, could not be cured; the dear woman endured it resolutely and without complaint until her death in 1905.

A trip to Vienna and Budapest followed my days of rest in Berlin. With others I took part in a musical-dramatic academy in the imperial city. The designation "academy" was used in general for larger performances with a mixed program. This designation was already in use before the time of Beethoven and has continued up to the present day.

The program of the concert that took place on March 19 to benefit the German Aid Association consisted of two parts, the first of which presented some instrumental and vocal performances. Emile Sauret played the Violin Concerto by Mendelssohn, Frau Gomperz-Bettelheim sang an aria by Rossini and Schubert's "Erlkönig," and I contributed a few of my own compositions. The second part presented Mozart's "Schauspieldirektor."[81] Under the thoughtful direction of Josef Hellmesberger, this showpiece of roguish and charming humor produced a delightful effect. Among the cast members were Pauline Lucca, Albin Swoboda, and Gustav Hölzel. Leo Friedrich from the Burgtheater played the director.

Via Budapest, where on the 22nd I gave my "Hangversenye" (i.e., an evening piano recital) and was able to spend a very stimulating evening with Liszt and Sophie Menter at the home of Count Geza Zichy, I returned to Berlin in order to prepare for the approaching season in London and to see to it that the my composing pen did not completely become rusty. A few small things occurred, but they are not worth mentioning.

I do not remember much about the two seasons in London (1880 and 1881). According to my collection of programs, I played twice in the concerts of the Old Philharmonic Society and also in the Crystal Palace (Beethoven's E-flat Major Concerto and my own new one in C Minor, op. 56). In addition, there were a large number of afternoon and evening concerts *intra ex extra muros* in the capital. I stayed away from the social swirl, in which the foreign artist is easily carried away; yet I was not able to escape completely the duties and pleasantries of society without coming into discredit as an eccentric. Pleasant memories remain of the musical afternoons at the home of Mr. Eberstadt, who welcomed weekly the most select group of artists in his comfortable bachelor's home. There one met Joachim, Hans Richter, Sarasate, Frau Essipoff, Ignaz Brüll, and many others. Even Saint-Saëns, who at that time did not act anti-German, turned up regularly.

Alma-Tadema[82] provided a meeting place for the artists of the season in his fabulously furnished apartment. Whatever artistic taste and opulence of furnishings can achieve, the astounded eye could observe here. For his music room the artist had a grand piano built by the Broadwood Company, unusual and expensive, in keeping with the style of the magnificent room.

The inner surface of the piano lid offered a large smooth ivory surface. Each artist who had been granted the privilege to be heard on the instrument was asked by the host to immortalize himself by signing this spacious surface, which, however, was most uncomfortable for extensive writing. Josef Joachim, although "only" a violinist, as I was told, had struck a powerful C major chord at the inauguration of the instrument and made a show with his name as the first in the series.

Also in the splendid rooms of Lady Lewis and Mrs. Joshua, the elegant, dazzlingly beautiful sisters of the above-mentioned Mr. Eberstadt, one met the artists of the season; their Apollo Musagete, who was admired and idolized by the ladies of the house, was the blond hero Hans Richter.

I also maintained friendly contact with Villiers Stanford,[83] the excellent composer whose second job at the time was as organist in Trinity College in Cambridge. Mr. Stanford had invited me one day to a sports festival of the student body. They valiantly boxed, rowed, wrestled, ran, and played ball. Student duels, like those customary in Germany, did not take place; therefore one could go without looking at slashed or wrapped faces and could enjoy student sports without the smell of carbolic acid. Later they all gathered in the beautiful church sanctuary, where Stanford provided his listeners with an exquisite artistic treat through his extraordinary virtuoso organ playing.

Every evening at the common meal I was presented with an unusual sight. At the entrance into the dining hall a large, wide, and high fireplace was built into the transverse wall, above whose fire of coals half of an ox, a truly fine specimen of its species, was being roasted *coram publico* before its grand intended purpose. During the meal people had a good time, and the good youths, whose appetite appeared to be greatly stimulated as a result of their athletic activity, eagerly helped themselves. The half of an ox, which just a short time ago looked so good and was bursting with generous plumpness, had become a skeleton. By general request Stanford sat down once more on the organ bench and played Bach's D Minor Toccata and the Fantasia and Fugue in G Minor.

My English publisher, Mr. George Augener, in whose home I stayed as a guest the entire time during my London sojourn, was preparing at that time a Chopin edition, which was produced in his own music print shop. By chance I got a hold of some of the printed sheets that had been corrected by an "editor" and noticed with dismay that the text abounded with countless printing errors. I informed Mr. Augener of my discovery, which thank goodness was not too late. As a result the publication of the work was entrusted to me. I thought of dedicating the work that I had taken over to my publisher friend in return for his hospitality for several months. I refused unequivocally and stubbornly an honorarium offered to me, the sum of which I was to determine. Yet the kind man pressured me so long until I finally named a sum, the amount of which, as I believed, had to appear to him as fantastic and therefore not discussible. However, I was fooled. Smiling in a friendly way, my host indicated that my "fee" did not correspond by far to the sum that he considered suitable, and so he offered me double the honorarium that I had named. At that time English pounds were very popular, and so as the maiden Danae of old,[84] I endured the rain of gold without a murmur. The revisions took much more time by the way than I had first thought, in spite of the fact that I searched only for mistakes and reshaped some completely impossible fingerings for the piano.

Now it was summer and with it a time for rest and relaxation. I had become acquainted with most of the concert halls in Germany and England as well as with those of Vienna and Budapest. I knew by heart the names of all of the stations, one after the other, between Vienna and London and was familiar with the number of railroad crossing shacks and telegraph poles on this stretch. I thought now of dedicating myself with solemn passion to raising my two children. However, the nanny seemed not to be in complete agreement with my method of bringing up children and a few times protested appropriately. To be fair, I had to agree with her, and so I withdrew from the nursery, ill humored yet convinced of the inadequacy of my pedagogical talent, packed my suitcase, and soon was walking outside under the tops of the beech trees on Rügen.

Also in this year—1880—the blessed kindness of heaven presided over my family. On November 26, our third little girl was born; she received the name Marie Helmi Konstanze and was called "Marischka," the nickname of one of the small daughters of Hans Richter. My three small Graces now sang steadfastly very lovely vocal trios, whose intonation was not always totally correct, but produced by normally developed lungs. Reasonable people certainly could not take offense at the frequently occurring cacophony in the case of such small children.

Soon after Marischka's birth, in the beginning of December, I returned to Vienna. Princess Marie zu Hohenlohe, the wife of the first steward of the emperor, had invited me to participate in a "musical-declamatory academy" planned for a charitable purpose. A number of concerts in Vienna and Budapest were connected with this event. On December 11, I took part in the artists' evening of the Gesellschaft der Musikfreunde. On the following evening I performed my Second Piano Concerto (C Minor) with members of the Philharmonic under the direction of Gericke, which earned me an honorarium of two shiny gold pieces; this is the usual honorarium, which the fortunate composer receives at the performance of a new piece. This custom probably stems from the time of piecework contracts of long ago, when the ducat—as in present-day republican Austria—represented a fortune.

Josef Hellmesberger had invited me for the 16th to play in one of his quartet evening concerts. Brahms came to my room backstage during the intermission after my performance and said some kind words about my work. With well-meaning candor he added: "But that you shortened the adagio is a low-down trick; one does not do something like that, and it is better not to write things that one can not take on." I could not deny this argument, thanked him for the kind reprimand, and promised not to repeat the mean trick.

Soon thereafter I performed the Piano Quartet in Budapest and also performed an evening piano concert there. Both concerts were attended by Liszt, who became a witness to a very funny episode. Through Dunkl, a music dealer friend of mine and owner of the well-known music publishing house Roszavölgyi & Co., I had received an invitation to visit a very wealthy family in Budapest with a good musical reputation, but whose family head launched lively, but not always happy, political activities. I accepted the invitation, which had arrived in correct form, and found myself during the evening in a select, aristocratic society. The charming daughter of the family

The first page of the original manuscript of the Polish National Dances, op. 3, no. 1

The Polish Dancer, a caricature of Xaver Scharwenka

Franz Liszt, a caricature by George Henschel

Engagement photos of Xaver Scharwenka and Zenaide Gousseff, August 15, 1876

Xaver Scharwenka (1889)

Caricature of Scharwenka by Lindloff from Die Musik *(Deutsche Verlagsanstalt, Stuttgart)*

Philipp Scharwenka (brother)

An enigmatic postcard that was delivered to Scharwenka through the resourcefulness of the post office

Masked ball at the court of the Princess of Albania. In the middle photograph, daughter Lucie. Photos taken by the Princess of Albania

Caricatures of Scharwenka at the piano and as conductor, which appeared in Helsinki

On a walk with Felix Mottl in Tarasp, Switzerland

Childhood silhouette in color. Xaver Scharwenka (1915)

Scharwenka's "Cottage of the Muses" in Bad Saarow on Lake Scharmützel (Brandenburg, Germany)

happened to lead me to the opened Bösendorfer, which I was eager to show all imaginable honor. The evening passed perfectly. I must forgo describing the menu in order not to expand the size of the present book by the stipulated number of pages. My own concert took place the following evening. Liszt, who was also staying on the same floor of the Hotel Hungaria, wanted to pick me up. He was already sitting in my room and was enjoying a cup of tea with rum when the door opened, and a richly liveried servant of the above-named politician appeared and handed me a large triple-sealed letter. From the envelope I took a thank-you note, in which was enclosed a fifty-florin note with "admiration and appreciation of my musical achievement." At first we were speechless; then Liszt joined me in a roaring duet of laughter, the cause of which the startled footman who looked in certainly did not have the faintest notion. After our laughing fit had subsided, I sat down at the desk and drafted the following answer, which I handed to the servant to deliver to his master.

Dear Sir!

Thank you very much for the great recognition, with which you so kindly acknowledge my modest achievement with the payment of the 50 florins. I ask you respectfully to donate this sum, which I herewith return to you, to the poor people of Budapest, and in doing so I would like to express my painful regret that the needy will not receive a more generous donation.

Please accept, etc.

The success was an unexpected one. All the humor sections in the papers of the city attacked the art Maecenas,[85] about whose generosity I had told a few reporters, and treated him unmercifully.

For the next weeks I chose Vienna as my headquarters, enjoying the pleasantries of the imperial city with leisure and devotion. I sent for my wife from Berlin, and we settled comfortably in the Hotel Müller. Prince Hohenlohe placed his box in the opera house at our disposal any time and gave us ample opportunity to become acquainted with the aristocratic society of Vienna. We maintained regular contact with Brahms, Hellmesberger, Bösendorfer,[86] among others; we attended the theater and balls, and we were incredibly happy. Every week there was a friendly stag party at a late hour in an old smoky bar, to whose regular guests, in addition to Bösendorfer, Baron Erlanger, and Eduard Schelle, Daniel Spitzer[87] of the *Wiener Spaziergänger* also belonged. I had read with immense pleasure the latter's humorous articles, brimming with printed poison, which at that time had already appeared in a book, and was extremely happy to become acquainted with this entertaining fellow who I assumed was overflowing with jokes. How surprised and disappointed I was when on the first evening together, I became acquainted with a taciturn, sour-faced looking gentleman, who slowly chewed on his roast beef with onions. Spitzer hardly participated in the conversation; whether he was listening or pensively preparing a new *Spaziergang* and gathering material from our conversations could not be determined from this stony guest.

On the occasion of a ball in the Hofburg, a small, very pleasant courtesy was shown me, which might appear worthy of mention only as a result of an episode connected with it a decade later.

During a dance intermission I strolled with my wife past the orchestra of the court ball, directed by the "handsome Ede" (Eduard Strauss).[88] At that moment one of the cellists, who presumably had performed in my concert, as a delightful joke played the first theme of my Piano Concerto:

I expressed my thanks for this gesture with a friendly greeting to the orchestra. I related this small, in itself insignificant episode many years later in New York on the occasion of a pleasant German evening of drinking beer, which a few prominent musicians had organized in my honor in the Liederkranz.[89] After my story a handsome, distinguished gentleman stood up and said: "Professor, that was I." There was universal camaraderie and toasts with due ceremony after this confession! Now I could personally thank this dear brother in Apollo—it was Victor Herbert, the operetta composer who had achieved great respect in America and who was an excellent cello virtuoso.[90] Sincerest greeting, Herbert, if you get to see these lines.

The year 1881 brought much that was eventful and most gratifying. I was expected in St. Petersburg for concerts in the middle of March. On the trip there, with my wife along to support the head of the family, we arrived on the evening of the 13th in Vilna, where the Russian locomotive was granted a full hour to recover. After the tiring trip and in anticipation of the wonderful days in St. Petersburg, we enjoyed a bountiful buffet there. However, our joy had been in vain. An old Polish servant in the rest room whispered secretively to me in his language: "Do you know yet that the emperor was murdered?" In that first moment, since I had just come from Germany, I thought of our dear old emperor whom I had just seen the day before. To my remark about this, the old Polack replied that he *naturalnie* had meant the Russian czar. The news had not yet spread in the restaurant, and my inquiry with the stationmaster was denied absolutely; he declared the news to be empty gossip, and so I proposed to continue the trip to St. Petersburg. My wife, however, hurried into the telegraph office to do some investigating. Also there, there was a friendly but firm denial. When my wife informed the telegraph official that I intended to give concerts in St. Petersburg and that our trip would be totally useless should the news be confirmed, the official responded that he would not go! This sufficed for us. We carried our luggage to the hotel and returned the following day to Berlin, when the news of the murder of Alexander II had been officially confirmed and the military had taken an oath to the new czar. Now I could allow myself a few weeks of rest and peace. I closed the grand piano and the inkwell and devoted myself, as a passionate smoker, to the nerve-calming study of blowing smoke rings, which I brought to a high degree of mastery.

Completely rested and prepared, I could now look forward to the strains that awaited me at the meeting of composers in Magdeburg. There, under the direction of the young Arthur Nikisch,[91] my Second Piano Concerto in C Minor was performed, which through his clear form and even melodic lines of conducting held its own successfully alongside the tumultuous Antar Symphony of Rimski-Korsakov and a few other ultranew German outpourings. Liszt was in the best of moods. His own works—the Hungarian Coronation Mass, the Mountain Symphony, and Death Dance—found excellent interpretations, and the master was paid homage bordering on idolatry. During the rehearsal-free morning hours his rooms were never free of visitors, and there was always music being played. At that time a musically very clever spoof had appeared in print: Variations on the so-called Cutlet Theme:[92]

The player on the right had to perform the theme, while the partner on the left (this designation without a political connotation, please) had to take over the variations. Each of the ladies present—my wife among them—was asked by Liszt to sit down at the piano with him for the cutlet chopping. My wife was the first in line. I asked the kind master to play in very strict time and rhythm, since my wife would never give up. This frivolous, in part groundless, suspicion of my better half drew a mild rebuke on the part of the good doctor who always valiantly championed the sacred rights of women. My wife beamed and fearlessly started playing; however, she showed that she was not equal to the complicated rhythm of the cutlet theme. Liszt gave in. I shouted with joy!

After this fun at the piano *à quatre mains*, an unpleasant incident occurred. A beautiful, young blond woman from the group of those present approached Liszt shyly with her sheet music in hand and asked whether she could sing something. Most obligingly the master offered to accompany her on the piano. The singer placed the handwritten copy on the music frame of the piano and asked the master to transpose the song to a key higher—it was the well-known "Im Herbst" ("In Fall") by Robert Franz. The singing began. Probably as a result of the poor notation, Liszt got confused in the sequence of chords; he jumped up angrily, hurled the music across the piano, and angrily snapped at the singer, pale with fright, "It is an unparalleled insult to place such an illegible scrap of paper in front of me; I will not stand for that in the future." Flashing with anger, the master glanced around the group, as if to require our consent for his certainly explainable, yet somewhat very temperamental outburst. We all stood quietly and waited for this embarrassing scene to end. Soon, however, the gentleman in Liszt won the day. Following his good heart, he approached the sobbing nightingale and tried to stem her flood of tears with reassuring words.

The busy year of 1881 brought me my first royal honor: an appointment as Royal Imperial Austrian Chamber Virtuoso. It might be interesting to become acquainted with the document that notified me of this pleasant event because of its antiquated curial style. It said:

By His
Majesty the Emperor of Austria,
Kings of Bohemia
And Apostolic Kings of Hungary, etc.
Our most gracious Lord
Granted the favor to the
Pianist in Berlin
Herr XAVER SCHARWENKA.

His Royal and Imperial Majesty has signified his pleasure most graciously to grant you by royal decree on the 29th of August the title of Royal Imperial Chamber Virtuoso.

You will be informed herewith of this gracious decree.

Moreover, His Royal and Imperial Apostolic Majesty remains affectionately yours with royal, imperial, and archducal favor and grace.

Given in Vienna, under the imprint of the secret seal of His Royal and Imperial Apostolic Majesty, on the 30th day of the month of August of the year of one thousand eight hundred and eighty-one.

The Royal Imperial First Steward
(signed) R. Prince zu Hohenlohe
(seal)
By the personal order of His Royal and Imperial Apostolic Majesty.
(signature illegible)
Royal Imperial Privy Councillor

The Conservatory. Anton Rubinstein. The Young d'Albert. Concert Tours in Holland, Scandinavia, and Russia. Liszt in Karlsruhe

My summer activity was devoted in large part to the organizational work necessitated by my plans for the establishment of a music conservatory. In a stately house on 136/137 Potsdamerstraße there were suitable rooms both for the institute and also for my private residence. I had succeeded in securing a number of excellent teachers. In addition to my brother Philipp, who had taken over the direction of the theory and composition classes and who loyally assisted me also in managing the administrative business, the following names are to be mentioned:

Dr. W. Langhans—Music History
Albert Becker—Counterpoint
Philipp Rüfer—Ensemble and Score Playing
Prof. Wilh. Jähns—Rhetoric
Frl. Marie Schmidtlein—Voice
Otto Leßmann—Voice and Methodology
Frau Marianne Scharwenka—Violin
Joseph Kotek—Violin
Heinrich Grünfeld—Cello
Martino Röder—Italian

On October 9, an opening ceremony with music took place in rooms of the institute, for which Karl Wittkowski had written a stirring prologue that Professor Jähns solemnly delivered. The conservatory soon attained a place in the foremost rank of German music institutes, which it maintains laudably even today. A number of very promising, talented young people had entrusted themselves to my management. The first public student performance took place in Philharmonic Hall on January 29, 1883, with the Philharmonic Orchestra. Among the accomplishments, the performances of Fräulein Emma Koch and of young Vianna da Motta especially stood out. The future brought both of them ample recognition. Gustav Ernest, the subsequent Beethoven biographer, directed an overture that he had composed.

The faculty assembled once a month for an informal discussion in the rooms of the conservatory. The serious debate about artistic and educational questions was usually followed by a cheerful postlude, at which King Gambrinus[93] presided. One of the most cheerful people was Albert Becker, whose most significant work—a mass in B minor—had caused a great and well-deserved sensation.

Guests from other areas of the arts often appeared at our monthly symposia in the conservatory. My friend Skarbina, Professor F. A. Leo (called Shakespeare Leo), Wilhelm Scholz, the brilliant artist of the *Kladderadatsch*,[94] and other dear friends, who contributed to the good fellowship. On an especially festive evening Wilhelm Scholz produced an amusing "enigmatic inscription," which may find space here and be deciphered by the kind reader familiar with Latin (see figure 3.5).

Philipp Rüfer brought enjoyment through his performance of a Chinese opera, for which he had written the text and the music.[95] Although we did not have a complete command of Chinese, we were not confused about the course of the plot. Rüfer had a vocal range from double B up to D two octaves above middle C and knew how to transfer his delighted listeners, supported by his phenomenal facial expressions and virtuoso skill of pantomime, to the Middle Kingdom.

Josef Kotek, an excellent violinist who unfortunately died so prematurely, imitated and characterized various animals on the violin: the donkey, the rooster, the cackling hen, the quacking goose, among others.

There was many a happy surprise for the students of the institute. Thus the young Eugen d'Albert[96] dedicated an evening piano recital to them in the hall of the institute. In addition to one of his own suites, he played two rhapsodies by Liszt, the A-flat Major Polonaise by Chopin, and Tausig's Nachtfalter (Night Moth) and Halkafantasie.

Shortly thereafter Anton Rubinstein paid a visit to the conservatory. The great master requested some student performances and finally sat down at the piano himself. He performed for us his F Minor Barcarole, some pieces from Schumann's Kreisleriana, and at my request Bach's Chromatic Fantasia—incomparably beautiful!

Figure 3.5 Enigmatic Inscription: "Du, Xaver, komm. Essen ist da!" (You, Xaver, come. The food is here!)

In December I accepted an invitation for an extended concert tour in Holland, where I performed my B Minor Piano Concerto. A lot of pleasant memories are associated with this lovely, interesting trip, which among other things brought about my acquaintance with the composer and conductor Jean Verhulst,[97] who deserves a great deal of credit for cultivating music in Holland. The warm-hearted old gentleman, who was enthusiastically devoted to his profession, could not do enough in working out the orchestral parts of my work, which he accompanied superbly in the Hague and Amsterdam. His enthusiasm went so far in the Felix Meritis[98] concert in Amsterdam that he passionately embraced me *coram publico* at the conclusion of my Piano Concerto. After the performance there was a very pleasant gathering of congenial people. Oysters were in season! One can obtain this food, which a civilized Dutch person cannot do without, ready to eat—that is, with the beard removed and the meat loosened, so that diners only have to slurp or swallow it without too much effort. As on the podium, so Verhulst was also an accomplished master at the restaurant table, with the difference that for musical tempos he had the most sensitive feeling, but with regard to oysters, however, he was always in a strange hurry, which turned into a continual *alla breve* with the second dozen. Although I myself am rather quick, I could not keep up with the older virtuoso—Verhulst beat me by two dozen oysters.

In Rotterdam I became acquainted with Friedrich Gernsheim;[99] he directed the concerts of the Eruditio Musica[100] there, which flourished under his energetic and intelligent direction. Gernsheim became a dear friend of mine; I stayed at his home and enjoyed a few days of quiet, homey, and cozy togetherness. Later in Berlin the ties of friendship became even stronger and lasting.

For some time the idea of a larger orchestral composition was haunting those cells of my brain reserved for music; it soon took on a more concrete form, finally crystallizing into a symphony, and on Christmas Eve of 1882 I gave myself a present of the completed score, op. 60. The giver and receiver had the same joy.

To my inquiry with Liszt regarding a performance of the new work at this year's meeting of composers, I received the following lines from the master from Budapest:

My dear Scharwenka!

Your kind message pleased me very much; best wishes to mother and children.

With regard to the symphony, the program is already overfilled, and I am not in charge of determining it. Kindly check with Riedel, who is in charge of organizing it.

With kind regards,

| | Yours faithfully, |
| Budapest, 8.3. | F. Liszt |

In the spring I made a short trip to England. Shortly thereafter I went to Switzerland for a longer stay, first to Zurich, where the meeting of composers of the Allgemeiner Deutscher Musikverein was convening. Here we had the joy—my wife was with me—of being able to greet Liszt. He was no longer the same—the burden of his seventy-one years weighed on him noticeably, and it seemed as if the adulation of his loyal *feminini generis* no longer gave him as much pleasure and satisfaction as last May.

In Zurich we became acquainted with a very interesting couple, Herr and Frau von Stockar, who annually made their summer home in Chateau Stutz, situated closely to Triebschen[101] on Lake Lucerne. On their recommendation we also took lodging there, and in pleasant and stimulating company we enjoyed the splendors, which the great master builder of the world in extravagant abundance wrapped like a belt around the shore of this indescribably beautiful, legendary jewel of a lake. Herr von Stockar, who lived in Zurich, could tell us a lot of interesting and intimate details about Richard Wagner's time in Zurich. What was known about this great man in exile from books and other written records came to life through the storyteller's revelations and completed the picture of the master that at that time was not yet as well known as today to the general public in such clearly drawn outlines. Also the old ferryman, who took us almost every day from Stutz across the lake to Lucerne, chatted entertainingly about the boat trips with Wagner, Hans Richter, Friedrich Nietzsche, and other notable personalities of the Wagnerian circle who visited Triebschen.

It was the first time that the wonders of the high mountains revealed themselves to me, and my happiness would have been complete if an old, neglected stomach illness had not made itself noticeable very painfully the first night of our stay in Stutz; it finally forced me to say a premature farewell to the mountains. We returned home via Strassburg, where I consulted Adolf Kussmaul, the famous doctor.[102] He prescribed a course of treatment in Karlsbad, which, however, did not get rid of the pain. Only the often-repeated visit to the Tarasp mineral springs,[103] however, alleviated this stubborn malady, even though it did not completely eliminate it.

With Emile Sauret, who had taken Gustav Holländer's place in our subscription concerts and who at the same time took over the instruction of the advanced violin classes at my conservatory, I had arranged a concert tour to Scandinavia at the beginning of the new year (1883). We first gave six concerts in Copenhagen. The good old King Christian IX—the "father-in-law of Europe"—on the occasion of a Royal Concert pinned the beautiful Order of Dannebrog on our manly chests. As a result of the document written in French, I had then become a "Chevalier." What a sound that has! Something like "Ritter Gluck!"[104] Should I acquire armor, a double-edged sword, and a proud warhorse? I was very happy about this first medal. So was Sauret, who celebrated the happy event on the evening of our "decoration day" with so much Pommery champagne that on the following morning one could not wake him, and he overslept the departure of the small steamship, which was to take us to Aarhus. Several concerts in Odense, Horsens, Randers, and more followed. Then at the end there was an afternoon concert in the immediate circle of the royal family. At the announcement that I would soon go to St. Petersburg, the queen gave me a letter for her daughter that I was to deliver personally; the address read: "To the Empress of all Russians."

Our next destination was Stockholm, where we arrived early in the morning half done in after a strenuous night trip. At the train station a dignified old gentleman awaited us—he was the orchestra valet—and escorted us directly to the orchestra rehearsal in the Royal Theater. The arrangement there was odd in that my Bechstein stood alone on the stage; however, the orchestra, contrary to our practice, was in the orchestra pit, which certainly did not seem favorable for the sound of the piano. It was very interesting for me to hear that my piano stood on the spot where Gustav III fell victim to the bullet of the lieutenant and assassin Ankarström during a masked party. I was also shown the small side room—today fixed up as the artist's room—where the mortally wounded was at first moved.

From Stockholm, where we gave six concerts, we went to Oslo.[105] The trip had to be interrupted in the evening, because at that time night trains did not run in Norway. We had to stay overnight at a small border station on Norwegian territory. The train station attendant answered our request for a small, warming tonic for the heart—grog, cognac, or aquavit—with a sympathetic shrug of his shoulders. As we learned from one of the fellow passengers, alcoholic liquor could not be sold. However, this knowledgeable Theban led us to an inconspicuous wall cabinet, opened it, and let us view a well-assorted supply of all kinds of beautifully labeled bottles and fine crystal glasses. We refreshed ourselves thoroughly after the strenuous trip, placed the required kroner and öre in the cupboard, closed it, and, inwardly warmed up and accompanied by a knowing smile of the attendant, went to bed comforted. Yes, liquor could not be sold at the Norwegian train stations!

In the United States of America the production of alcoholic consumables had been forbidden for some time; likewise the import of the beverages of the devil, such as champagne, Bordeaux, Rhine and Moselle wine, and so on. The poor people cannot even treat themselves to a small glass of pilsner. *Aqua pura*, improved with a dash of lemon, is now served at the restaurant table. Cheers!

Oslo and its magnificent surroundings were resplendent in their wonderful winter adornment; we thoroughly enjoyed the frozen splendors on our concert-free days. Sauret, the eternally happy, kind Frenchman from the south, who spoke German quite fluently yet with an unmistakable accent, was a pleasant, fun-loving travel companion. I will never forget when, armed with his Stradivarius, he turned up by me and performed an operatic scene or a Handel aria. The recitative, the aria with endless coloratura passages, imitations of the orchestra—all in extreme caricature—were presented in such striking Handelian style that a good deal of surprise at so much technical, vocal, and mimic ability was mixed with my unrestrained amusement.

After we had given six concerts in Norway's capital, we returned to Berlin, where our agent presented us with the statement of the financial results of our concert tour. I have had more pleasant moments in my life! It seemed to us as if the various agents, on account of a more convenient calculation, had shared the concert receipts generously with themselves and us.

The year concluded pleasantly with the premiere of my symphony under my direction in the Koncert Foreningen in Copenhagen on December 1 (repeated on the 5th), and the performance of my Second Piano Concerto, under the direction of Joachim, in one of the orchestral concerts of the Royal Academy of the Arts in the Berlin Singakademie on December 14 (repeated under the direction of Rudorff in Stettin on the 15th).

The year 1884 had an auspicious beginning: On February 14, my small home orchestra, which up to then consisted of an alliance of three, expanded to a quartet; stated bluntly, my fourth little daughter was born and was named Isolde. The expressions of sound of the new little citizen of the world were significantly more moderate and melodic than those of her female predecessors, and indeed the young creature early on revealed a very commendable sense for melodious musical sound and rhythmical precision.

On March 3, the first Berlin performance of my symphony took place in a Philharmonic concert, conducted by Wüllner.[106] In the same concert Hans von Bülow played Raff's Piano Concerto in C Minor. During the final rehearsal Bülow was the cause of a very amusing interlude. The good-humored master found, when he wanted to sit down at the piano, that the piano stool was too low—adjustable stools were not invented yet—and so he had Wüllner hand him a score to use to raise the seat. However, when he noticed that he held the score of my symphony in his hands, which was to have the honor of raising him up, he placed the volume carefully on the bench, pulled out a pristine handkerchief, and unfolded it carefully over the score with an engaging smile and a graceful sweep of the hand toward me. The orchestra and the few listeners—at that time there were still no public dress rehearsals—found this funny scene most amusing, which induced me to ask the mischievous master loudly and for all to hear if he perhaps was concerned about his nice new trousers? Now the laughing was on my side.

In May I went to Leipzig to hear Goldschmidt's *Helianthus*;[107] Liszt had come with a few of his faithful followers from Weimar. On the day after the performance, as I sat in my hotel room at afternoon coffee, there was a knock on my door, and to my "come in," four young men entered my room; at first they apologized for the intrusion. Then they introduced themselves in order: Moritz Rosenthal, Emil Sauer, Arthur Friedheim, and Bernhard Stavenhagen. As I learned, they were Liszt's students and had come from Weimar with the master; they had found my name in the hotel register and wanted to meet me. I thanked them for the honor shown me, ordered coffee, cognac, and cigars, and invited the happy quartet to a splendid dinner in Aeckerlein's Cellar. Later on during the evening, we visited a different pub, where the revelry reached its high point. In the course of our extremely lively discussion, we noticed suddenly that one dear fellow was missing. Rosenthal had slipped away unobserved. After a lengthy search, we found him in a quiet room to one side, where he was practicing passages in sixths with solemn seriousness on a worn-out piano. Yes, my dear Moritz, you really and honestly did do that, and the astounded world was soon to discover that this labor of love was not in vain.

Later Sauer stayed in Berlin for some time and was often a welcome guest in our home. He soon gave an orchestral concert in Berlin, in which he played my First Piano Concerto with extraordinary success. I soon lost sight of Friedheim. Only later in America did I see him again; it was similar with Stavenhagen, who there became acquainted with the score of my just-completed opera *Mataswintha* and who decided to perform the work at the Hoftheater in Weimar, where in the meantime he had become the number one conductor. He kept his word. The first performance took place on October 4, 1896.

After the *Helianthus* days in Leipzig, I withdrew to my retreat in Berlin and started on a larger revision. A Hamburg publisher had come to me with the request to produce an edition of Schumann's piano pieces. I devoted myself with great joy to this task, which in addition to a careful textual revision included corresponding indications of phrasing and fingering, and sacrificed for it almost two to three hours of work per day for two years. Because of an illness, I had to exceed the stipulated delivery date by fourteen days, whereupon the agent felt obliged to reduce the agreed-upon, very limited honorarium. My claim initiated with the court in Hamburg had the outcome that the defendant was ordered to make immediate payment—seizure in the case of noncompliance or inability to pay—and I was given the right legally to publish the judgment in the newspapers, which was not exactly complimentary for the defendant. I received my money, but dispensed with the publication of the nasty business.

For the summer I accepted an invitation to Marienlyst; I was supposed to play there three times, for which the management of the health spa offered me as compensation, in addition to a considerable honorarium, a villa for me and my family with completely free living expenses. That was worth considering! Here I continued my studies in fishing for flounder, which I had begun in Sassnitz with Brahms, under the expert instruction of the director of the health spa and finally achieved outstanding skill in the field.

During the three winter months I concertized in Russia and Finland. I remember with particular fondness the evenings in St. Petersburg at the homes of Auer, Davidoff, and Anton Rubinstein, in which I became acquainted with many well-known and interesting personalities. At times there were passionate cards games. Rubinstein took part *con passione*; he needed the card games whist and ecarté, as he convincingly assured us, simply as a means to calm his exhausted nerves. The stakes were kept within moderate limits, and the games, in which I participated only as kibitzer, proceeded always *piano ma con amore*, only interrupted from time to time by a *sforzato* of one of the players. On one of the evenings—at the home of Davidoff—the three played Rubinstein's B-flat Major Trio for the enjoyment of those present.

My memory also likes to wander back to the afternoon concerts at the home of Grand Duke Konstantin, the most artistic, well-educated, and intelligent of all the Romanovs. A passionate friend of music, he bowed his cello with great skill and participated tirelessly and most successfully in the performance of chamber music. The grand duke sight-read Bronsart's Trio right from the music that I had brought along one day. An enormous organ was installed in the grand hall of armor in his castle, which Naprawnik often demonstrated for us. An exquisite evening meal followed the music, which provided an opportunity to become acquainted with the famous wine cellar of our noble host; I was especially impressed by a Crimean wine from his own vineyard. The letter, which the Danish queen had sent along for her daughter, I unfortunately could not hand over personally. Both majesties lived shut off from the people around them, almost like prisoners in the Gatschina.[108] So I handed the letter, on the advice of a highly placed court official, to Prince Dolgorucki with the request that it be conveyed to her majesty. Whether it reached the hands of the empress, I do not know; I never heard anything more about it.

From St. Petersburg I went to Moscow. Max Erdmannsdörfer conducted the concerts of the Imperial Music Society there after the tragic death of Nicholas Rubinstein.[109] There I also played my First Piano Concerto and, following that, several evening recitals. Accepting an invitation from the Mother Superior of the Smolnoj-Institute, I devoted an evening full of Beethoven, Chopin, and Liszt to the pupils—exclusively of the feminine gender. The huge hall of the institution, which was under imperial protection, offered a fabulous view. On the seats, arranged in a semicircle amphitheater style, sat two thousand girls in silent anticipation, all in the same attire—white with a colorful sash. When I stepped up on the podium, the sparkling group stood up and greeted me with a silent bow, which made a much deeper impression on me than the most ear-deafening applause. After my performances there was tea, cake, and sweets; even a cut glass bottle with rum was presented to me for the tea—it had been requested as "medicine" from the institutional pharmacy!

Then followed a series of concerts in Finland and the Baltic provinces. On December 23, we were again in our home in Berlin, and my wife, who had shared the joy and pain—particularly the former—could then decorate the Christmas tree in time for the children.

From the year 1885, the composers' festival in Karlsruhe has remained vividly in my memory. There I saw Liszt for the last time. His appearance was alarming and his spirits varied greatly; an insignificant little thing could upset him greatly and an innocent-seeming word could provoke him. The indulgence he showed for particular individuals, even totally unworthy ones of his group, was strange and continued until his death a year later. He, the world conqueror, had become weak—weak to the point of helplessness. This became apparent, among other things, in one of the festival concerts, in which his least talented favorite female student was supposed to play the A Major Concerto. There was a catastrophe in the orchestra rehearsal: Already by the twelfth measure, the performer and orchestra were no longer together. They started from the beginning again; Felix Mottl[110] was conducting and tried his utmost. However, again the performer was thrown off course. Liszt, who was sitting in the first row, whispered some instructive comments to his favorite student during the involuntary break, after which they began for the third time. But nothing helped; they could not come together! Finally the orchestra refused to continue to play; Mottl laid down his baton, and the unlucky favorite student seemed to be finished for this life. But no—things progressed differently. Liszt had a rather long and, as it appeared, very heated conversation with the director, and the unbelievable happened; at the festival concert in the evening the kind-hearted Mottl accompanied the Piano Concerto on a second piano. It is only due to his phenomenal skill in accompanying that the "performer who could not play correctly" was not immediately ridiculed.

Together with Fräulein Emma Koch I played Liszt's *Concert pathétique* for two pianos in one of the festival concerts, and the next evening I heard the "Dies irae" from Berlioz's *Requiem* for the first time; it made such an overwhelming impression on me that I resolved to perform the entire work in Berlin.

The festival concluded with a splendid noon meal at the home of the grand duke, to which the male solo players of the festival concerts were invited. The enjoyment of the delicious food and the finest liquors was severely marred by the performance of a military band in the adjoining room. While the best condiment of a common meal is the conversation with one's neighbors, here one could hardly hear one's own words, and so I made myself understood with my two neighbors largely through sign language, expressive gestures, and many "toasts" presented with strong intonation and the clink-ing of glasses. Liszt, who sat on the right side of the grand duke and across from me, spoke little and showed little taste for the joys of the banquet. Ap-parently he was suffering a lot.

Of the events worth mentioning of this year, I can list my appointment as royal professor and the performance of my symphony by Theodor Thomas in New York.

With my head filled with great plans, I entered the year 1886, which first of all was devoted to my work on the Schumann edition, and in the course of which the world had to mourn the death of a truly great man. Franz Liszt died on July 31 in Bayreuth. A rich life, accompanied by unprecedented suc-cesses, was extinguished; a great, kind human being, an artist by the grace of God, who accomplished the best of his time, had left us.

Grave and cradle—close together. On September 11, our son and heir was born; he was named Philipp after his uncle.

Orchestral Concerts. The Berlioz *Requiem*

Now came a very exciting time. During the summer I had made plans to arrange a series of orchestral concerts; they were to take place in the course of the winter in two series of four concerts each in the Konzerthaus, Leipzigerstraße No. 48, the hall in which Bilse[111] had formerly given his ex-traordinarily popular concerts. Even Richard Wagner had used this hall when he wanted to improve the financial resources of his Bayreuth under-taking through concert performances. The concert hall was built on the spot where formerly there was the "Hall of the Muses," a dance hall of a distinctly plain style and run according to the Parisian practice. The "muses" who fre-quented the place and whose mythological numbers surpassed the hundreds, for the most part enjoyed the fatherly attention of the authorities. The Berliner loves rich-sounding names, especially when they stand in crass con-trast to the nature of their intended purpose. A bar with the most ordinary entertainment, in which the country bumpkin can admire the cancan for a lot of money, is called the Orpheum. Even the music hall in the upper Friedrichstraße was a dance hall of questionable reputation. The Halls of Apollo or Amor are like the Orpheum above. This fine-sounding list could be expanded considerably.

The Konzerthaus now served more noble purposes. My orchestra, in part recruited from the old orchestra of Bilse and in part expanded to seventy-eight members by new appointments, was now well trained through gen-eral rehearsals, followed by section rehearsals for string and wind players separately. Prepared in this way, I was able to inaugurate my series of concerts on October 13. The program of the first evening was the following:

1. Les Préludes
2. The 137th Psalm   Liszt
3. Dante Symphony
4. Elegiac Song
5. Eroica Symphony   Beethoven

Siegfried Ochs had placed his chorus at my disposal. From among the soloists, who supported me by their participation, I mention Sofie Menter, Therese Malten, Heinrich Gudehus, Amalie Joachim, Teresina Tua, and Hermann Ritter (alto viola in the Harold Symphony).[112] The last concert was devoted exclusively to Berlin composers. There I had stirred up a hornet's nest! To my regret I was not able to permit all Berlin composers to be heard in a time span of two hours, and so those whose works were not performed vowed bloody revenge; dagger, bullet, poison—thank goodness I am alive. Only two unfavorable reviews spoke of my mean, unfriendly attitude.

My next goal was a worthy performance of the *Requiem* by Berlioz. The preparations for this demanded a lot of time. First of all the standard choral music in France with three or six voices without alto had to be arranged for four or eight voices, which is commonly used here. By blending the deeper soprano parts with the higher tenor parts of the work a new, fourth voice emerged, which enhanced the choral effect quite significantly. Then it meant that a chorus had to be created ad hoc. I succeeded through continual and unrelenting recruiting to bring together 250 musically trained, female voices. Tenors and basses I took from the cathedral choir, the choral society for teachers, and some other male choruses. The entire chorus totaled about 420 voices. After eight months of conscientious practice I could proceed to action in December. The Philharmonic Orchestra was expanded to 150 musicians, 118 for the main orchestra, the rest for the four side orchestras. The performance took place on December 30 in Philharmonic Hall with Prince Wilhelm and his wife in attendance. The prince, on whose head the imperial crown was placed six months later, said to me after the performance: "If I could maintain order among my hussars in Potsdam, as well as you maintained order among your groups of singers, string-players, and horn-players, I would be satisfied." At the same time His Royal Highness honored me with a handshake that cracked my bones.

The performance came off splendidly and so successfully that a few days later it was repeated in the same place, and on January 27 there was a third performance in the Victoria Theater.

The conservatory that I founded flourished; soon the available rooms were no longer adequate to accommodate the number of students. So I decided to purchase my own building and found a suitable site in Potsdamerstraße No. 31a. The new rooms, to which a lovely, spacious hall belonged, were dedicated on my birthday in 1888 with an impressive celebration, which my brother arranged and for which he had written a prologue; it follows here in reverent memory of my dear departed brother.

> Only a few years ago there was planted
> A tender shoot with the hand of a skilled gardener;
> It was to sprout, to grow strong,
> And to blossom anew for the glory of the noble art.
> With ardent care the planter's eye clung
> Also with hope to the young sprout,
> Which expanded and developed and grew and shot up,
> Cared for with faithful, untiring love.
>
> For a group of guardians had
> Joined the master to form an intimate union,
> They helped loyally and kept good watch
> With clear sharp eyes at every hour,
> They kept safe from danger the noble sprout,
> Protected its tender youth from storms,
> Watered it when it wanted to grow weary,
> And supported it when it swayed in the wind.
>
> And as it struggled to grow ever higher,
> Mightily strengthened in the quickly passing years,
> Then it revealed its noble being
> And its planter's strong and noble stock.
> With every spring it sets new, strong limbs
> And branches from those last sprouted,
> To unfold a crown of leaves
> In full array, it never allows him to rest.
>
> Now he stood there, a proud, strong trunk,
> In the fresh, green leafy garment of spring,
> And through the branches darted happy little birds,
> They warbled their song in every land

And attracted fellow songsters from far and wide
To live here under its roof.
It was buzzing and teaming lively on all limbs,
The cheerful space was almost too confined.

With astonishment at the rapid, wild growth
The master watched, the pain of concern seizes him,
For the further development of his dear one,
For whom the topsoil was long since too thin.
A new garden he must prepare,
Spacious and roomy and fitting as a place,
For the high and luxuriant trunk that sprouted,
And to hold the groups of assorted singers.

So the new garden was prepared,
From the old, small place was removed
The tree with roots, trunk, and crown of leaves,
So that it would have more room to grow.
And strong and powerfully it soars upward and higher,
It shows anew its power to sprout,
Anew it produces its leaves, blossoms, and fruits
For the joy of all and for the glory of the master.

The performance of some of my works by the teachers followed this. Then came the surprise of the evening: congratulatory delegations from the elementary, middle, and upper classes, from the foreign students, publishing companies, and piano factories, from the riding club to which I belonged, and finally the unexpected arrival of the three Magi! (My birthday falls on the Festival of the Magi.)[113] A scenic performance of Schumann's *Carnival*, invented by my brother Philipp, formed the conclusion of the festival. Wilhelm Berger, the subsequent conductor in Meiningen and student of my brother, performed his duty at the piano, and the characters of the carnival passed before our amazed eyes in real impersonation. Among the particularly impressive numbers were the Lettres dansantes, which were represented by five charming female students who were dressed as "sandwich men." They wore the letters of my first name on their chest and back, swirled gracefully around, and then arranged themselves on the concluding beat so that their position produced the name Xaver. Chopin—resembling a portrait—was represented by a young Finn, who walked into the hall with a silent keyboard. My outstanding sister-in-law Marianne played Paganini both as a violinist and as an actress. The Davidsbündler March came at the end, during

which there was a downright—but of course only make-believe—brawl between the Philistines and the Davidsbündler.[114]

It was a magnificently successful festival. A thousand thanks to you beyond the grave, dear brother!

About this time I read Dahn's *The Struggle for Rome*.[115] The episode of
King Witichis and Mataswintha aroused my interest, and I thought I had
found useful opera material. After I had received Dahn's permission, I
sketched out a scenario; it received the warm approval of the author. Then I
arranged with a friend of mine, Dr. Ernst Koppel, who undertook to complete
the text, and soon I was in possession of a finished libretto. The next three
years were devoted mainly to work on the opera.

Soon after the performances of the *Requiem* death knocked on our door.
Our dear little Marischka became a victim of scarlet fever; she died on February 9 at the age of eight. Since also her older sister came down at the same
time with the insidious illness, both children had to be taken to the hospital
in order to avoid the danger of infecting the young students of the conservatory. In this year Germany saw three emperors on the throne: in March Wilhelm I died, and in June Friedrich III.

Even though I was exhausted from working at my desk, I sought relaxation
on the podium; a variety in work is always relaxing. As a passionate early
riser, I was able to indulge moreover my nonmusical inclinations: hunting
and horseback riding. Through my four-legged friend Caesar, I became acquainted in detail with the environs of Berlin. Related to this passion of mine
is a good joke that Moritz Moszkowski told. To the question directed to him
as to why Scharwenka rode so much, he snapped back: "Probably music does
not bring in enough!"[116]

Visit to New York. The First Concert Tour in the United States

The following winter's extended concert tours took me to Southern Germany,
Belgium, Austria, and Hungary. The year 1890 brought about a complete
change in my outward life. That year I received a visit from a young man who
on behalf of Behr Brothers, the recently founded piano factory in New York,
presented me with a piano from their factory as well as an invitation to delight the owners of the firm with a visit as their guest. That intrigued me
tremendously. An ocean voyage! It was a fantastic prospect for this landlub-
ber who, except for the Müggelsee and Wannsee, had only gotten to know the
Great and Little Belt and the English Channel. With pleasure I accepted;

soon thereafter I packed my trunk, insured my life—each finger extra—embraced my mother, wife, children, and whatever else presented itself to say goodbye, and steamed off into the wide blue sea. Oh, how wonderful! For twelve days no letters, for months no piano lesson—indeed during this time I was even able painlessly to do without the tax collector—only a sunny sky, blue sea, limitless horizon, and heavenly rest; it was all too beautiful.

In New York one of the co-owners of the company met me and first escorted me to the hotel, then to his wonderful country estate in Hastings-on-Hudson, across from the so-called "Palisades." There I spent delightful days, and there the plans developed that ultimately led to my temporary move to America. As the first step for this, a concert tour through the United States for the coming winter was undertaken.

Shortly before my trip home I was given a very special honor. At the suggestion and invitation of Anton Seidl,[117] the artistic world of New York gave a reception for me followed by a banquet in the Brighton Beach Hotel. Probably 120 artists and other prominent figures of the city were present. The words of greeting, which Seidl as the master of ceremonies directed to the audience, are repeated here because of their humorous rendering.

Gentlemen!

If I wanted to honor the musician Scharwenka, I would have to give a speech at least an hour long. But that would not at all be necessary, since probably all of you who more or less belong to the "trade" know Mr. Scharwenka as a musician as well as I do. Therefore, I want to confine myself to honoring Scharwenka the man, to be sure an honorable man. A man who comes to America to play the piano out of enjoyment and not to rake in as many dollars as possible, without a doubt must be an honorable, even an extremely honorable fellow. Nevertheless, I hope in the interest of all of us as well as in that of the music-loving public, that in the next years he will cast off this high sense of honor and in addition to the man, he will show us Scharwenka the musician. As long as he is still high minded, however, I raise my glass and drink to the health of Xaver Scharwenka, who for the time being is still an honorable man!

I quote this speech from the New York *Figaro* as well as the following notice that is found a few paragraphs further on: "In the mean time Anton Seidl had invited all those present to his concert in the large concert hall, where the guests found their way en masse. The orchestra greeted Scharwenka at his entrance with a fanfare, which was followed by the tumultuous applause of the audience that filled the hall."

Of the other speeches from the banquet table, I was most interested in that of Mr. Prochazka, the publisher of a music paper. From his speech, spiced with humor, I learned some interesting facts about the fate of a few of my compositions in the United States. The speaker had collected statistical material about the reprints, which my works, in particular my Polish Dance, op. 3, no. 1, had enjoyed. Unfortunately at that time the works of foreign authors were unprotected by copyright. Had this dance been protected, I would have received royalties of ten cents per copy, and as the speaker had determined precisely, it would have amounted to ninety thousand dollars. At that time a fortune! Today a sum of seventy-two million tattered paper mark bills. I felt hot and cold. Among the guests was also Mr. Schirmer, head of the well-known music publishing house. The dear old man invited me the following day to see his large and grand establishment. I gladly accepted the invitation, and with rightful pride Mr. Schirmer took me through all the floors of his very impressive music house. "Here the collections are found," he said, "here the engraving takes place, here the printing, etc." "And on which floor is the reprint shop?" I dared to ask. Had he not heard the question or had he not understood my question? I did not receive an answer; yet the friendly gentleman insisted on inviting me to a splendid lunch at Delmonico's.

Filled with very pleasant impressions and happy hope for the winter campaign in America, I returned home at the end of August.

I used the fall mainly to expand my program and to arrange some scenes of my opera that I thought of performing over there. I returned to America for the second time at the end of December (1890).

My dear old mother had expressed the wish to accompany me, and so on Christmas Day we began the trip on the steamer *Saale*. A magnificent Christmas tree, which seemed to beam the last greeting from home, decorated the evening dinner table. Many a teary eye was seen; also my heart ached—it was just the hour when my wife and children were gathered around the Christmas tree at home and certainly missed their father. Then Captain Richter, who cared for the ship and passengers in a self-sacrificing manner, began to speak. In a simple and heartwarming way, he knew how to cheer up the guests at his table, whose faces were distraught, partly by homesickness and partly as the result of a certain involuntary swaying, and to arouse a true Christmas atmosphere. The stewards brought Pommery champagne, the ship's band played the choral "This Is the Day the Lord Has Made," and soon we were in good spirits—as far as the surly, agitated Neptune, who was always increasingly at odds with dear, convivial Bacchus, allowed.

The trip was extremely stormy; for days the *Saale* worked its way through mountains of waves and snowstorms toward its goal, which it only reached with a three-day delay. Completely covered with ice from the tips of the mast to the waterline, she presented a fantastic sight. Soon after its arrival, the newspapers published pictures of this vessel, which was decked out like in a fairytale.

I took lodging in the Normandy Hotel near the Metropolitan Opera, while my mother was given accommodations with the Behr family. The first days of my stay in New York were taken up mainly with reporters and photographers; also many former students came to greet their former "dear teacher."

It was really heartwarming how the dear young people expressed their affection and their fondness, and not only through word and gesture, no: they brought flowers, fruit, cigars, tobacco, books, candy, and similar symbols of friendly sentiments to my hotel room. One of them even brought me a wonderful leather suitcase, another an alarm clock, and a third one powerful opera glasses—it would not have surprised me if a particular fan had presented me with a dress suit or a pair of boots.

My first concert took place in the Metropolitan Opera House on January 23, 1891, which was repeated the next day at the same place with the same program. It was splendidly prepared and consequently came off very favorably. I played my First Piano Concerto and the Concerto in E-flat Major by Beethoven and in between some solo pieces. In addition two scenes of my *Mataswintha* were performed with Antonie Mielke in the title role and Heinrich Gudehus as Witichis; the orchestra and chorus of the Metropolitan Opera were under the memorable direction of Anton Seidl. Then at an almost uninterrupted fast pace, my extensive, well-prepared concert tour of the United States followed. The tours, especially the train trips, always gave me pleasure and relaxation. In the so-called state room, a separate room on the train acquired for a modest surcharge, one can find all that is required for a journey of several days: armchairs, sofa (both could be made into beds), table, chair, and—last but not least—one's own bathroom with warm water and all imaginable amenities for the nourishment and needs of the body. I always had my handy typewriter with me, and so I could take care of correspondence in peace during the trip. A dining car with an exceptionally plentiful menu, as well as an observation car with a library and other "spirituous" beverages at the end of the train, provided ample diversion. My manager, Mr. John Lavine, a model for his difficult, responsible profession, looked after my physical well-being with touching devotion and took care of the concert business in an exemplary manner.

From New York my route led first to Washington, D.C., where I gave two recitals. There I found an invitation to the White House from President Harrison, with whose family I spent a very stimulating evening—without music! Only on the following day, when I was making my farewell visit, did Mrs.

Harrison ask me to play something for her and her grandchildren, which I did gladly. After I had counted off the eastern states, my itinerary took me to Chicago, where I played my two piano concertos under Theodor Thomas and gave some recitals.

Among the places worth seeing in this huge city, Armour's impressive plant made a big impression on me. There daily about one thousand well-fed steers, three thousand plump pigs, and about two thousand fattened sheep end their earthly existence. The victims for slaughter are driven up an inclined surface right from the train cars to the top floor of the six- to seven-story large building. Having arrived here, they are killed and cut up, and the individual parts, depending on their use, are moved through doors in the floor to the lower floors, from where as a finished product they are guided to their next destination. In a large adjoining building, whose rooms are kept at a freezing temperature, there is a long series of streets in which, in place of houses, animal carcasses cut in half hang—arranged according to age. For the next days I became a confirmed vegetarian!

My next destination was St. Paul, Minnesota. On the trip there I came down with the flu, which held me in its clutches for fourteen days. When immediately after my arrival the news of my illness became known in the city, Mr. Severance, one of the prominent people of St. Paul, had his family doctor inquire whether I would like to exchange my dreary hotel room for one of the comfortably furnished rooms of his villa on Summit Avenue. On my only too-willing acceptance, a heated ambulance drove up, which took me under doctor's care to my kind, unknown host. There I found true humanity, and the extremely favorable impression that I had gotten up to then of the Americans intensified to genuine admiration through the many signs of kindness and affection, which I received amply there and elsewhere.

My condition was worse than I suspected; for two nights the physician stayed in the house, and when I sat down at the keyboard for the first time, I had difficulty orienting myself; I felt like a beginning student, and it took a rather long time until I could venture forth in public.

After a side trip to Duluth on Lake Superior, my itinerary took me to Omaha. There my former student Mr. Jones, director of the conservatory, awaited me. With well-deserved pride he led me through the rooms of the institute, which had a very comfortable appearance. The view from one of the rooms situated toward a side street was not so pleasant. There my astonished eyes saw the body of a Negro, lynched a few hours earlier, swinging from a pole—an unaccustomed sight for someone from Central Europe. Other countries, other customs. However, the "colored" gentleman was immoral; he had assaulted a noncolored woman probably as the result of sudden color blindness, and so "poor Jonny" had to atone for his crime in the uncomfortable position, which even a properly built gallows would not have made more bearable.

My friend showed me more sights, and he escorted me to an Indian camp a few kilometers out of the city, where the attempt was being made to train the "Redskins" as soldiers. The commandant of the company had the copper-colored soldiers perform some drills; they performed so miserably and comically that I could scarcely resist laughing. The government soon realized that Indians were not suitable for training, and so the sons of the prairie, after unsuccessfully completing their year of military service, moved back to their native hunting grounds, where like their ancestors they could swing their tomahawks and blow the smoke of their pipe to the great spirit.

I also moved homeward, however, first to New York for the time being. My decision was firm; I wanted to move to America. The necessary preparations for this and negotiations were soon taken care of by the Behr Company, and I returned to Berlin in April, while my mother remained in New York.

Notes

1. The square piano or *Tafelklavier* was common in the eighteenth and nineteenth centuries in Germany. The strings were arranged parallel to the keyboard.

2. Theodor Kullak (1818–1882), Polish-born pianist, composer, and teacher, studied under Czerny in Vienna and in 1846 was appointed pianist to the Prussian court in Berlin. There he founded the Tonkünstler Verein in 1844, the Berlin Musikschule with Stern and Marx, and in 1851 the Neue Akademie der Tonkunst, often referred to as Kullak's Institute. By 1880 this conservatory was the largest private music school in Germany, with one hundred teachers and eleven hundred students.

3. Richard Wüerst (1824–1881), German music teacher, composer, and court conductor in Berlin, taught composition at Kullak's conservatory.

4. Berlin was often referred to as the "Metropolis or Capital of the German Intelligentsia" and as "Spree-Athen" or the "Athens on the Spree River."

5. Ebenezer is the name the Old Testament prophet Samuel gave the stone, which he set up at Shen to commemorate the victory over the Philistines (1 Sam. 7:12).

6. Adolf Menzel (1815–1905) was a German realist artist, known for his historical paintings, drawings, and wood engravings.

7. Heinrich Dorn (1804–1892), German composer and conductor, studied music in Königsberg and Berlin and coedited the *Berliner Allgemeine Musikzeitung*. While he was conductor of the Leipzig Opera, Schumann studied counterpoint with him. At the urging of Liszt, Dorn conducted *Tannhäuser* at the Royal Opera in Berlin in 1855; this was the first opera by Wagner to be performed in the city.

8. It is unclear why Dorn was called "old Grimmbart," a mythological troll or gnome.

9. Julius Stern (1820–1883), born in Breslau, founded the Sternscher Gesangverein in Berlin and served as its conductor from 1846 to 1874. Together with Kullak and Marx, he founded the Berlin Musikschule in 1850. It became known as the Stern Conservatory in 1857 after the other founders left.

10. Carl Tausig (1841–1871), Polish virtuoso pianist and composer, was a favorite student of Liszt and a close friend of Richard Wagner, for whom he developed plans to raise funds for the Bayreuth Theater.

11. Anton Rubinstein (1829–1894), a Russian composer, educator, and piano virtuoso known for his perfect technique, founded and directed the St. Petersburg Conservatory.

12. Hans von Bülow (1830–1894), piano virtuoso, conductor, composer, and critic, was one of the most important musical figures of the nineteenth century. He completed his piano training under Liszt, and in 1857 he married Liszt's daughter Cosima. He worked closely with Richard Wagner and conducted the premier performances of *Tristan und Isolde* (1865) and *Die Meistersinger von Nürnberg* (1868). This close collaboration with Wagner ceased, however, when his wife left him for Wagner; and although he continued to interpret Wagner's music, he became a strong supporter of Brahms. He developed the Meiningen Orchestra into a model orchestra, whose precision playing resulted in a totally new sound experience. He also served as conductor of the Hamburg and Berlin orchestras and was renowned for his extraordinary memory that allowed him to learn quickly entire orchestral and piano scores by heart.

13. Karl Moor is one of the main protagonists in Friedrich von Schiller's first drama *Die Räuber* (1781) from the period of German literature known as Storm and Stress (1770–1784). His famous last words as he leaves the stage are: "dem Mann kann geholfen werden" (that man can be helped).

14. A gold coin issued by Frederick the Great in 1741.

15. Carl Reinecke (1824–1910), pianist, composer, and conductor, served as court pianist in Denmark and taught at the conservatory in Cologne before moving to Leipzig to teach at the conservatory and to conduct the Gewandhaus Orchestra.

16. Johann Wolfgang von Goethe, who studied in Leipzig, called the city "little Paris" in his tragedy *Faust.*

17. The Gewandhaus, a former guildhall in Leipzig, was made famous by the concerts conducted there by Felix Mendelssohn. The orchestra, begun in 1743, eventually was called the Leipzig Gewandhaus-Konzerte.

18. Robert Franz (1815–1892), a gifted songwriter, was born in Halle, where he became city organist and conductor of the Singakademie and orchestra. His first book of songs was well received by Liszt and Schumann. During his lifetime he published over 250 songs.

19. Scharwenka describes here how he pulls his compositions from his travel bag to present them to Breitkopf & Härtel in the poetic language taken from the fourth line, first stanza, of Friedrich von Schiller's (1759–1805) ballade "Die Bürgschaft" (1799). In this ballade, which Franz Schubert set to music in 1815, Damon is caught

with a dagger concealed under his clothing by the guard of Dionysius, the tyrant of Syracuse.

20. Bote & Bock was a well-known music publishing firm in Berlin founded in 1838 by Eduard Bote and Gustav Bock.

21. Moritz Moszkowski (1854–1925), pianist and conductor born in Breslau, studied in Berlin at the Stern Conservatory and at Kullak's Neue Akademie der Tonkunst, where he then taught piano for over twenty-five years. In 1897 he moved to Paris and turned to composing. He became wealthy as a result of his popular piano music, but he suffered financial ruin through bad investments after World War I and died in poverty.

22. During the eighteenth century, Weimar was often referred to as "Ilm-Athen," that is, the "Athens on the Ilm River." This was especially true after Goethe took up residence there.

23. Liszt returned to Weimar in 1869 and took up residence in the small, two-storied Hofgärtnerei on the edge of the ducal gardens.

24. According to the Treaty of Frankfurt that concluded the Franco-Prussian War (1870–1871), France agreed to pay Germany reparations of one billion dollars over three years and ceded Alsace and a large part of Lorraine.

25. A central district of Berlin.

26. Scharwenka describes here the "Gründerjahre," the years of economic boom and financial speculation in Germany (1874–1914) that followed the defeat of France in the Franco-Prussian War and that promoted the rapid industrialization of Germany.

27. Heinrich de Ahna (1835–1892), Austrian violinist and violist, was a member of the Joachim Quartet (1869–1892).

28. Josef Joachim (1831–1907), born in Hungary and one of the most influential violinists of his time, was a friend of Mendelssohn, Brahms, and Schumann. He served as concertmaster under Liszt in Weimar and in 1869 founded the Joachim Quartet in Berlin.

29. Scharwenka makes a pun on the German word *Kater*, which means both tomcat and hangover.

30. Louis Köhler (1820–1886) published his two-volume work, *Systematische Lehrmethode für das Klavierspiel*, in 1858. He spent most of his life in Königsberg, where he conducted the Sangverein and was the director of a music school.

31. Duysen pianos were built in Berlin starting in 1857 by Deutsche Piano-Werke and after 1928 in Braunschweig, Germany.

32. Scharwenka playfully uses "Durch die Felder, durch die Auen," the title of an aria in the opera *Der Freischütz* by Carl Maria von Weber (1786-1826).

33. Otto von Bismarck (1815–1898), first chancellor of the German Empire from 1871 to 1890, was known as the Iron Chancellor. His son Herbert wanted to marry Princess Elisabeth of Carolath, but Bismarck opposed the marriage because the princess was a divorced Catholic and ten years older than his son.

34. Alexander Moszkowski (1851–1934), founder of the satirical *Lustige Blätter* in Berlin and brother of the pianist and composer Moritz Moszkowski (1854–1925),

based his parody *Anton Notenquetscher am Klavier* on a scene of a piano student from Goethe's *Faust*. Scharwenka's brother Philipp drew the humorous illustration for the work. Alexander Moszkowski composed variations on a theme in the style of famous composers from J. S. Bach, Czerny, and Clementi to Liszt.

35. Friedrich von Schiller (1759–1805) wrote the poem "Das Lied von der Glocke" in 1797.

36. Line from the ballad "Der Ring des Polykrates" (1797) by Friedrich von Schiller.

37. Adelina Patti (1843–1919) was born in Madrid but raised in New York City, where she made her operatic debut at the age of sixteen. She soon acquired an international reputation for her vocal range and clarity and became one of the most famous operatic singers of her time as well as one of the most highly paid in history. She became associated with the song "Home Sweet Home," which she sang at the White House in 1862 for President and Mrs. Lincoln, who were mourning the death of their son Willie. She lived most of her life on her estate in South Wales. She was asked to sing for most European heads of state, including Queen Victoria, for whom she performed for over twenty-five years. One of her most famous singing roles was that of Violetta Valerie, the heroine in *La Traviata*.

38. Ernesto Camillo Sivori (1815–1895), Italian virtuoso violinist and composer, was Paganini's only student and was renowned for his pyrotechnic playing.

39. The Carl Stangen Travel Agency in Berlin, the oldest German chain of travel agencies, was founded in Breslau in 1863 and was purchased by Hapag-Lloyd in 1905.

40. Pablo de Sarasate (1844–1908) was a well-known Spanish virtuoso violinist and composer, who concertized all over Europe and North and South America. Best known of his compositions are the Zigeunerweisen op. 20 and his four books of Spanische Tänze (21, 22, 23, 26).

41. Rügen is the largest German island in the Baltic off the coast of Mecklenburg-Vorpommern.

42. "Playing in the Waves" (1883), an oil painting by the Swiss artist Arnold Böcklin (1827–1901), shows mythological figures swimming with humans. Böcklin spent most of his life in Italy and together with Feuerbach belonged to the group of artists called the "German Romans," who tried to incorporate idealist philosophy in their art.

43. Ludwig Barnay (1842–1924), born in Budapest, became famous on the German stage for his good looks and sonorous voice. He directed theaters in Berlin and Hannover, was cofounder and director of the Berlin Theater, and founded the Association of German Actors in 1870.

44. George Henschel (1850–1934), born in Breslau, developed a successful musical career as singer and conductor in England, where he became a citizen and was knighted in 1914. In 1881 he became the first conductor of the Boston Symphony, and in 1886 he began the London Symphony Concerts.

45. "Auf geheimem Waldespfade" ("On a lonely forest path"), a poem by Nikolaus Lenau (1802–1850), was set to music by Robert Franz, Hans Erich Pfitzner, Henri Marteau, Charles Tomlinson Griffes, Othmar Schoeck, and Alban Berg.

46. Krampas is a resort on Rügen near Sassnitz.

47. Scharwenka may be making a wordplay here on *Brahms* and *brahma,* a breed of large Asian rooster. Brahms is a real "rooster" when he wakes him with the statement "that the rooster has crowed for the third time"; that is, it is three o'clock.

48. Richard Wagner (1813–1883) completed *The Ring of the Nibelung* or the Ring Cycle in 1869. *Siegfried* is the third of four operas in the cycle.

49. Austrian alpine region.

50. An Italian cheer, equivalent to the English "Long live the princess."

51. Count Helmuth von Moltke (1800–1891) was a Prussian field marshal, whose brilliant strategies led to Prussia's victory over France in the Franco-Prussian War (1870–1871).

52. An ornate style of furniture designed by French cabinetmaker André Charles Boulle (1642–1732).

53. Councillor of commerce, a title conferred on a distinguished businessman.

54. Wiatka or Vyatka, capital of the Kirov oblast, is located eight hundred kilometers east of Moscow on the Vyatka River and was renamed Kirov in 1780.

55. The Germans referred to Dresden as their "Florence on the Elbe."

56. The legend of the Pied Piper of Hamelin, who rid the town of Hamelin, Germany, of its rats in 1284, was used by Goethe, the Grimm brothers, and Robert Browning.

57. Although not identified by first name, this undoubtedly was Franz Fischer (1849–1918), the cellist and court conductor in Munich, who also conducted Wagner's *Parzifal* in Bayreuth.

58. Heinrich Grünfeld (1855–1931), a cellist born in Prague and brother of pianist Alfred Grünfeld (1852–1924), taught the cello at Scharwenka's conservatory in Berlin for eight years. In 1866 he was appointed court cellist to Emperor William I of Prussia.

59. Hermann Ritter (1849–1926) studied at the Neue Akademie der Tonkunst in Berlin. While studying music, art history, and philosophy in Heidelberg, he became interested in the development of the viola and commissioned what he called a "viola alta" from Karl Adam Hoerlein, a violin builder in Würzburg. The five-stringed viola alta became known as the "Ritter viola" and was greatly admired by Wagner, who had six Ritter violas in his orchestra.

60. The glass and iron Crystal Palace was built in Hyde Park in 1851 to house the Great Exhibition, which was to show Great Britain as the leader in the industrial revolution. At the end of the exhibit, the building was moved to Sydenham Hill in South London, where in 1936 it was destroyed by fire.

61. Edward Dannreuther (1844–1905), pianist, writer, and teacher, was born in Strasbourg but grew up in Cincinnati, where his family established a piano factory. He eventually settled in London, where he taught at the Royal College of Music and in 1872 founded the London Wagner Society.

62. Liszt was made an abbé, a member of the French secular clergy, in Rome in 1865.

63. The grand ducal Order of Sachsen-Weimar, like the Legion of Honor, is worn on a red ribbon.

64. Norderney is the largest of the East Frisian Islands off the North Sea coast of Germany.

65. Franz Wilhelm Abt (1819–1885), German conductor and composer, studied music in Leipzig and developed an international reputation in choral conducting. He conducted all over Europe and in 1872 was invited to conduct in the United States. Vocal music remained his lifelong interest, and he wrote more than three thousand pieces of music.

66. Scharwenka makes a play on words in German by saying that the child had "Hand und Fuß," which means literally it has "hands and feet," but figuratively that it is well done or made.

67. August Manns (1825–1907), born in Stolzenberg, Germany, conducted at the Crystal Palace in London for forty-two years. During his tenure, he conducted over twelve thousand concerts, and his Saturday afternoon concerts became a popular and affordable source of classical music. He became a naturalized British citizen in 1894 and was knighted in 1903.

68. The Gürzenich Orchestra of Cologne takes it name from the historic festival hall built in Cologne on the Gürzenich family property from 1441 to 1447. The Gürzenich Orchestra began performing concerts in the hall in 1857 and premiered works by Brahms, Mahler, and Richard Strauss.

69. Ferdinand Hiller (1811–1885), German pianist and composer, was a pupil of Hummel in Weimar and as a child played in Goethe's home. In 1843–1844 he replaced Mendelssohn as conductor of the Gewandhaus Orchestra. From 1850 until his retirement in 1884, he conducted the Gürzenich concerts and reorganized the music school in Cologne.

70. A pun on "Gürzenich" and "Kürzenich," meaning "unabridged, not shortened."

71. John Ella (1802–1888), an English violinist, critic, and concert manager, founded the Musical Union (1845) to promote high-quality chamber music performances. He pioneered extensive program notes with musical examples and recommended the reading of miniature scores during concerts.

72. Gustav Holländer (1855–1915), violinist, composer, and teacher, studied violin with Joachim. After the directing the Gürzenich Orchestra and teaching at the conservatory in Cologne, he returned to Berlin and became head of the violin faculty at Kullak's Neue Akademie der Tonkunst. He served as director of the Stern Conservatory in Berlin from 1885 until his death.

73. Emile Sauret (1852–1920), French violinist and composer, concertized in the United States between 1874 and 1906. He taught at the Neue Akademie der Tonkunst in Berlin and in 1890 became a professor at the Musical College in London. In 1903 he left to teach at the Musical College in Chicago, but returned to Europe in 1906. In 1908 he returned to London, where he was appointed a professor at Trinity College of Music.

74. Reference to the "Siegessäule," the column in Berlin commemorating Germany's victory over France in the Franco-Prussian War of 1870–1871.

75. Hans Richter (1843–1916) was born in Hungary, studied at the Vienna Conservatory, and began his conducting career in Austria. In 1876 he was selected to conduct the first complete performance of Wagner's *Der Ring des Nibelungen* in Bayreuth. After assisting Wagner with a series of concerts in London, Richter remained in London to direct the Hallé Orchestra (1899–1911) and the London Symphony Orchestra (1904–1911) until failing eyesight forced him to retire.

76. Josef Hellmesberger (1828–1893), Austrian violinist and conductor, was violin professor and director of the Vienna Conservatory and conducted the Gesellschaft der Musikfreunde in Vienna from 1851 to 1859. In 1849 he founded the Hellmesberger String Quartet, which for many years was regarded as the leading string quartet in Vienna.

77. Eduard Hanslick (1825–1904) was one of the most influential Viennese music critics of the nineteenth century. He studied music with Tomasek and then received a law degree from the University of Prague. He was the music critic at the *Neue freie Presse* until his retirement and held a position at the Austrian Ministry of Culture. He championed the music of his close friend Brahms but rejected the music of Wagner, which led to the "War of the Romantics" in the nineteenth century.

78. (Karl) Eduard Schelle (1814–1882) was a critic and music researcher in Vienna.

79. Ofen, the German for Buda on the right bank of the Danube, was combined in 1873 with Pest on the left bank to form Budapest.

80. William Cusins (1833–1893), English pianist, organist, conductor, and composer, studied under François Joseph Fétis. He edited the piano works of Robert Schumann and was knighted in 1892.

81. Mozart's "Der Schauspieldirektor" ("The Impresario"), based on a libretto by Gottlieb Stephanie (1741–1800), is a "Singspiel" or German comic opera that intersperses spoken dialogue with arias. The one-act comedy is a satire of the difficulties faced by an impresario when casting an opera with two vying prima donnas and was premiered before Emperor Joseph II in Schönbrun in 1786.

82. Lawrence Alma-Tadema (1836–1912), born in Friesland, settled in England and achieved great success as a classical painter of scenes from antiquity. In 1876 he became an English citizen and was knighted in 1899 on the occasion of Queen Victoria's eighty-first birthday.

83. Charles Villiers Stanford (1852–1914), English composer and teacher, studied with Carl Reinecke in Leipzig and was organist at Trinity College, Cambridge (1873–1892). He was knighted in 1901.

84. Zeus visited Danae, a princess of Argos, in the form of a shower of gold.

85. Maecenas, a Roman statesman (8 BC), was a generous patron of literature.

86. Although Scharwenka does not name Bösendorfer by first name, he is undoubtedly referring to Ludwig Bösendorfer (1835–1919), the son of Ignaz Bösendorfer, the founder of the Austrian piano company. When Ludwig Bösendorfer took over

from his father, he expanded the business but strongly resisted the piano construction innovations introduced by Steinway and Chickering between 1860 and 1890.

87. Daniel Spitzer (1835–1893) was a well-known Viennese satirist and feature writer; a collection of his humorous articles was published in a book with the title *Wiener Spaziergänger*.

88. Eduard Strauss (1835–1916), a successful Austrian composer and conductor, was a younger brother of Johann Strauss (1825–1899), who composed over four hundred waltzes.

89. The local choral society.

90. Victor Herbert (1859–1924), Irish-American cellist, composer, and conductor, was born in Dublin and studied at the Stuttgart Conservatory. He and his wife immigrated to the United States in 1886, when the Metropolitan Opera Company hired him as first cellist and his wife to sing the soprano role in the American premier of Verdi's *Aida*. After conducting the Pittsburgh Symphony Orchestra from 1894 to 1904, he turned to composing.

91. Arthur Nikisch (1855–1922), Hungarian conductor and violinist, played in Wagner's orchestra at the dedication of the Festspielhaus in Bayreuth. He was appointed conductor of the Boston Symphony in 1889 and then held positions at the Budapest Opera, the Leipzig Gewandhaus, and the Berlin Philharmonic.

92. The reference here is to the simple waltz for piano known as "Chopsticks," written by the sixteen-year-old British girl Euphemia Allen under the pseudonym Arthur de Lulli and published in London and Glasgow in 1877 under the title "The Celebrated Chopsticks Waltz Arranged as a Duet and Solo for the Pianoforte." In 1879 Borodin, Rimski-Korsakov, Cesar Cui, and Anatoli Liadov published their variations titled "Paraphrases on the Cutlet Polka" ("Koteletten Polka"), written originally for Borodin's daughter Gania. The second edition of "Paraphrases" in 1880 included variations on "Chopsticks" by Liszt.

93. King Gambrinus was the reputed inventor of beer.

94. The *Kladderadatsch*, a political-satirical weekly, was published in Berlin by Albert Hoffmann and David Kalisch from 1848 to 1944. Since 1970, it has been published in Bonn.

95. Philipp Rüfer (1844–1919), pianist and composer, studied at the Liége Conservatoire and became music director in Essen (1869–1871). In 1871 he went to Berlin to teach at the Stern Conservatory, then taught at the Kullak Conservatory from 1872 to 1875, and then returned to the Stern Conservatory.

96. Eugon F. C. d'Albert (1864–1932), a Scottish-born pianist and composer, was a student of Liszt and spent most of his life in Germany.

97. Jean (Johannes) Verhulst (1816–1891), a Dutch composer and conductor, studied in Leipzig and became a close friend of Schumann. On his return to the Netherlands, he was appointed court conductor and directed numerous orchestras, including the Felix Meritis, and became a major influence in the musical life of his country.

98. The Felix Meritis, in Amsterdam at Keizersgracht 324, is the oldest concert hall in the Netherlands.

99. Friedrich Gernsheim (1839–1916), a German pianist, composer, and conductor, studied piano with Moscheles in Leipzig. He taught at the Cologne Conservatory, conducted in Rotterdam, and then accepted a teaching position at the Stern Conservatory in Berlin.

100. The Collège Eruditio Musica was founded in 1792 by Johann Wilhelm Wilms (1772–1847) and five other musicians as a self-governing orchestra in Amsterdam and achieved considerable success.

101. Triebschen is the villa on Lake Lucerne belonging to King Ludwig II of Bavaria, where Wagner lived when he was forced to leave Munich in 1865.

102. Adolf Kussmaul (1822–1902) was a well-known German internist, who studied medicine in Heidelberg and Vienna and received his doctorate in Würzburg. He taught medicine in Heidelberg, Erlangen, Freiburg, and Strassburg. His name is still associated with certain medical diagnoses or tests, for example Kussmaul aphasia, Kussmaul coma, Kussmaul respiration, and others.

103. Tarasp is a resort with thermal baths in the Engadine Valley of the Swiss Canton Graubünden.

104. This is an ironic reference to Christoph Willibald von Gluck (1714–1787), German composer of operas during the Classical period, who was knighted by Pope Benedict XIV in 1756 and awarded the Order of the Golden Spur. Thereafter, Gluck used the title "Ritter von Gluck" (Sir von Gluck) or "Chevalier de Gluck."

105. Scharwenka uses Christiania, the older name for Oslo.

106. Franz Wüllner (1832–1902), composer and conductor born in Münster, held conducting positions in Munich, Dresden, Berlin, and Cologne, where he was associated with the Gürzenich Orchestra and spent the last twenty years of his life. He directed the premier performances of Wagner's operas *Das Rheingold* and *Die Walküre*.

107. The opera *Helianthus* (1884) was composed by Adalbert von Goldschmidt (1848–1906), a Viennese banker, who changed careers to write music and poetry. His music dramas were heavily influenced by Wagner.

108. The Gatschina, the summer residence of the czar, is located about forty kilometers outside St. Petersburg.

109. Nicholas Rubinstein (1835–1881), brother of Anton, was also a brilliant pianist and music teacher. He founded the Moscow Conservatory in 1864 and was its director until his death.

110. Felix Mottl (1856–1914), an Austrian conductor, became known for his performances of the operas of Wagner and Berlioz in Karlsruhe and Munich. In 1903–1904 he conducted at the Metropolitan Opera in New York.

111. Benjamin Bilse (1816–1902), musician, composer, and conductor, formed a successful orchestra in his home town of Liegnitz, Silesia, which in 1865 became known as the Bilsesche Kapelle and gave a series of popular concerts in Berlin. In a dispute with Bilse in 1882, fifty-four musicians left the orchestra and with the help of concert agent Hermann Wolff founded the Berlin Philharmonic Orchestra. According to Scharwenka, their concert hall in the Leipzigerstraße was a former dance hall, but other sources indicate it had been an ice-skating rink.

112. The "Harold Symphony" refers to Berlioz's symphony *Harold in Italy* (1834), which features orchestral scenes for solo viola.

113. January 6 or Epiphany commemorates the arrival of the three wise men from the East to pay homage to the infant Jesus.

114. The Davidsbündler or League of David, named after the biblical King David who played music and slew the Philistines, were characters created by Robert Schumann who appeared in his journal *Neue Zeitschrift für Musik* and defended the tradition of classical music composition. These characters also appear in Schumann's *Carnival*, especially in its concluding March of the Davidsbündler against the Philistines.

115. Felix Dahn's (1834–1912) novel *Der Kampf um Rom* (1878) portrays the invasion of Rome by the Goths in the sixth century. It became one of the most popular German novels of the nineteenth century.

116. This is a wordplay on the German verb *abwerfen*, which means literally to be thrown from a horse or means figuratively to yield enough income.

117. Anton Seidl (1850–1898) was born in Budapest and studied at the Leipzig Conservatory. Hired by Wagner, he helped prepare the first fair copy of *The Ring of the Nibelung* and participated in the first Bayreuth Festival in 1876, and on Wagner's recommendation he became the conductor of the Leipzig Stadt-Theater. In 1885 he succeeded Leopold Damrosch (1832–1885) as the conductor of the German Opera in New York, and in 1891 he became the conductor of the New York Philharmonic, a post he held until his death.

CHAPTER FOUR

~

New York, 1891–1898

Preparations for the Move. Mexico (Missouri), Cincinnati, Chicago, and the Phony Namesake. Death of My Mother

The summer was completely filled with work that accompanies a move. I sold my house and settled the business of the conservatory, whose management Dr. Langhans took over. My family was only to follow me in the space of a year. My brother Philipp gladly agreed to my suggestion to go with me to New York for a few years and to teach the music theory classes at the conservatory to be founded there and which to some extent was thought of as a branch of the Berlin institute. Also Paul Oehlschläger and Fräulein Hella Seydell, two experienced instructors, joined us.

Not long before our departure an inquiry came from Anton Rubinstein whether I would be willing to move to St. Petersburg to take over the administration there of the Conservatory of the Imperial Russian Music Society, founded by him. The position, as I knew from experience, was a very respected and pleasant one and not weighed down at all by too much work. I had to decline, because I was committed to America. However, I would not have pursued the offer in any case, because the director's salary was so low that it would only have been enough for cigarettes and postage stamps. However, the possibilities, besides also earning one's daily bread, were very great, as I learned from a reliable source.

I had hired Mr. Emil Gramm as the business manager of the New York Institute, who, together with the Behr Company and with the effective assistance of the tireless, loyal John Lavine, had prepared everything most satisfactorily; and so the conservatory was able to open at the beginning of October in the splendid rooms of a building fixed up for this purpose at 81 Fifth Avenue. In the meantime I had rented a spacious house with a large garden in Brooklyn, which I had comfortably furnished for my family, who was expected within a year's time.

The year passed with strenuous teaching and concert activity. The institute flourished, and even though the separation from my wife and children and the longing for my dear homeland cast many a dreary shadow over the bright present time, I felt satisfied and fortunate, especially since I had resolved to spend the four summer months in Germany every year.

In June 1892 I returned with my brother to Berlin; he could not get used to the American "air" and asked me to relieve him from his position. At the same time he expressed the desire to take over the management of the Berlin conservatory, to which I agreed. In September I began the trip to New York with my family. I had reservations on the *Normannia*, which sailed from Hamburg. On the day of our departure from Berlin, I was warned by friends about going via Hamburg, since individual cases of cholera had been reported from there. Unfortunately I did not heed the advice, which I was to regret bitterly, because the rumor was confirmed—Hamburg was completely infected, and we tried of course to leave as quickly as possible. Two days after our departure on the *Normannia* cholera broke out, to which some passengers fell victim; the bodies were buried at sea during the night without singing or bands. Our ship was quarantined for fourteen days in the outer harbor of New York, during which time the most terrible scenes took place on board.

Finally we were permitted to land. The trip of the *Normannia* had caused an enormous sensation in New York, and the welcome at the pier developed into a heartrending ceremony for the unfortunate people who had died. A very special honor was bestowed on me. Conductor Nathan Franko[1] and his orchestra, who had waited for hours for the arrival of the ship, welcomed me with a greeting that I could hear from onboard. The program consisted of several of my own compositions.

Totally exhausted we arrived at our home, where we were greeted most cordially by neighbors, whose names we did not even know. Half of Henry Street gathered around us, and all—among them prominent people of the city—offered us their help. Again, true humanity! It was heartening.

Shouting with joy, the children ran through the house and into the garden, whose fruit trees they stripped with expertise. After they had recovered somewhat from the enormous strains of the journey, they were enrolled in school, soon found pleasant playmates, and after a short time felt completely at home. Also our old German servant and his wife, who worked as our cook, became accustomed to the new circumstances; only they had difficulties with the English language, and it took quite a while before *Broadwei* became *Broadway, Huse* became *house*, and *Me-at* became *meat*.

The following summer (1893) I spent in Germany again, mostly in the company of my brother. We visited Switzerland and the Tyrol; later I went to Ruxmühle, thoroughly enjoying the solitary beauty and heavenly peace of the Polish forests. That did me a lot of good after all the trouble of the last years.

Soon after the start of the winter semester in New York, my manager introduced me to Mr. Yancey, the president of Hardin College, in Mexico, Missouri, a well-accredited school in the western part of the Union.[2] A music conservatory was connected with this college, which accepted only female students and whose curriculum included all scholarly subjects. Mr. Yancey asked me to serve as the judge at their public performing contest, taking place soon.

These performances formed the high point of the season for this small town; they took place in the Grand Opera House and for weeks became the exclusive talk of the town. The winner received a thousand-dollar piano! On one of my trips to the West I performed my duties. If you have never attended such an affair, you cannot imagine the course of events and the storm of feverish excitement the awaited results unleash. When the name of the female winner was announced after the performances, there were such ear-deafening, blood-curdling screams and yelling, such frantic shouts of joy from a thousand voices, that the walls threatened to burst. Rising to a boiling point, this anticipation and excitement looked for and found an outlet; the relatives and friends of the winner stormed over benches and chairs onto the stage, embraced, kissed, and congratulated the speechless lucky one so energetically that the tormented victim finally fainted on the piano bench. Fortunately, one of the teachers, who was considered a strict teetotaler, had on him a flask with a liquid that strengthens the nerves, the sale of which had been strictly forbidden in the United States for some time, and soon the heavily tested but successful contestant opened her beautiful eyes.

Before my departure Mr. Yancey expressed the wish to keep me at the college on a longer basis, that is, for four weeks every year I should teach and supervise at the conservatory. I liked the idea, especially since my planned stay there was scheduled for the spring. During the rest of the year Mr. Oehlschläger was to function as my substitute. Since the financial questions had been resolved very generously, I accepted the position gladly with the respectful title of General Director. The wonderful weeks that I spent in this small town, situated about one hundred kilometers west of St. Louis, were restful and socially very stimulating.

I won enthusiastic admirers of my art among the blacks, who are great fans of music as is well known. During the evening hours a sizable group of our black brothers gathered regularly in front of the windows of my hotel room on the ground floor, from which I offered the enchanted listeners a small musical treat. Partly because they had great difficulty pronouncing my name and partly probably out of loving gratitude for the enjoyment that I provided, they called me "our professor." One such seasoned pipe smoker confided to my wife, who accompanied me once, that "our professor" could walk the most deserted, isolated streets of the city in the dead of night, and nothing bad would happen to him. I took real pleasure in my black music fans.

One of the noteworthy "podium incidents" of 1893 was a performance that my former student Benjamin Guckenberger[3] in Cincinnati had prepared artistically and laudably in honor of his "dear old teacher." With the choral society Orpheus under his direction, he performed a series of my works, among them scenes and choruses from my opera *Mataswintha*. The festival was introduced by an orchestral serenade, which prominent Germans of the city had performed in front of my hotel. The orchestra was followed by members of Orpheus and a large crowd of people. It was very festive; the president of the society gave a speech, to which I gave a moving response. A solemn social function followed the final concert, at which Heinrich A. Rattermann, the highly deserving poet of German culture and language in Ohio, presided.[4] Cordial greetings and belated warmest thanks, dear Benjamin.

In the course of the year, to my great regret, I had to sever my connection to the Behr Brothers. Their concert grand pianos were so sharply attacked by the press that the well-meaning directors of the company suggested that I look around for a different means of expressing my piano soul. After I had played a Knabe piano for a while, I came to an agreement with William Steinway. Then I had what I needed. In their establishment on Fourteenth Street (Steinway Hall), the company set up a splendid studio for me, as a result of which I moved the rooms of the conservatory to the upper city (Sixty-eighth Street) and consequently had two sites for teaching, located far from each other. Meanwhile I had also moved my home to Manhattan, because the commute between Brooklyn and my place of work in time became too complicated and time consuming.

During my first concert tours in the United States, I learned that the public and some of the Western press questioned my identity. A pianist using my name had given concerts for quite a while before I appeared in America. It came out by chance that an individual by the name of Ernst Hoffmann had carried out this shameless deception. After the discovery of this unprecedented impertinence, the newspapers published a picture of the wrongdoer with the following advice:

The False Scharwenka
Old acquaintances of Ernst Hoffmann (a piano teacher, former conductor of music clubs, and dowry speculator, who perpetrated his various arts under the musically rich-sounding name of Scharwenka and who also under this name married a Miss Gutmann, whom he abandoned after two days without paying for the chuppah and the rabbi) assume that windy Ernst took off for the windy city of Chicago. Perhaps the good picture of him above will track down even other "brides," who bear the name of one of the musical demigods of New York without any benefit.

The audacity of this scoundrel went so far that he appeared one day at my home and tried to blame his exploits on an adverse financial situation and asked me for a recommendation so he could be admitted to the Odd Fellows Lodge. I rang my servant, and soon thereafter Hoffmann found himself standing alone on Madison Avenue.

At the beginning of summer I went to Berlin as I did every year. There in the Kroll Concert Hall, before a full house, I performed my opera, which in the meantime had been completed. Emil Götze sang Witichis with incomparable beauty. The rest of the summer was devoted to my dear old mother, who had returned to Berlin the year before. The farewell from my beloved mother was moving, because I suspected that I would never see her again. My premonition had not deceived me; on December 17, the devoted eyes of my mother closed forever.

To the richly blessed areas of endeavor that awaited me in America, a new one was added. Director Schemmel, of the conservatory connected with the University of Tennessee in Nashville, asked me to enter into a similar relationship with this institute as existed with Hardin College. After lengthy negotiations I agreed to come to Nashville annually for ten days. However, I only performed my duties there twice; the city was too "dry" for me, although water was available abundantly; however, I was not converted to becoming a hydrophile there. As a result of my—to be sure forced—abstinence, and in recognition of some of my other good attributes, I was awarded an honorary doctorate.

Mataswintha in Weimar and New York. Commodore Vanderbilt. Choral Festival in Philadelphia

In the course of the winter Bernhard Stavenhagen[5] concertized in the United States. On the occasion of a visit at my home, he saw the score of my opera. He asked for the piano arrangement and the text, took both with him to his hotel, returned the next day, and surprised me with the joyful news that he wanted to perform *Mataswintha* right at the beginning of the season in Weimar, where he had become the conductor. He kept his promise: On October 4, 1896, the premiere performance of my work took place in the Hoftheater in Weimar. For this reason my entire family had come to Europe with me. Before my departure for America, I accepted an invitation to the Imperial Russian Music Society in Moscow to conduct one of their orchestral concerts. For this I needed a passport, and this circumstance gives me the opportunity to recall with the greatest admiration the highly developed, model institution of the Prussian tax officials. As you know, every Prussian has the privilege of paying taxes, and those citizens who have moved their residence to a foreign country also enjoy the privilege, after leaving their native soil, of being able to pay for two more years. In the turbulence of my moving I had neglected to make use of this privilege. As I now innocently applied for a passport—six years had passed since my move to America—my really unintentional damage to the tax treasury became known. I received the passport against payment of the back taxes, which exceeded the Moscow honorarium not insignificantly. I was very proud of the Prussian administrative machinery that functioned so perfectly.

An important change had occurred in the administration of the Berlin conservatory. Thinking that I probably would not return to Berlin for permanent residence, I had transferred the exclusive rights and privileges connected with the conservatory to my brother. Hindered in his artistic work considerably by the burden of administrative duties, Philipp withdrew from the business management of the institute and came to an agreement with Dr. Hugo Goldschmidt, a music author and singing teacher, who was then responsible as director. Soon thereafter Karl Klindworth, who ran a small, very well-known piano school in addition to his work as a conductor, approached Dr. Goldschmidt with the idea of a merger.[6] As a result of the completed merger, the new school was named the Klindworth-Scharwenka Conservatory. For the time being, Goldschmidt remained as the sole autocrat, while Klindworth directed the piano department, and my brother took over the theoretical instruction.

The performance of my opera in Weimar and the lovely impressions that I received during the summer spent in Europe gnawed at my heart greatly, there in the corner, where the longing for the old homeland and for the inextinguishable love of the fatherland is located. With somewhat mixed feelings I returned to New York with my family. The constant monotony of performing and teaching did not satisfy me anymore; I longed for an artistically more satisfying field for my spare energy. My New York friends, with William Steinway at the head, teamed up and decided to start a Bach Society, whose management was to be entrusted to me. But the conferences, committee meetings, planning, newsletters, and similar preparations finally took so much time that I was already determined to return to the land

> Where my dreams wander,
> Where my dead will rise again,
> The country that speaks my language.[7]

So the nice plan fell into the water, there where it is deepest. As a small compensation for the dashed hopes I can list the performance of my *Mataswintha* at the Metropolitan Opera House.

Before my departure for Germany, I set out in the company of my faithful manager Lavine for concerts in the far West via Chicago, Minneapolis, St. Paul, Denver, and Salt Lake City to California. A very strange experience left me with a strong and lasting impression. During the trip the train rolled through a desolate rocky region. Since I felt like smoking, I left my window seat in the parlor car and went to the smoking compartment. Scarcely had I arrived there when a terrible crash and rumbling noise ensued, as if a bomb had hit. And indeed something similar had happened, only no explosion followed. We rushed into our compartment and saw to our horror that a very heavy boulder, which had broken away from the rock stratum, had flown through the wide window, smashing the frame, and had completely crushed my seat. A merciful stroke of good luck; in this case my need to smoke had saved me from certain death. The smart Lavine wanted to exploit the incident for a large advertisement. Of course, I vigorously opposed this, which the manager found incomprehensible and very unfortunate.

After the conclusion of this trip, which was strenuous but rich in wonderful impressions of nature, I went to Mexico (Missouri) to my black friends and soon recovered there from the stress of performing. The contrast between the turmoil of the last weeks and the undisturbed and tranquil peace that encompassed me there stirred and drove me to new work. After completing my duties at Hardin College, I retreated to a quiet hideaway on Long Island and there outlined the rough draft of my Third Piano Concerto (in E-sharp minor, published as op. 80).

In this idyllic tranquility Mr. Henry Wolfsohn[8]—America's Hermann Wolff[9]—surprised me. He brought me an invitation from Commodore William Vanderbilt, who was about to arrange a large celebration in his villa on the ocean (in Newport, Rhode Island) to honor his friend Theodore Roosevelt. This financial giant had expressed the desire to have the evening embellished by my performances on the piano—as Wolfsohn expressed so nicely. I accepted. The evening proceeded splendidly. Among other things,

Vanderbilt had engaged the entire Philharmonic Orchestra, whose members all appeared in Rough Rider uniforms, made just for this occasion. Remember that Roosevelt had organized a cavalry regiment called the Rough Riders at his own expense in the Spanish-American War. At that time he was running for governor of New York, was elected vice president of the United States in 1900, and after the assassination of Mr. McKinley in 1901 became president.[10] The old commodore knew what he was doing!

Now there was only one more obstacle to remove before my trip to Europe; it was the choral festival held in Philadelphia in June, which I had undertaken to review for the *New Yorker Morgen Journal*.[11] About ten thousand singers participated in the competition. From all parts of the Union the German song-loving minstrels came and could be heard either in individual groups or in their imposing entirety. In order to inform its readers as fast as possible about the individual stages and the result of the choral contest, the *New Yorker Morgen Journal* had a direct telegraph connection set up between the printing press and the press room of the enormous choral hall. My reports were set in New York immediately, printed, and sent out so quickly that the morning issue of the newspaper in Philadelphia could appear at the same hour as in New York (six o'clock). An amazing achievement!

After a short farewell visit at the home of my children, who were spending the summer in the Catskills, I began, with the completed sketch of my Piano Concerto, my trip to Europe in order to begin, among other things, my move back to Berlin.

I had chosen a slow steamer in order to work on the instrumentation of my concerto during the crossing. In a quiet corner of the dining room I had set up my workplace and was not disturbed by my fellow passengers. Only one of them, a butter wholesaler from Baltimore, favored me with his attention. After he had looked at me with interest for a while, he asked me what I was doing. "I am writing musical notes," I replied. "Well, well," answered the kind man, "why are you going to such trouble? That's not worth it. One can buy notes so cheaply these days." Since I could assume that an explanation of my activity would remain futile, I promised him to take his words to heart; only he should not take offense if I completed the work I had begun. He was content with this explanation.

My brother was very happy when I informed him of my decision; however, for the time being it was to be kept secret.

My stay in Europe did not last long. I quickly made the arrangements for my permanent return to the place of my long-standing productiveness. Dr. Goldschmidt greeted with joy my willingness to be associated again with the Klindworth-Scharwenka Conservatory. Klindworth, however, as I learned later, opposed my appointment with all his might and finally said it was a choice between him or me. Dr. Goldschmidt chose "him," and Klindworth actually left, bought himself a small country place near Oranienburg, grew cabbage, turnips, and legumes, indispensable delicacies for a real vegetarian. Until today it has remained inexplicable to me that he gave me the cold shoulder on the occasion of my return to the institute, which I had founded and built up. We had formerly been friends and associated a lot with one another; I liked the cultured man and fine musician very much.

With great joy I remember my trip from Berlin to New York accompanied by my wife. We chose the passage via Genoa. There we boarded the steamer *Fulda* and went out into the Mediterranean, shimmering like a sapphire, first to Naples, where the steamer took on board eight hundred Italian immigrants. Soon there was the sweet smell of spices and tuberous plants, the odor of which is perceived as perfume in the ghettos of the Galician cities. We had an eight-hour stop in Naples; we left the ship and saw what the limited time permitted us to see. Vesuvius was so kind as to honor us with terribly beautiful fireworks; we could still see the glare of the fire on the night sky long after our departure.

After taking care of my domestic affairs in New York and entrusting the conservatory to the care of my friend and colleague Emil Gramm, I also said good-bye. The farewell was very difficult for me. I had enjoyed many friendships, and I was able to reciprocate sincerely and cordially. I had lost two of my best friends through death shortly before my departure: William Steinway and Anton Seidl. Both died in the harness. Seidl, who lived on Sixty-eighth Street across the street from me, had come down with food poisoning from eating fish, which caused his death in a matter of a few hours. His funeral was worthy of a king. The casket lay in state among palms and flowers on the stage of the Metropolitan Opera House, flanked by members of the Philharmonic Orchestra. A thousand mourners filled the gigantic auditorium. The moving celebration culminated with the performance of the funeral march of Beethoven's *Eroica* and the final movement of Tchaikovsky's *Symphonie Pathetique*. Twelve of the most respected musicians of the city served as pallbearers.

Shortly before my departure from New York my friends gathered for a farewell celebration. A thoroughly German drink from the shores of the river, "which they are not to have,"[12] a few speeches in a melancholy and affectionate tone, many good-byes and "Wiedersehen"—and I went on my way into the future. By the way, the above-mentioned "Wiedersehen" was no delusion and also no teacher's trick, because in the coming spring I was contractually obligated to work at Hardin College, which also took place. My wife and some of the children stayed in New York for the time being; they were to follow at the end of December.

Notes

1. Nahan (or Nathan) Franko (1861–1930), an American violinist and conductor, was born in New Orleans and as a child prodigy toured with Adelina Patti. He was concertmaster of the Metropolitan Opera Orchestra from 1883 to 1907. In 1904 he became the first American-born conductor of the Metropolitan.

2. Hardin College and Conservatory of Music, the former Baptist Audrain County Female Seminary, was renamed in 1873 after benefactor Charles H. Hardin, who served as governor of Missouri (1872–1874). By the time Hardin College closed in 1932, it had educated over five thousand young women.

3. Benjamin Guckenberger founded the Birmingham-Southern College Conservatory of Fine and Performing Arts in Birmingham, Alabama, in 1895.

4. Heinrich A. Rattermann (1832–1923), a German-American author, poet, and historian, came to Cincinnati in 1846 and founded the German Mutual Insurance Co. For many years he edited *Der Deutsche Pionier*, a well-known historical journal published by the German Pioneer Society in Cincinnati.

5. Bernhard Stavenhagen (1862–1914), German pianist and composer, was one of Liszt's last students and gave the oration at Liszt's funeral. He conducted in Weimar and Munich and taught piano at the Geneva Conservatory.

6. Karl Klindworth (1830–1916) studied with Liszt and then spent fourteen years in London as a pianist and conductor. After meeting Wagner, he prepared the piano scores for Wagner's *Ring*. He taught for fourteen years at the Moscow Conservatory after the death of Nicholas Rubinstein and then returned to Berlin to conduct the Berlin Philharmonic and found his own conservatory in 1854. This school merged with Scharwenka's conservatory in 1893.

7. This is taken from a song by Georg Philipp Schmidt (1766–1849) titled either "Des Fremdlings Abendlied" or "Heimweh" and set to music by Franz Schubert.

8. Henry Wolfsohn's Musical Bureau in New York was the oldest concert management firm in the United States, and in 1904 he organized Richard Strauss's first American tour with the Pittsburgh Symphony and its conductor Victor Herbert. In 1930 the Wolfsohn Musical Bureau became part of the Columbia Concerts Corporation.

9. Hermann Wolff (1845–1902), born in Cologne, edited the *Neue Berliner Musikzeitung* (1878–1879) and *Musikwelt*. In 1880 he established his concert agency in Berlin, and in 1882 he helped the fifty-four musicians who defected from Benjamin Bilse's orchestra organize a new orchestra, which he managed and named the Berlin Philharmonic Orchestra.

10. Scharwenka mistakenly refers to the president as Kinley instead of McKinley.

11. The *New Yorker Morgen Journal* was a popular and well-financed German-American newspaper owned by William Randolph Hearst, who hoped to enter the ethnic newspaper market in New York with it.

12. The drink is undoubtedly Rhine wine. The reference to the Rhine River comes from the poem by Nikolaus Becker in 1840, "Sie sollen ihn nicht haben den freien deutschen Rhein," written when France was threatening to make the Rhine its border. The kings of Prussia and Bavaria honored Becker, and Robert Schumann, among many other composers, set the poem to music in the same year.

CHAPTER FIVE

~

Back in Berlin, 1898

Concerts. Illness. Hardin College

On January 27, 1899, after an interval of seven years, I appeared again before Berlin audiences. Among other things I played my new Piano Concerto, no. 3, and the Chopin Polonaise with its preceding Andante spianato,[1] which I had orchestrated.

A new concert tour to Finland followed the Berlin venture. Soon after my return I came down with a serious illness, which confined me in bed for six weeks. American newspapers announced my death, and even in Berlin such a rumor circulated. My physician and loyal friend, Professor Dr. Salzwedel, however, snatched me from the greedy hands of death, to be sure with the help of the most bitter medicine that I ever had to swallow: I was not permitted to smoke! That was difficult. However, another good friend helped me out of this distress. Professor Philipp Rüfer came every afternoon at three o'clock, sat down at my bed of pain, and smoked there for two hours. So I had a small compensation for the forbidden pleasure. Also a woman friend of my parents, who was from Samter and as old as the hills, showed up to say her last farewell. Gasping for breath, she dropped into the armchair next to my bed and talked and talked so pitifully that I thought I was hearing funeral bells. I thought the end was really near. I was strengthened in this belief by the following conversation that the well-meaning lady now began with a voice choked with tears: "Oh, my dear professor, how absolutely wretched you look! Like the very sufferings of Christ! What is wrong?" With a weak voice and few words I described to her my condition. The old lady, whimpering, said, "Oh God, oh God, just like my late husband. How sad! Unfortunately that will not get better; my late husband passed away from that. In the last weeks he had to struggle terribly. Well, console yourself, dear professor, we all have to die eventually." And she began sobbing.

Completely disheartened, I stammered that I could wait and that I was in no hurry. I added that since yesterday I was being tormented by very excruciating, stabbing pains near the kidneys.

The old lady animatedly told me: "See, my dear professor, just like with my late husband. Two days before his death he got such terrible pains near the kidneys and then—"

Those were the last words that the old lady spoke, because my daughter Zina, who had heard her very comforting words, took the consoler by the arm and carefully but firmly led her to an adjoining room. I remained alone with my excruciating pains. Was I really so close to marching off to the great army? Fortunately, Rüfer came soon and blew away my gloomy thoughts with powerful puffs of his Upman cigar.

As violently as the illness had appeared, so just as quickly I recovered. In spring I boarded a ship again, and the strong breezes of the Atlantic soon blew away the last traces of my physical weakness. I arrived "on the other side" fresh and as if newly born, greeted by my many friends with an indescribably hearty "hello" and "how do you do?" After a short stay in New York, I went to Mexico, Missouri, to my black friends, who welcomed "our professor" at the train station with frenzied howls of joy. Oehlschläger, my substitute at Hardin College, had rented himself a charming, roomy little house and purchased a horse and wagon; and so we were able to make pleasant trips into the virgin forests of the surrounding area.

At the beginning of June I again crossed the ocean—for the twenty-second time—and went first to London, where I played my new Piano Concerto under the direction of old August Manns in the Crystal Palace. It was an embarrassing situation because Manns had become so deaf that while conducting he placed his left hand next to his ear to direct the sound and had to bend the upper part of his body far into the orchestra. Of course I also gave some recitals in London and out in the provinces.

I spent the summer with my family in Tarasp, where I underwent treatment annually until 1915. I lived in Fontana, a small village, three hundred feet above the spa hotel. A Capuchin monastery is located there, with whose residents I maintained friendly contact. In the beautiful, wonderfully situated church, which offers a marvelous view of the entire Lower Engadine Valley, is a new organ; at that time it was not yet paid for. I decided to contribute my small part to the cost, and so I arranged several church concerts over the years—I played the organ fairly well—and was able to contribute a very tidy sum to the organ fund. On Sundays I was the duly appointed organist for the service. My kind landlord, Aloys Cagienard, who was a shining example of his profession and had the best Veltliner wine[2] in his cellar, trained and directed the choir. Female singers from among the guests at the Tarasp spa enhanced the church service with solos—among them Frau Professor Blanck-Peters and Fräulein Marie Berg—and so the attractive sanctuary was usually not large enough to hold the number of worshipers. Also Rosa Poppe, the adored heroine of our Royal Theater who was married to Dr. Leva, the spa doctor in Tarasp, often attended our performances, as did Baron Leopold von Rothschild, the London patriarch of the dynasty. Felix Mottl also climbed up to my quiet hideaway; he was very sickly. The picture here (see photo 10 in the photo spread) is the last photograph taken shortly before his death.

For the year 1900 my election as a full member of the Royal Academy of the Arts in Berlin must be mentioned; a year later I was appointed to the Senate. In the spring of the same year the composers' festival took place in Heidelberg. Under the direction of Philipp Wolfrum[3] I played my Third Piano Concerto, the instrumentation of which had amazed the butter dealer from Baltimore so much. The festival turned out to be rather dull. Liszt was missing; Wolfrum was conducting!

The Music Teachers' Federation.
The Klindworth-Scharwenka Conservatory

Among the musicians in Berlin who took pride in their profession there had been agitation and growing unrest for some time. The city was so flooded with music schools of the lowest quality that it seemed advisable to confront this annoying situation and to stop the gradually worsening state of affairs. With this goal in mind, a number of brave men and women in leading positions came together and formed a committee to discuss first of all the groundwork or the bylaws of a proposed association for the betterment of the music teaching profession. In these preliminary meetings, which I convened, Professors Gustav Holländer, Richard Schmidt, Gustav Kulenkampff, and music director Mengewein participated. In addition, there were Frl. Anna Morsch, the tireless fighter in the battle against the musician proletariat and certainly the most diligent worker in our field of activity; Frl. Dr. Olga Stieglitz; Frl. Maria Leo; and others. After many discussions, this newborn entity was baptized with the name of the Music Teachers' Federation. After publication of the bylaws, we turned to the general public, but the press did not effectively support us in a sufficiently deserving manner. A larger meeting was called, and the final version of the bylaws was presented. The majority at the meeting declared their cooperation and became members and showed their confidence in the present leadership by electing the executive board from among them. Accordingly, I was elected as president, Holländer as vice president, and Frl. Morsch as the secretary. Also the other ladies and gentlemen among the current organizers now belonged to the executive committee.

Conferences were chosen as the most effective form to publicize the efforts of the association. The idea proved to be very fortuitous. The first Music Education Conference took place in Philharmonic Hall and the following meeting in the large chamber of the Reichstag Building. In order to attract the attention of the authorities to our efforts and to awaken their interest in the federation's plans for reform, invitations were sent to the agencies concerned: the Ministry of Education, the City Council of Berlin, and the Royal College of Music. Our call found a hearing. The minister of education sent Josef Joachim and Adolph Schulze as representatives, and the mayor Dr. Reicke and city school superintendent Fischer represented the City Council. All the men greeted the federation and its goals with warm and approving words. Dr. Reicke, in a splendidly organized speech, promised to support actively our efforts, as far as reasons of state permitted. All the important conservatories of the empire had sent representatives, of whom I will mention only Councilor Dr. Kliebert, director of the Royal School of Music in Würzburg; Prof. Iwan Knorr, representative of the Hoch Conservatory in Frankfurt a.M.; Prof. Julius Klengel of the Royal Conservatory in Leipzig; and Ernst Paul of the Royal Conservatory in Dresden, among others. Almost two thousand participants said they would attend the conference, but only thirteen hundred could be invited. Much useful work was accomplished during the three days of deliberations, including lectures with discussions, presentations, and demonstrations of new instructional material, development of courses of instruction in individual subjects, drafts of testing regulations, and so on. From the program of the third conference, which lies before me, I mention the following names and talks:

Prof. Dr. Max Dessoir: Music and Its Cultural Significance in the Present
Dr. Karl Stork: Music and Its Cultural Significance in the Past
Prof. Jacques Dalcroze: Training in Rhythm
Dr. J. Katzenstein: An Experimental Investigation of Chest-Voice and Falsetto
Ludwig Riemann: The Reintroduction in Notation of "B" instead of "H"
Prof. Georg Rolle: Review of Boys' Schools

Following all of these lectures were discussions that sometimes turned out to be very interesting and stimulating.

If I am not mistaken, I organized four such conferences, but each time I was greatly relieved if I did not have to cancel my closing speech because of a hoarse voice. The days required a lot of effort. From 9:00 a.m. to 1:00 p.m. and from 3:30 p.m. to 7:30 p.m. daily one had to keep eyes, ears, and mouth ready; a carafe of water was the only respite and a bell had to be used for those cases, when more than five speakers tried to speak at the same time, which, however, happened rarely. At this point I would like to mention most gratefully Count Ballestrem, the president of the Reichstag at that time, who most graciously had placed the chambers of the Reichstag at our disposal; likewise the director of the Reichstag, Councillor Jungheim, for all his efforts on our behalf.

After a few years, I resigned from the office, which I had come to like. This was shortly after Gustav Holländer had resigned from his position and from the federation. There was fierce agitation within the executive committee for tightening the regulations of the examination board, which in my opinion were strict enough. A blatant case of the strictest interpretation of one of the rules caused me to follow Gustav Holländer. Prof. Kulenkampff took my place.

Certainly it was not my intention to leave out the names of many outstanding women and men who deserve mention with regard to the federation and the conferences. May those not mentioned graciously excuse this unintentional omission and blame it on my memory, which soon will have been functioning for seventy-three years, and therefore is probably no longer absolutely reliable. Each reminder forwarded to me from the concerned group—even if it deals with other corrections—I will gladly take into account in an anticipated reprint of this book. May it happen soon. *Quod deus bene vertat*.[4]

Into this busy period, which I devoted to the Music Teachers' Federation and to the conservatory, came my first journalistic activity. The *New Yorker Staatszeitung*[5] asked me for reports of the important events in the musical life of Berlin. The most important ones had to be sent by cable. I remember that the editors of the paper wanted a telegram after every act of the performance of the opera *Roland* by Leoncavallo. I also supplied extensive reports for the *Monthly Musical Record* in London. In the long run, however, this work was not to my liking. Listening to music every evening, and not always good music, and then *stante pede* have to write about it after one had drilled students for five to six hours—no: "Let him who likes it, put up with it."[6] Not I!

Before my departure from the Music Teachers' Federation an important change in the administration at Klindworth-Scharwenka Conservatory had occurred. As the result of a stubborn ear ailment as well as his literary endeavors, Dr. Goldschmidt was hindered in devoting his active interest to the conservatory, which was necessary to maintain the position of the institute and which it could justly claim to hold and maintain. Since it was my very own undertaking and was closely connected with my name, I looked for a way to raise it from its existing low status. I prevailed on my brother to work with me on all aspects of the institute, which was beginning to show signs of a decline. The management of the business required a person of greater organizational skills and business knowledge than the current director was able to muster. In Robert Robitschek, who had managed branches of the conservatory for a few years with great skill, I believed that I had found the right man.[7] I had not been mistaken. Dr. Goldschmidt stepped down from the administration, and a three-member directorate, which consisted of me and my brother and the work-happy Robitschek, now ran the conservatory. We drew up big plans for the future, which were realized on a grand scale through the far-sighted views of the newly acquired directors and their energetic initiative. Robitschek saw to it that we got a new home, which met all the requirements that a large music school must confront. We are indebted to his initiative for the construction of the Blüthner- and the Klindworth-Scharwenka Hall. In 1906 the twenty-fifth anniversary of the conservatory was celebrated, in which forty-five teachers and one thousand students of the institution took part. At the beginning of 1914, I left my position, and since 1917, the year my dear brother died, Robitschek managed the business of the conservatory alone. *Vivat, floreat, crescat.*

My teaching, my many concerts, and the work required by the Music Teachers' Federation did not permit me any spare time for creating music. Except for an "Emperor Cantata," which I wrote at the request of the Senate of the Royal Academy of Arts for the birthday celebration of the emperor in 1901, in the first years after my return from America I was busy with revisions and wrote a few works of a purely instructional character: *Master Class of Piano Playing*, 4 vols. (*Meisterschule des Klavierspiels*, 4 Bände); *Contributions to Finger Training* (*Beiträge zur Fingerbildung*); *Studies in Playing Octaves* (*Studien im Oktavenspiel*); and *Methodology of Playing the Piano* (*Methodik des Klavierspiels*). In addition, Breitkopf & Härtel entrusted me with editing the *Handbooks of Teaching Music* (*Handbücher der Musiklehre*).

My Fourth Piano Concerto. Bucharest. Carmen Sylva

Not until the year 1908 was I moved to purchase a book of score paper, which willingly offered me its nice, smooth surfaces for its long-neglected use. It again became a Piano Concerto with Orchestra—my fourth (F minor), which was published by Leuckart in Leipzig. My talented student Martha Siebold played the first performance of the work; her excellent performance received the highest recognition from the press and the general public.

The performance was attended by the artistic Princess Wilhelm zu Wied, the later Princess of Albania who was at home in all areas of art and who also produced art of the finest taste. At the suggestion of this refined lady, who like her art-loving husband, immediately showed her warm interest in me and my family and has remained loyal up to the present, I adorned this new work with the name of Queen Elizabeth of Rumania, her close relative. The queen thanked me with kind words and invited me to visit Bucharest. In my daily interaction with this noble woman, who fulfilled her duties as mother of her country in such an inimitably selfless and loyal manner and nevertheless found time for poetry (Carmen Sylva),[8] I spent memorable hours. On my departure I received expensive articles of Rumanian workmanship—blouses, ornately made handbags, rugs, and the like, with which to delight my wife and children on my return. The king honored me by awarding me the Officer's Cross of the Rumanian Crown.

In a happy mood and without malice, I wrote a report to a friend in Berlin about my impressions of Bucharest. I was very surprised to read this letter in the *Berliner Lokalanzeiger* on my return trip at the Lemberg train station.[9] Since it contains a few explanations to the lines above, it follows here:

After a 38-hour trip through the snowfields of Silesia and Galicia, I arrived here last Friday evening with a two-hour delay and was welcomed at the train station by Herr Dinicu,[10] the director of the orchestra, and three professors from the conservatory. After convincing myself in the hotel that I had survived the Galician railway tracks without harm to my body, I first undertook a tour, accompanied by my welcomers, to find a suitable restaurant, where I could offer my stomach, which had become somewhat distrustful during the trip, a satisfying supply of things for my metabolism during the time of my stay here. Expressed more clearly: I looked for and found a suitable restaurant in an eatery on the Main Street and immediately put it to the test. The food was excellent, and the beer—a kind of Pilsen—was much better than our domestic beer (except for Bavaria). Only the wine, made from grapes grown on the slopes of the Carpathian Mountains, I did not really like; it is a mildly sour wine that is improved and made more palatable by adding water. Whether this blending is already done before bottling, I cannot say. In any case, I found it peculiar when the innkeeper, a friendly Austrian, assured me that his wines were absolutely pure. They were, as he added by way of explanation, decanted personally under his direction. Well, there you are! Bucharest is a modern city and has water works and sewers. *Sapienti sat!*

The following day—on Sunday—a royal servant brought me an invitation for tea in the evening with her majesty. I went to the palace at 6:30 and was most kindly received by the noble woman, who for the first time had left her bed after a five-week illness. After a quarter hour of lively conversation, during which I was able to deliver greetings from the Prince and Princess zu Wied and present the considerable proceeds from a Carmen Sylva evening in Berlin, the queen got up (until then she was lying on the chaise lounge) and led me (I had been looking around admiringly from my seat) through the rooms, which testified to the highest artistic taste. She called my attention to individual works of art, among which a large Rembrandt, a Ribera, and a grandiose seascape particularly stood out. Then we stopped in the music room. The charming lady-in-waiting, Madame de Bengescu, prepared tea, caviar sandwiches (not much bread, a lot of caviar) were served, and also a crystal bottle of rum was placed before my seat. I drank it of course mixed with tea. The queen expressed the wish to hear some music right away. After languishing for five weeks, this was an easily explainable wish, as the noble woman revealed. In the meantime my highly gifted young friend, the pianist Emil Frey, had arrived.[11] So we sat down at the grand pianos (Bechstein and Blüthner) and played my Piano Concerto dedicated to the queen, which Frey was to perform the following day in the Athenaeum with an orchestra under my direction. After our performance, which the queen listened to with shining eyes, she read aloud some of her poems with moving expression, and the way in which the noble woman knew how to portray the content of the verses in their characteristic variety was extraordinarily enthralling. I understand the love, which this unique woman is shown by all, even by those who have not had the good fortune of knowing her, because she only receives what she has lavishly bestowed in inexhaustible generosity from the cornucopia of her rich, noble heart. My invitation for tea the next day had to be cancelled, because the queen felt exhausted and was urged by her doctor to rest and take it easy. For today the entire orchestra is summoned to the palace, where I will direct my Piano Concerto in a separate performance. On Sunday Frey played it in the Athenaeum and had a sensational success. The day before yesterday we had tea at the home of the crown princess, where the crème de la crème of the capital gathered. Here we also performed the Concerto. The crown princess is a very beautiful, blond, stately figure, of regal stature, and winsome charm; she was flanked by her two lovely princesses, the older one about thirteen, the younger one eight years old, two sweet children. The music salon is of dazzling splendor and decorated with exquisite art works. Here, too, there are Bechstein and Blüthner pianos.

Yesterday I again had tea with her majesty. On this occasion I could wear the *Croix du Commandeur de la Couronne Roumanie*, which his majesty had awarded me. This is a medal, which one must put on carefully, because if one pulls on the ribbon of the medal too hard when putting it around one's neck, one could be strangled. And one tries to avoid that, provided there are no compelling reasons. That I performed well as conductor is shown by the fact that I was invited to direct the next large symphony concert in the Athenaeum; I will perform Beethoven and Wagner.

Two Concert Tours through the United States and Canada. Gustav Mahler. The Chinaman in the Bedroom. Dr. Cook, the North Pole Explorer

In the following year (1910) an enticing temptation in the form of an American agent approached me again to persuade me to go on a concert tour through the United States. Since I do not possess the steadfastness of the long-suffering Odysseus, after some hesitation I accepted the call of the sirens, which I was willing to do all the more since my wife agreed to accompany me. Also my small dear "Mungo," a charming toy dog, gallantly decided to go along.

Yet before we began the trip, I purchased for my family a sizable piece of property with green areas and a vegetable garden to the one side of the Hotel Trubel in Bad Saarow on Lake Scharmützel, on which I had a country home built in the style of a mountain house (see photo 12 in the photo spread). The building material consisted of American pinewood, and also in other ways the beautiful land "Dollarika" contributed financially to the realization of a long-cherished wish.[12]

In October we crossed the big pond, and in New York I began my concert tour with the performance of my new Piano Concerto. At that time Gustav Mahler[13] was the conductor of the Philharmonic Orchestra. He conducted my work in an accomplished manner and a week later also Beethoven's Concerto in E-flat Major. There, unfortunately, he was a different man. It certainly can be attributed to his ill health—the early signs of the great master's death a half-year later—that he forced the tempi almost to the limits of what was technically possible in the music. His beat throughout the first movement was without exception *alla breve*, so that I was able only with the greatest difficulty to follow this feverishly speeding baton. My strong accenting of individual beats did not help; I had to ride along with the chase if a catastrophe was to be avoided.

I stayed in the United States for five months. In addition to the great music centers of the country, the concert tour took me chiefly to the South. There is nothing particularly noteworthy to be mentioned about it. The audiences showed me the same friendly interest as formerly, and to the dear old friends I added new ones.

A lovely evening in a large college near New Orleans has remained a very pleasant memory. I gave a recital there, after the conclusion of which the charming young women delighted me with a fitting gift for the celebration of my sixtieth birthday: a floral arrangement in the shape of a lyre, which consisted of sixty thousand violets handpicked by the young ladies of the school.

Once more I went to America (1912), this time visiting primarily the eastern states and Canada. Again my wife accompanied me, and also my daughter Lucie joined us. Because Mungo howled so pitifully at our departure and looked at me with such unspeakable sorrow, I took the black little toy dog along on the trip; it found room in my wife's muff.

I would like to relate two interesting episodes of this trip. In Calgary, a city in the far west of Canada—the shining, snow-covered peaks of the mountains can be seen from there—I came to my hotel late in the evening. I was alone and had to be content with a small room, which in addition to the door to the corridor had another door to an adjoining room, which could not be locked. Exhausted from the twenty-four-hour train trip, I soon went to bed, after I had bolted the door and, as always, placed a loaded revolver on the night table. I soon fell asleep; however, I was awakened after sleeping a short time by a suspicious noise. I jumped up, and in the light of a dark lantern I saw a real live Chinaman and another figure next to my bed. In a flash I grabbed for my weapon, but the Chinaman stopped me and calmed me down with a very subdued voice. It was the night porter, who had opened my door with his master key in order to ask permission to give the small adjoining room as lodging to a strange gentleman who had just arrived and had not been able to find a room in the city. I agreed, and the night passed without other incident except for some very loud snoring next door.

On the return trip to New York I gave a concert in Winnipeg. As I was getting ready to walk from the room backstage into the hall, a man stormed in and asked whether among the letters that lay on the mantel I had noticed one addressed to Mr. Cook. I was able to confirm this. To my question whether the addressee was perhaps related to the famous North Pole explorer Dr. Cook,[14] I received the answer in an unassuming tone: "I am he." Then we chatted for a little while, but the audience began to get restless, and so I took the brave man, who had been privileged to have lunch on the northernmost point of the earth's axis, along into the concert hall, where he listened attentively to my performance. After the concert we spent a long time together and became friends, which we sealed according to good German custom with a strong drink and not ice water! It had gotten quite late, long past midnight, when another guest entered the otherwise empty dining room of the sumptuous Alexander Hotel. The late arrival, a tall, stately figure, had also been at the concert; he walked to our table, introduced himself as Mr. van Westrum, and courteously asked permission to sit down at our table. The conversation became very interesting. Dr. Cook talked about his North Pole expedition in the most fascinating manner, and van Westrum about his grand plans—he is the inventor of Westrumit,[15] named after him—and when he started to talk about his student days, he became very excited. One bottle followed another; the empty room provided excellent acoustics for the constant popping of the corks. When Mr. van Westrum told us that he had studied in Jena and was an active member of the Franconia Fraternity, I mentioned my son Philipp, who also was a Franconian in Jena and as such had been known far and wide as a fencer. Van Westrum's eyes lit up. Oh, the glory of the old student fraternities! After I had enumerated other good attributes of my son—for example, that he did not want to show me the university building during my chance visit in Jena—van Westrum was beside himself with joy. "Please have him come to see me," he said eagerly. "Please have him travel to America; he will make his fortune with me." I agreed, and actually soon thereafter my son went to Washington. He joined the Westrum Company and after a short apprenticeship was given the directorship of a Swiss branch of the company.

I then traveled through Canada toward the east. In Toronto I met my wife. My train was delayed fourteen hours; the tracks were closed for this period of time as the result of a terrible train crash. Those were anxious hours for my wife, who had to wait for such a long, scary time for my arrival. On the return trip to New York we visited the ice-clad Niagara Falls and after that made a side trip to Washington to visit my daughter, who had been welcomed cordially into the family of a dear girlfriend; she stayed there through the summer.

My vacation soon came to an end, and I had to think about returning home. In March (1913) we were back on the shores of the Spree River. Up to then I had crossed the ocean twenty-six times, and the possibility of increasing this number exists today as I write these lines. This is still undecided.

The Federation of German Performing Artists

In Berlin I found new duties in addition to my established professional work, the most important of which was the founding of the Federation of German Performing Artists. In order to serve a good cause, I take the liberty of directing the following "open letter" to my publisher.

Dear Doctor!

With the assumption and with the wish that this book through some lucky chance may get into the hands of as many as possible performing artists of Germany, permit me to express the request to publish in full the following passage, which is relevant to this federation and which, as I am aware, does not really fit into the framework of this biographical work because of its propagandistic intent. With regard to the economics, about which the publisher naturally has to be concerned as to the quantity of his publications, my request may seem perhaps unjustified or even pretentious; however, it is my urgent wish that information of the purpose and goals of the federation may find the widest possible dissemination in interested circles.

In order to be able to give a clear and true picture of the goals and of the development and growth of our federation, I have asked the chairman of the board of directors, Dr. Rudolf Cahn-Speyer, for a report, which he has kindly placed at my disposal.[16] Since I have nothing to add, may it find a place here with the permission of the author in its original form.

On this occasion I cannot fail to mention on behalf of the executive committee, whose presiding chairman I had the honor of being, the extraordinary services that Dr. Cahn-Speyer rendered to the federation through his distinguished organizational ability and his vast knowledge and competence and with his tireless work.

The report states:

The Federation of German Performing Artists was founded in Düsseldorf on April 16, 1912. Decisive for the founding was the recognition that the performing artist was formally and effectively without rights: formally because legal provisions and regulations did not exist that took into consideration the nature of this profession; and effectively because the economic dependency of the performing artist on concert agents and business men, often both combined in one person, was too great for the artist to have dared only to rely on those rules in the civil law code, which in the course of interpretation could be applicable in his favor, especially the rule about termination of contract due to the violation of good morals.

The young federation wanted to confront this abuse in both of its forms, on the one hand, by contact with the responsible authorities and by public agitation, and on the other hand, by organizations, through whose help artists were to be made independent of their agents.

The leadership of the federation at that time, which did not possess any practical experience in this field of activity, in particular made the mistake from the very beginning of counting on an evolution and a structure that could only be the result of years of work. As a result, disappointment and distrust were awakened, and in addition, a financial situation was created that was indefensible.

Out of these circumstances arose the recognition that reform was necessary; in October 1913 the decision to move the federation to Berlin was made, and the management placed into the hands of other people, who today are still in the majority at the head of the association.

While these reforms were prepared, a group of dissatisfied members undertook secession and founded the Professional Society of Practicing Artists. In order to give this new association standing right away from without, Professor Xaver Scharwenka was elected as president, and he accepted the election without being informed adequately about the opposing relationship of the two associations.

When, however, Professor Scharwenka was able to view the facts, he recognized immediately how damaging the existence of two associations for the same profession must be. The authorities did not want to recognize any one of the two as having jurisdiction, and the artists did not know which one they should join. Therefore, Professor Scharwenka insisted in the fall of 1913 that merger negotiations be started. These, however, encountered serious difficulties. Only when the outbreak of World War I had reinforced the need for unity, and when Professor Scharwenka declared that he would resign from his office if the negotiations remained fruitless, did the merger take place on September 15, 1914.

In the meantime the Federation of German Performing Artists had not been inactive. After the reorganization in October 1913, it temporarily had to give up for all practical purposes its work for the independence of artists from the concert agents. On the other hand, it succeeded in being consulted by the police authorities in Berlin, who up to that time did not have an official ruling for the business activity of the concert agents for this purpose. The result was that the validity of the employment law for concert agents was established, and that the Prussian minister for trade and industry issued an administrative regulation in the form of an order on March 9, 1914, about how concert agents were to conduct their business. Even if the regulations were inadequate from the viewpoint of the federation, they were a first step in an uncharted course to create order in these situations.

Under pressure from the war, the federation had to change its activity and focused entirely on wartime relief. Even before the merger with the Professional Society and at its suggestion, the federation had participated in the founding of an Aid Alliance for Musicians and Performing Artists of Greater Berlin, which had as its goal the collection of funds for financial support, used clothing, and the distribution of food stamps for soup kitchens for the poor and the middle class. With the assistance of numerous relief committees made up of ladies of Berlin society, among them Frau Scharwenka, the Federation of German Performing Artists in October 1914 founded a "soup kitchen for artists," in which the needy performing artists and their families received good and inexpensive meals in rooms suited to the needs of artistically sensitive people. Originally limited to about 80 people, the artists' soup kitchen soon had to be enlarged. It moved into rooms, very kindly made available by the Provincial-Gross Lodge of Hamburg[17] in the Emserstraße, and there finally 500 to 600 people were fed daily, in the course of which also members of other related professions generously were admitted. This kitchen was the only one of all the relief kitchens in Berlin established with private funds that survived the entire war; indeed it remained in operation until spring 1920.

At the same time the federation objected to the increasing exploitation of artists for charity performances. It was largely responsible that the Federal Council issued a decree in 1915 appointing an Imperial commissioner for war relief, who, together with subordinate agencies, had to supervise this area according to specific rules.

Moreover, during wartime the activities of the federation came to a standstill, especially because it used all of its resources for relief purposes and because a substantial part of the federation's administration was inducted into the army.

Immediately before the armistice was concluded in September 1918, the federation proceeded to realize its goals in a practical way. It founded a "Concert Department," which had been planned for a long time and which, as a charitable employment agency, was to free the performing artists gradually from concert agents by taking over those business activities for the benefit of all, which the concert agents performed for profit with repeated instances of abuse. Abuses, as they frequently occur in the case of agencies, are not possible in the federation because the administrative people are elected annually in a free election by the artists and work completely in an honorary capacity. The fees are without exception lower than those of the agencies, and all discounts, which benefit the federation as the bulk purchaser of ads and the like, are credited to the artists in full. Therefore the federation is not interested like other companies in having the artists make unnecessary large advertising orders, since it does not earn anything on them.

These are the principles according to which the Concert Department was founded in 1918 and which have remained in force until today. The business offices were located in the building in which Professor Scharwenka also had his apartment, so that he could constantly keep an eye on the business operations. At the founding there was the sure prospect of official support; however, this did not come about when circumstances changed after November 1918. Nevertheless, it was possible not only to keep the organization going, but also to expand it. In the 1921–1922 season the federation made arrangements for 165 concerts and recitals, and its contacts for engagements stretched throughout Germany and the foreign countries accessible to us.

Also connections to the authorities were further developed. The federation was constantly consulted, especially by the Berlin police authorities. It received authorization to send a representative together with the Society of German Composers to the provisional Imperial Economic Council, and it took and takes part prominently in the deliberations in the Imperial Ministry of Labor. The goal here is to create a new labor law according to #157 of the constitution. In it there are to be safeguards for performing artists so that the interests of their individually different professions are not ignored by simplified legislation and that burdens, such as compulsory insurance, are not imposed on them.

Furthermore, the federation could state its opinion advantageously on various tax questions, for example on merging the value-added tax with the income tax deduction, on the luxury tax on musical instruments, and especially on the entertainment tax. The federation is largely responsible that the tax on concerts and recitals, which seriously threatened concert life, was reduced to a bearable rate first in Berlin and then in the entire empire. It is also represented in the Foreign Trade Commission.

So the Federation of German Performing Artists under the methodical leadership of Professor Scharwenka succeeded in acquiring more and more the trust of the authorities and the artists themselves. Only recently did the Federation of Performing Artists of Munich demonstrate this by joining the federation immediately when it was founded as a local chapter. The federation has succeeded in having its voice heard where it is necessary and in having its members feel safe under its legal protection; this is also expressed by the fact that some of the best-known names of German musical life are to be found on the executive committee and the board of directors of the federation. Let us name only Prof. Karl Klingler, Prof. Friedrich E. Koch, Prof. Stephan Krehl, Prof. Télémaque Lambrinno, Prof. Mayer-Mahr, Prof. Siegfried Ochs, Prof. Ferdinand Pfohl, Director Robert Robitschek, Director Prof. Dr. Max von Schillings, Prof. Dr. Georg Schumann, and others. So the hope and the trust seems justified that the Federation of German Performing Artists will be more and more in a position to fulfill its mission as a professional organization and therewith contribute to the support and advancement of our German musical life.

The Final Chord

Then came World War I, and with it the fate of artists took a disastrous turn for the worse. Shall I report on the suffering that descended on the profession, the creators, performers, and teachers? It is a disgrace, and still there is no end to the misery. Whoever has not looked into the hearts of the many thousands who were thrown out of their career path, who has not observed the discouraged, the starving, the ruined, and the destitute, can hardly imagine the destruction that the war brought about in the realm of the fine arts.

My artistic activity was focused primarily on participating in charity concerts and on other charitable functions. Also my trips to the eastern and western front served similar purposes. Occasionally there were a few evenings of artistic uplift within our bleeding fatherland. I played my piano concertos in Dessau, Rostock, Schwerin, Oldenburg, and even in 1918 in the Berlin Opera House with the Royal Orchestra.

In Oldenburg I made a small faux pas in front of the grand duke, which caused great amusement. After the performance of my Piano Concerto, the general manager, Herr von Radetzky, an old, dear family friend, appeared in my dressing room and asked me and conductor Boehe to follow him to the loge of the grand duke. The nobleman was in the company of his two young daughters, two charming young girls of about sixteen and fourteen years of age. The grand duke said a few kind words to me, reached into his coat pocket, and handed me an elegant small box, out of which shone the Gold Medallion for Art and Science. After expressing my thanks, I put the small box in the back pocket of my tailcoat, while the grand duke turned to the conductor, whom he honored with the title "professor." Meanwhile the princesses approached me, the oldest of whom offered to pin the medal *brevi manu* on my chest. I reached into my coat pocket and handed the lovely creature the small box just as the grand duke turned to me. At the same moment the silvery sound of laughter emanated from the young girls. With her arm raised and her eyes sparkling cheerfully, the princess rushed to her father with the words: "Just look, papa, what you gave the professor," and with resounding laughter in which we all joined, she presented the grand duke with a Swedish matchbox. The riddle was solved immediately; I had reached into the wrong coat pocket and handed over the small box without looking at it at the moment the grand duke spoke to me. Later I met the two lovely royal children again at the home of their mother in Schwerin, where the comical incident evoked happy memories.

An evening filled with artistic honors I owe Moritz Rosenthal.[18] The great piano master, who had often played my Concerto in B Minor, now also took my Concerto in F Minor, op. 82, into his repertoire. After he had successfully performed it first in Brünn, he invited me to the forthcoming performance in Vienna with the request to direct the work there. It was a splendid feat of Rosenthal, who celebrated a veritable keyboard orgy with passion and verve and had a tumultuous success. A week later I gave my own concert, in which, in addition to some other works, I performed my Cello Sonata, op. 46; the Variations, op. 48; and the two Songbooks, op. 88 (with Maria Mora von Götz).

At the suggestion of the Federation of German Performing Artists, my fiftieth anniversary as a performer was celebrated in the Singakademie, exactly on the day (November 29) when I had given my own first concert at the same place. Alfred Klaar honored me with a prologue stirringly recited by Miete Möller; Claudio Arrau played my Variations, op. 48, and Frl. von Götz sang my Songs, op. 88. At the conclusion my Piano Quartet, op. 36, was performed. The day after a banquet was held, at which my friends from musical and social circles came together. Not long thereafter, on January 6, 1920, I was able to celebrate my seventieth birthday.

In March of the same year I left for concerts in Sweden and Denmark. My return came during the days of the Kapp putsch,[19] in the aftermath of which I had to suffer a lot and almost lost my life. Coming from Copenhagen, the travelers arrived in Warnemünde in the afternoon, where they learned that travel by rail was completely stopped. We—that is, my three compartment companions and I—decided that it was way too boring in wintry and dreary Warnemünde, and to leave by any other means, be it to Lübeck or Hamburg, from where we hoped to get a connection to Berlin. In Warnemünde a "council" from the groups of fishermen had been organized; I do not remember its official name. Our solution was to get away from there. For a fabulous price we found a car that was to bring us to Hamburg; it was confiscated by the council. We even rented an airplane to Berlin; it was seized by the council shortly before our takeoff. Finally we chartered a miserable small fishing boat that was to bring us to Lübeck. For the payment of a few thousand marks we received permission from the council for the trip, in addition to which we had to pay the owner of the boat fifteen hundred marks per passenger (there were four of us). At ten o'clock at night, in pitch darkness, the trip began. We had barely reached the lighthouse when heavy gunfire from shore opened up, which was intended for our boat. We threw ourselves flat on the deck—there was no cabin—and in this position awaited whatever was to follow. We did not have to wait long. A small motorboat followed our peaceful fishing boat, whose driver ordered us to stop. When our simple boat had stopped, four guys stormed on board, who with drawn revolvers screamed at us, "Hands up!" In the light of a dark lantern they searched us scrupulously, rummaged through our suitcases, and inspected our pants pockets, wallets, and handbags. The council found nothing suspicious; nevertheless we were not allowed to continue our trip, and loaded down with our luggage, we had to leave the boat and travel out of breath and stumbling the long way to Warnemünde in the pitch black night. There good "advice" was expensive; it cost us several thousand marks and a lot of sweat, but it did not help. During our march the gunfire started up again; this time it was meant for a small steamship that was looking for the harbor, but the "blue beans" whistled menacingly past us. It had become midnight by the time we arrived in Warnemünde, and we were taken like criminals to the police station of the council, where we were searched again and questioned. After four hours in the badly smelling room, we were finally released. The following day a train went to Berlin, which we reached about midnight. But I was not to get to my family that evening. The streets around the Stettin train station were cordoned off with wire; so I had to spend the night in a hotel across from the train station. I only arrived at home the following morning.

At the time I was also active literarily; I was commissioned by the Ullstein Publishing Company to write a biography and study of Felix Mendelssohn; the work is supposed to be published shortly.

I am coming to the conclusion. As I noticed when I last paged through this account, I have spoken little of my family and my friends. So may my last words then concern those, who have brightened and filled my life with sunshine through their love and devoted affection.

Without serious storms my small ship of fate sailed through the sea of life; and if on occasion it took the wrong course, then providential navigation steered it back in the right direction. I was spared catastrophic and painful events. Naturally one who is advanced in years has many a dear grave to tend. However, cruel, relentless death demanded tribute from those trusting souls who were dear to me and who could not escape him, at a time when with one exception, he felt that he had the right to make his claim.

My parents died when they had reached the biblical age. Death liberated my dear brother at the age of seventy from a pernicious, very painful illness, which he endured resolutely and without complaint.[20] Of my five children, the third daughter, Marischka, departed this life at the age of eight; it was the first and last heartache that this small, sunny individual caused us.

My oldest daughter devoted herself to art; she studied with Franz Skarbina[21] and achieved considerable skill, especially in painting portraits. Her most successful work so far in the view of experts is the portrait of her father, which she painted for the hall of the Klindworth-Scharwenka Conservatory. A copy of it is supposed to be hung in the concert hall of the same name.

My second daughter, Zenaide, is married to Judge Charmak of the regional court

> and reigns wisely,
> by the hearth,
> and teaches a girl
> and restrains a boy.[22]

(To tell the truth, I unfortunately was forced to correct Schiller—who speaks of an unnamed multitude of children—to correspond to the real circumstances.)

Isolde, my third daughter, possesses a remarkable musical talent, which expresses itself in performance in a well-defined feeling for rhythm and a self-confident capacity for expression. As my partner on the second piano, she has often performed with me in concerts with splendid results. Recently she married the country judge, Judge Knauer.

My son Philipp threw himself into the study of law, however, without having missed out on the opportunity to become acquainted *ex fundamento* with the glories of fraternity life. After completing his studies, as I reported, he went to America and from there to Switzerland. Then came the war, which he took part in from beginning to end. He returned home safely as a lieutenant in the Air Force with the Iron Cross First Class on his chest and now holds a high position in the Civil Service. Last but not least—but who may speak of his wife? For as is well known, it is the best women of whom nothing is said. According to that we ought to remain silent. However, it would be impolite and ungrateful if I were not to say that she was a faithful and devoted companion in life and still is; a lady in the full sense of the word.

Most of my friends lie under the sod: Bruch, Gernsheim, Rüfer, Kiel, the old and the young Dorn, Emile Sauret, Wilhelm Blanck, Otto Leßmann, and many others from related fields of art. In my lasting memory I treasure the fact that I was able to become acquainted with many great masters of the previous century and had the good fortune of getting to know some more closely.

Notes

1. The orchestra opens Chopin's Grande Polonaise Brilliante in E-flat Major, op. 22 (1831), with the preceding Andante spianato (1834). Chopin performed the two together in Paris in 1835 and published the two together in 1836.

2. White wine produced primarily in Austria from Veltliner grapes.

3. Philipp Wolfrum (1854–1919), organist, composer, and conductor, taught music at the University of Heidelberg and founded the Bach-Verein. He worked intensively for the revival of Bach and published a two-volume monograph of Bach. Similarly, he promoted the works of Liszt and headed the group that published Liszt's complete works.

4. Latin for "May God grant his blessing."

5. The *New Yorker Staatszeitung*, founded in 1835 and referred to as the *Staats*, became the largest German newspaper in New York and is still published today as a weekly.

6. The line "das ertrage, wem's gefällt" is quoted from the German translation of Mozart's opera *Don Juan* (1787) by Friedrich Rochlitz.

7. Robert Robitschek (1874–1967), born in Prague, was a student of Dvorak. He conducted the Prague People's Theater before going to Berlin to direct the Tonkünstler Orchestra (1902–1904). From 1904 he was associated with the Klindworth-Scharwenka Conservatory, where he became one of the three directors with Xaver and Philipp Scharwenka. After Philipp Scharwenka's death in 1917, Robitschek served as director of the conservatory until he was forced to retire in 1937 because he was non-Aryan. He composed orchestral and chamber music, songs, piano pieces, and the opera *Ahasver*. He died in St. Paul, Minnesota, in 1967. In 1937 Philipp's son Walter Scharwenka (1881–1960) became the director of the conservatory and also taught organ. One of his organ students was former German Chancellor Helmut Schmidt.

8. Carmen Sylva was the pseudonym under which Queen Elizabeth of Rumania (1843–1916), born in Neuwied, Germany, wrote extensively in German, French, English, and Rumanian.

9. Lemberg is German for the Polish city Lwow.

10. Grigoras Dinicu (1889–1949), Rumanian composer, violinist, and conductor, is well known for his virtuoso violin piece *Hora staccato* and the popular music concerts that he conducted from 1906 to 1946 in Bucharest.

11. Emil Frey (1889–1946), Swiss pianist and composer, studied at the Geneva Conservatory and the Paris Conservatoire, where he won the *premier prix* for piano in 1906. He toured successfully in Europe and South America and taught in Zurich until his death.

12. During the first decades of the twentieth century, America, with its booming dollar economy, was called "Dollarika." Scharwenka refers to the fact that his earnings from his musical endeavors in America helped finance his country home.

13. Gustav Mahler (1860–1911), Austrian composer and conductor, was director of the Vienna Hofoper from 1897 to 1907. In 1907 he signed a contract to conduct the Metropolitan Opera, and his first performance was *Tristan und Isolde* on January 1, 1908. In fall 1908 he returned to conduct both the Metropolitan Opera and the New York Symphony Orchestra. At the end of the season he was asked to conduct the newly reorganized New York Philharmonic. In 1909 he became the principal conductor of the Philharmonic and took it on an American tour in 1910. He died in Vienna on May 18, 1911, of endocarditis.

14. Frederick A. Cook (1865–1940), American polar explorer and physician, accompanied Robert E. Peary as surgeon on an expedition to Greenland in 1891–1892. In a subsequent expedition to the Arctic, he claimed to have reached the North Pole in April 1908, a year before Perry reported reaching it. Perry accused Cook of fraud, and Cook was forced to give up some of his honors. Later he was involved in an oil-drilling scheme in Texas and spent five years (1925–1930) of a fourteen-year sentence in prison.

15. Westrumit was a mixture of oil, ammonia, and water that was sprayed on race-tracks to keep the dust down.

16. Rudolf Cahn-Speyer (1881–1940), Austrian composer and conductor, studied music in Leipzig and Munich, where he received his doctorate. He conducted in Kiel and Hamburg before being appointed as a professor in 1911 at the Klindworth Conservatory in Berlin.

17. A lodge of the Freemasons.

18. Moritz Rosenthal (1862–1946), a virtuoso pianist and interpreter of Chopin's music, was born in Lemberg, studied with Liszt, and eventually settled in New York.

19. Wolfgang Kapp (1858–1922), a right-wing politician, led an armed uprising in Berlin in 1920 with the goal of restoring the German monarchy. His seizure of the government was ended by a general strike. After fleeing to Sweden, he returned to Germany and died in 1922 before coming to trial on charges of treason.

20. Philipp Scharwenka died on July 16, 1917, in Bad Nauheim, a well-known health spa near Frankfurt am Main. His most famous students were the conductors Oskar Fried and Otto Klemperer.

21. Franz Skarbina (1849–1910) was an artist born in Berlin and trained in Paris, where he came under the influence of the Impressionists.

22. The line is taken from Schiller's "Das Lied von der Glocke"; here Scharwenka changes "girls" to "girl" to fit the number of children in his daughter's family.

~

Catalog of Scharwenka's Works

This catalog of works was assembled by Scharwenka for his autobiography and is reproduced here with English translations of most of the titles. Although Scharwenka listed his study of Mendelssohn's life and works, the Ullstein Publishing House has no record of it in its files. The Scharwenka Society also has never been able to locate any materials related to this project, and one must assume therefore that Scharwenka for reasons beyond his control either never completed the study or that his manuscript was lost.

Opus Number	Work	Original Publisher
1.	Trio für Klavier, Violine und Violoncello, Fis-Dur (Trio for Piano, Violin, and Cello, F-sharp Major)	Breitkopf & Härtel
2.	Sonate für Klavier und Violine, D-Moll (Sonata for Piano and Violin, D Minor)	Breitkopf & Härtel
3.	Fünf polnische Tänze für Klavier (Five Polish Dances for Piano)	Breitkopf & Härtel
4.	Scherzo für Klavier, G-Dur (Scherzo for Piano, G Major)	Breitkopf & Härtel
5.	Zwei Erzählungen am Klavier, Des-Dur, F-Dur (Two Legends for Piano, D-flat Major, F Major)	Breitkopf & Härtel
6.	Sonate für Klavier, Cis-Moll (Sonata for Piano, C-sharp Minor)	Breitkopf & Härtel
7.	Polonäse für Klavier, A-Moll (Polonaise for Piano, A Minor)	Breitkopf & Härtel
8.	Ballade für Klavier, H-Moll (Ballade for Piano, B Minor)	Breitkopf & Härtel

Opus Number	Work	Original Publisher
9.	Drei polnische Tänze für Klavier, Cis-Moll, C-Dur, B-Moll (Three Polish Dances for Piano, C-sharp Minor, C Major, B-flat Minor)	Breitkopf & Härtel
10.	Vier Lieder für eine mittlere Stimme mit Klavierbegleitung (Four Songs for Medium Voice with Piano Accompaniment)	Breitkopf & Härtel
11.	Tarantelle für Klavier, F-Moll (Tarantella for Piano, F Minor)	H. Heiser
12.	Polonäse für Klavier, Cis-Moll (Polonaise for Piano, C-sharp Minor)	H. Heiser
13.	Walzer für Klavier, As-Dur (Waltz for Piano, A-flat Major)	H. Heiser
14.	Barcarole für Klavier, E-Moll (Barcarole for Piano, E Minor)	Augener & Co.
15.	Drei Lieder für eine mittlere Stimme mit Klavierbegleitung (Three Songs for Medium Voice with Piano Accompaniment)	Breitkopf & Härtel
16.	Polonäse und Mazurka für Klavier (Polonaise and Mazurka for Piano)	Breitkopf & Härtel
17.	Impromptu für Klavier, D-Dur (Impromptu for Piano, D Major)	Breitkopf & Härtel
18.	Menuett für Klavier, B-Dur (Minuet for Piano, B-flat Major)	C. Simon
19.	Scherzo con duo Intermezzi für Klavier, D-Moll (Scherzo con duo Intermezzi for Piano, D Minor)	C. Simon
20.	Drei Klavierstücke, A-Moll, D-Moll, A-Dur (Three Pieces for Piano, A Minor, D Minor, A Major)	C. Simon
21.	"Nordisches" für Klavier, vierhändig, F-Dur, C-Dur (Something Nordic for Piano, Four Hands, F Major, C Major)	C. Simon
22.	Novellette und Melodie für Klavier, F-Moll, F-Dur (Novellette and Melody for Piano, F Minor, F Major)	Praeger & Meyer
23.	Wanderbilder für Klavier, H-Dur, B-Dur (Travel Pictures for Piano, B Major, B-flat Major)	Praeger & Meyer
24.	Aus alter und neuer Zeit. Vier Klavierstücke, vierhändig (From Old and Recent Times, Four Piano Pieces for Four Hands)	Praeger & Meyer
25.	Zwei Romanzen für Klavier, G-Moll, As-Dur (Two Romances for Piano, G Minor, A-flat Major)	Praeger & Meyer
26.	Bilder aus Ungarn für Klavier, Cis-Moll, B-Moll (Pictures from Hungary for Piano, C-sharp Minor, B-flat Minor)	Praeger & Meyer
27.	Sechs Etüden und Präludien für Klavier (Six Etudes and Preludes for Piano)	C. Simon
28.	Sechs Walzer für Klavier (Six Waltzes for Piano)	Breitkopf & Härtel

Opus Number	Work	Original Publisher
29.	Zwei polnische Tänze, Cis-Moll, H-Moll (Two Polish Dances, C-sharp Minor, B Minor)	Breitkopf & Härtel
30.	Valse-Impromptu, F-Moll (Valse Impromptu, F Minor)	Praeger & Meyer
31.	Valse Caprice für Klavier, A-Dur (Valse Caprice for Piano, A Major)	Praeger & Meyer
32.	Konzert für Klavier und Orchester, B-Moll (Concerto for Piano and Orchestra, B-flat Minor)	Praeger & Meyer
33.	Romanzero für Klavier (Romanzero for Piano)	Praeger & Meyer
34.	Zwei polnische Tänze für Klavier, H-Moll, Cis-Moll (Two Polish Dances for Piano, B Minor, C-sharp Minor)	Breitkopf & Härtel
35.	II. Valse Caprice für Klavier, A-Dur (II. Valse Caprice for Piano, A Major)	Breitkopf & Härtel
36.	Zweite Sonate für Klavier, Es-Dur (Second Sonata for Piano, E-flat Major)	Breitkopf & Härtel
37.	Quartett für Klavier, Violine, Bratsche, und Violoncello, F-Dur (Quartet for Piano, Violin, Viola, and Cello, F Major)	Praeger & Meyer
38.	Im Freien. Fünf Tonbilder für Klavier (Outdoors. Five Tone Pictures for Piano)	Augener & Co.
39.	Bilder aus dem Süden für Klavier, vierhändig (Pictures from the South for Piano, for Four Hands)	Augener & Co.
40.	Zwei polnische Tänze für Klavier, B-Moll, Es-Dur (Two Polish Dances for Piano, B-flat Minor, E-flat Major)	Augener & Co.
41.	Suite de danses für Klavier, vierhändig (Suite of Dances for Piano, for Four Hands)	Augener & Co.
42.	Polonäse für Klavier, F-Moll (Polonaise for Piano, F Minor)	Augener & Co.
43.	Album für Klavier (Album for Piano)	Augener & Co.
44.	Zwei Walzer für Klavier, vierhändig, D-Dur, Es-Dur (Two Waltzes for Piano, for Four Hands, D Major, E-flat Major)	Augener & Co.
45.	Zweites Trio für Klavier, Violine, und Violoncello, A-Moll (Second Trio for Piano, Violin, and Cello, A Minor)	Praeger & Meyer
46.	Sonate für Klavier und Violoncello, E-Moll (Sonata for Piano and Cello, E Minor)	Augener & Co.
47.	Vier polnische Tänze für Klavier, B-Moll, G-Moll, B-Dur, E-Moll (Four Polish Dances for Piano, B-flat Minor, G Minor, B-flat Major, E Minor)	Augener & Co.
48.	Variationen für Klavier, D-Moll (Variations for Piano, D Minor)	Augener & Co.
49.	Zwei Menuette für Klavier, E-Moll, Es-Dur (Two Minuets for Piano, E Minor, E-flat Major)	Augener & Co.
50.	Fantasiestücke für Klavier (Fantasy Pieces for Piano)	Augener & Co.

Opus Number	Work	Original Publisher
51.	Zwei Klavierstücke: Tarantelle G-Moll; Polonäse Cis-Moll (Two Piano Pieces: Tarantella, G Minor; Polonaise, C-sharp Minor)	Augener & Co.
52.	Zwei Sonatinen für Klavier, E-Moll, B-Dur (Two Sonatinas for Piano, E Minor, B-flat Major)	Augener & Co.
53a.	Zwei Stücke für Klavier, F-Moll, E-Dur (Two Pieces for Piano, F Minor, E Major)	Augener & Co.
53b.	Drei Stücke für Klavier: Prärie-Rose, Western Daisy, Wild Primrose (Three Pieces for Piano: Prairie Rose, Western Daisy, Wild Primrose)	C. F. Trebbar, NY
54.	Ballerinnerungen: Walzer, Menuett, Polnischer Tanz (Memories of the Ball: Waltz, Minuet, Polish Dance)	Breitkopf & Härtel
55.	Huldigungsmarsch zur Krönungsfeier des Königs und der Königin von Rumänien (Honor March for the Coronation of the King and Queen of Rumania)	Bote & Bock
56.	Zweites Konzert für Klavier und Orchester, C-Moll (Second Concerto for Piano and Orchestra, C Minor)	Breitkopf & Härtel
57.	Variationen für Klavier über ein Thema von C. H. (Variations for Piano on a Theme of C. H.)	Bote & Bock
58.	Vier polnische Tänze für Klavier, Cis-Moll, B-Moll, C-Moll, D-Moll (Four Polish Dances for Piano, C-sharp Minor, B-flat Minor, C Minor, D Minor)	Augener & Co.
59.	Romanzero für Klavier, II. Teil (Romanzero for Piano, Part II)	Breitkopf & Härtel
60.	Symphonie für Orchester, C-Moll (Symphony for Orchestra, C Minor)	Breitkopf & Härtel
61.	Menuett und polnischer Tanz, F-Dur, B-Dur (Minuet and Polish Dance, F Major, B-flat Major)	Breitkopf & Härtel
62.	Album für die Jugend (Album for Young People)	Breitkopf & Härtel
63.	Drei Klavierstücke: Spanisches Ständchen, Barcarole, Tarantelle (Three Piano Pieces: Spanish Serenade, Barcarole, Tarantella)	John Church Co., NY
64.	Neuer Romanzero für Klavier (New Romanzero for Piano)	Breitkopf & Härtel
65.	Zwei Klavierstücke: Menuett, Scherzo (Two Piano Pieces: Minuet, Scherzo)	John Church Co., NY
66.	Zwei polnische Tänze, C-Dur, B-Moll (Two Polish Dances, C Major, B-flat Minor)	John Church Co., NY
67.	Zwei Klavierstücke: Im Zwielicht, Abendfriede (Two Piano Pieces: In the Twilight, In the Still of the Evening)	John Church Co., NY
68.	Drei Klavierstücke: Liebesliedchen, Scherzo, Zum Andenken (Three Piano Pieces: Love Song, Scherzo, In Memory)	John Church Co., NY

Opus Number	Work	Original Publisher
69.	Mazurka-Caprice für Klavier, G-Moll (Mazurka-Caprice for Piano, G Minor)	John Church Co., NY
70.	Serenade für Violine und Klavier, G-Dur (Serenade for Violin and Piano, G Major)	John Church Co., NY
71.	Vier Klavierstücke: Scherzino, Murmelndes Bächlein, Spinnrädchen, Valse mélancolique (Four Piano Pieces: Scherzino, Murmuring Brook, Spinning Wheel, Valse mélancolique)	John Church Co., NY
72.	Rhapsodie für Klavier, H-Moll (Rhapsody for Piano, B Minor)	John Church Co., NY
73.	Zwei Klavierstücke: Humoreske, Moment Musical (Two Piano Pieces: Humoresque, Moment Musical)	John Church Co., NY
74.	Zwei ländliche Tänze für Klavier (Two Country Dances for Piano)	John Church Co., NY
75.	Vier Kirchengesänge für gemischten Chor, Solo und Orgel (Four Chorales for Mixed Choir, Solo, and Organ)	P. L. Jung, NY
76a.	Polnische Rhapsodie für Klavier (Polish Rhapsody for Piano)	Breitkopf & Härtel
76b.	Valse Impromptu für Klavier, B-Dur (Valse Impromptu for Piano, B-flat Major)	Breitkopf & Härtel
77.	Beiträge zur Fingerbildung für Klavier, 3 Hefte (Contributions to Finger Training for Piano, Three Books)	Breitkopf & Härtel
78.	Studien im Oktavenspiel für Klavier (Studies in Playing Octaves for Piano)	Breitkopf & Härtel
79.	Zwei Gesänge für Männerchor: Sonnenlicht, Sonnenschein; Ein Stündlein wohl vor Tag (Two Chorales for Male Chorus: Sunlight, Sunshine; A Short While before Day)	Breitkopf & Härtel
80.	Drittes Konzert für Klavier und Orchester, Cis-Moll (Third Concerto for Piano and Orchestra, C-sharp Minor)	Breitkopf & Härtel
81.	Zwei Militärmärsche für Infanterie- bzw. Jäger-, Schützen-, Pionier- oder Kavalleriemusik, Manuskript (Two Military Marches for Infantry or Riflemen, Engineer or Cavalry Music, manuscript)	Breitkopf & Härtel
82.	Viertes Konzert für Klavier und Orchester, F-Moll (Fourth Piano Concerto for Piano and Orchestra, F Minor)	F. E. C. Leuckart
83.	Variationen über ein eigenes Thema, C-Dur (Variations on an Original Theme, C Major)	Peters
84.	"Eglantine" für Klavier ("Eglantine" for Piano)	Art Publ. Society, St. Louis, MO

Opus Number	Work	Original Publisher
85.	Zwei Balladen für Klavier, Fis-Moll, F-Moll (Two Ballades for Piano, F-sharp Minor, F Minor)	F. E. C. Leuckart
86.	Drei Klavierstücke: Nocturno, Serenade, Märchen (Three Piano Pieces: Nocturne, Serenade, Fairytale)	Peters
87.	Zwei lustige Stücke für Klavier, As-Dur, C-Dur (Two Merry Pieces for the Piano, A-flat Major, C Major)	Peters
88.	Acht Gesänge für eine mittlere Stimme mit Klavierbegleitung (Eight songs for Medium Piano Accompaniment)	F. E. C. Leuckart
89.	Sommertage am Achensee. Fünf Stücke für Klavier, Posaune und Pauken (Summer Days on Lake Achen. Five Pieces for Piano, Trombone, and Timpani)	Siegel

Works without Opus Number

Work	Original Publisher
Mataswintha, Oper; Partitur und Klavierauszug (*Mataswintha*, Opera; Full Score and Piano Score)	Breitkopf & Härtel
Tarantelle für Klavier, F-Moll (Tarantella for Piano, F Minor)	Reinecke Bros.
Sechs Tanzcapricen (Six Dance Caprices) Pfalzgräfin Jutta, Ballade für eine mittlere Stimme (Palatine Countess Jutta, Ballade for a Medium Voice)	Augener & Co. Praeger & Meyer
Meisterschule des Klavierspiels, 4 Bände (*Master Class for Piano Playing*, 4 vols.)	Breitkopf & Härtel
"An die blauen Jungs" für zweistimmigen Männerchor ("To the Boys in Blue" for Two-Part Male Chorus)	Breitkopf & Härtel
"The Day Dream" (Tennyson) für eine Singstimme ("The Day Dream" [Tennyson] for Single Voice)	C. Kegar & Co.
"Impromptu à la hongroise" und Marsch für Klavier nach Schubert (Impromptu à la hongroise and March for Piano after Schubert)	Breitkopf & Härtel
Ouvertüre für Orchester, C-Moll (Overture for Orchestra, C Minor). Manuskript, Jugendarbeit (Manuscript, early work)	Breitkopf & Härtel
Methodik des Klavierspiels: Systematische Darstellung der technischen und ästhetischen Erfordernisse für einen rationellen Lehrgang (*Methodology of Playing the Piano: Systematic Description of the Technical and Aesthetic Requirements for a Rational Course of Study*)	Breitkopf & Härtel
Felix Mendelssohn Bartholdy: Sein Leben und Analyse seiner Werke (*Felix Mendelssohn Bartholdy: His Life and an Analysis of His Works*)	Ullstein & Co.

Revised Editions

Work	Original Publisher
Robert Schumann. *Complete Piano Works*	Pohle, Hamburg
Frederic Chopin. *Complete Piano Works*	Augener & Co.; Schott, Mainz
Ludwig van Beethoven. *Variations and Choral Fantasy*	Breitkopf & Härtel

~

Discography

Compiled by Robert S. Feigelson

A comprehensive Scharwenka discography is provided in two sections. The first contains a list of some of Scharwenka's historic piano recordings. It covers both his own music as well as the works of other composers. It provides an excellent idea of the repertoire that appealed to him and the pieces he most likely performed in concert. According to Trenkner,[1] Scharwenka made seventy-six piano roll recordings for Welte-Mignon, Hupfeld, and the Philips Companies. I could not find more than a passing reference[2] to this large number and have included only the specific rolls I was able to find from a wide variety of sources. A complete compilation of these historic performances is beyond the scope of this book. Scharwenka recorded mainly in the periods 1905–1906 and 1910–1913. Like many other famous pianists of the time, Scharwenka thought that the Welte mechanical reproductive system accurately reflected his playing with respect to touch, tempo, and tonal quality. Surprisingly the subject of these or any other recordings was not discussed in his autobiography.

Scharwenka also recorded for a few other companies, including early 78 rpm recordings for Columbia Records. However, since many piano roll recordings were marketed under several brand names and also transferred to other audio media, it is difficult to trace the history of many of his recordings.

When long-playing 33 1/3 rpm records came on the scene in the early 1950s, some of these early piano rolls were rerecorded using the original piano roll equipment as the source. Thus modern recordings of the historic performances by Scharwenka and many other famous pianists and composers, such as Saint-Saëns, Busoni, Hoffman, and Debussy, were preserved. In the current age, piano roll recordings have been faithfully transferred to digital compact discs. Two of his recorded performances are included on the enclosed CD; one from an off-air tape from the 1970s radio program *Keyboard Immortals Play Again... In Stereo*, produced by Joseph S. Tushinsky (at the time owner of a very large collection of piano rolls), and the other from a currently available Nimbus compact disc.

The second section covers recordings of Scharwenka's musical compositions. It is divided into two sections: historic performances from piano rolls to early LP recordings and modern recordings from the late LP era up to currently available digital recordings. The bulk of the historic recordings are of his famous Polish Dance. This music has been transcribed and arranged for a surprisingly large variety of instruments and instrumental combinations, not all of which have been recorded. A transcription for solo guitar is one example. Modern recordings of Scharwenka's music have benefited from excellent sound quality and enthusiastic performances. A reasonable sample of these recordings can be heard on the enclosed compact disc.

Scharwenka's Recorded Performances

Collected Piano Performances
Franz Xaver Scharwenka Performs in 1906, Welte Legacy of Piano Treasures, North Hollywood, CA: LP RTN 685/ Fantasia for Piano, op. 49 in F Minor/Chopin, Etude d'Execution Transcendante, no. 9, Ricordanza/Liszt, Polish National Dance, op. 3, no. 1, in E-flat Minor/Scharwenka, Piano Sonata no. 27, op. 90, in E minor, First Movement/Beethoven, Valse in A-flat, op. 42/Chopin, Impromptu à la hongroise/Schubert, Fantasia or Caprice for Piano, Scherzo, op. 16, no. 2, in E Minor/Mendelssohn, performed on a Welte-Vorsetzer (1970).

Caprice (Fantasie), op. 16, no. 2/Mendelssohn
Welte Corp., Freiburg, Germany: Roll 232.
Franz Xaver Scharwenka Performs in 1906, Welte Legacy of Piano Treasures, North Hollywood, CA: LP, RTN 685 (1970). (See collected piano music.)

Erzählungen am Klavier (Two Legends), op. 5, no. 1, in D-flat/ Xaver Scharwenka
Welte-Mignon Corp., Freiburg, Germany: Roll 235 and C-235.

Etude d'Execution Transcendante, no. 9, Ricordanza/Liszt

Welte Corp., Freiburg, Germany: Roll 244 (recorded 1905?).

Telefunken, Hamburg, Germany: 10" LP, WE 28020 (from Welte-Mignon rolls) with Polish Dance, op. 3, no. 1, recorded in 1905 (1955).

Franz Xaver Scharwenka Performs in 1906, Welte Legacy of Piano Treasures, North Hollywood, CA: LP, RTN 685 (1970). (See collected piano music.)

The Compositions of Franz Liszt as Performed by the Legendary Masters of the Piano, limited centennial edition, Welte Legacy of Piano Treasures, Studio City, CA: LP, LCC 5860 and LCC 5861, recorded in 1906 (1986).

Fantasy-Impromptu in C-sharp Minor, op. 66/Chopin

Columbia Phonograph Co.: A5261, 12" 78 rpm (mx 30610-2), Col-Rena 254 (UK), recorded 27 December 1910, released in April 1911.

Welte Legacy of Piano Treasures: reissued by Reader's Digest, Pleasantville, NY: CD, RC7-206-3, also KRC-206, RC6-206-1, and RDK-6162/F (1992).

A Multitude of Pianists' Rare Recordings, from the Harry L. Anderson collection, with Scharwenka's *Polish Dance op. 3, no. 1*, IPAM Records, International Piano Archive at Maryland: CD, IPAM 1206, recorded in 1906 (2000).

The Art of the Piano: Its Performers, Literature, and Recordings, CD included with the book of the same name by David Dubai (Pompton Plains, NJ: Amadeus Press, under license from Arbiter Records, 2004).

Fantasia in F minor, op. 49/Chopin

Welte Corp., Freiburg, Germany: Roll 241.

Franz Xaver Scharwenka Performs in 1906, Welte Legacy of Piano Treasures, North Hollywood, CA: LP, RTN 685 (1970). (See collected piano music.)

Frühlingsstimme/Strauss

Columbia Phonograph Co.: 10" 78 rpm (mx 36545-1-2), recorded 30 January 1913. (Commercially released?)

Impromptu a la hongroise/Schubert

Welte Corp., Freiburg, Germany: Roll 250.

Berühmte Pianisten um die Jahrhundertwende: Aufnahmen von Einspielungen auf dem Welte-Mignon-Flügel in den Jahren 1905–1913, Telefunken, Hamburg, Germany: 12" mono LP, HT 32, recorded in 1905 (1950).

Telefunken, Hamburg, Germany: 10" LP, WE 28016, recorded in 1905 (1955) (from Welte-Mignon rolls).

The Definitive Piano: Welte-Mignon Piano Reproductions, Telefunken, Hamburg, Germany: 10" LP, WEV 28017, recorded 1905 (1960–1969?).
Franz Xaver Scharwenka Performs in1906, Welte Legacy of Piano Treasures, North Hollywood, CA: LP, RTN 685 (1970). (See collected piano music.)

Invitation to the Dance/Weber
Columbia Phonograph Co.: 12" 78 rpm (mx 36544-1), Col-Rena 401 (UK), recorded 30 January 1913.

Klaviersonate Nr. 23 in F-Moll (Appassionata): First Movement/Beethoven
Hupfeld, Leipzig, Germany: Roll 52790 (Andante con moto-presto).
Legendary Masters of the Piano, Recorded in 1905, The Classics Record Library, Camp Hill, PA: three-12" LP's, SWV 6633 (produced and manufactured for Book-of-the-Month Club Inc.) Los Angeles, CA (1963).
Welte-Mignon 1905: Berühmte Komponisten spielen ihre Werke, from Welte-Mignon Rolls, Telefunken, Hamburg, Germany: 12" Stereo LP, SLA 25057 (1971).
Berühmte Pianisten der Jahrhundertwende spielen Beethoven und Schubert, from Welte-Mignon Roll 236, Teldec, Hamburg, Germany: CD 8.43929, recorded 7 March 1905 (1988).

Klaviersonate Nr. 27 in E, op. 90/Beethoven
Welte Corp., Freiburg, Germany: Roll 236.
Franz Xaver Scharwenka Performs in 1906, Welte Legacy of Piano Treasures, North Hollywood, CA: LP, RTN 685 (1970). (See collected piano music.)
Welte Legacy of Piano Treasures, 1968–1969 Sampler of the Encore Release, Recorded Treasures Inc.: 12" Stereo LP, SLPR 1001, SLPR 1004 (1969).

Kreisleriana, op. 16, nos. 1–6/Schumann
Welte Corp., Freiburg, Germany: Roll 239.

Liebesnacht, op. 40/Philipp Scharwenka
The Aeolian Co., New York: 46 note organ roll 5147.

Liebestraum, no. 3/Liszt
Columbia Phonograph Co.: 12" 78 rpm, A5467,(mx 30608-2), Col-Rena 351 (UK), recorded 27 December 1910, released in June 1913.
Famous Voices of the Past: Famous Pianists, Rococo Records, Toronto, Canada: 12" mono, RR 2049 (1970s).

Marche des "Davidsbündler" contre les Philistin from Carnaval, op. 9, no. 21/Schumann
The Aeolian Co., New York: American Autographic Roll A-089.
The Aeolian Co., New York: Duo-Art Roll 5531, recorded 8 March 1905.

Mazurka, op. 16, no. 2/Xaver Scharwenka
The Aeolian Co., New York: Duo-Art Roll 5534, recorded 8 March 1905.

Mazurka/Xaver Scharwenka
The Aeolian Co., New York: Roll 4238.

Mazurka, op. 33, no. 4/Chopin
Welte Corp., Freiburg, Germany: Roll 240.

Nocturne in F-sharp, op. 15, no. 2/Chopin
Welte Corp., Freiburg, Germany: Roll 242.
Bedeutende Pianisten vergangener Zeiten, from Welte-Mignon rolls, Telefunken, Hamburg, Germany: 10" LP, WE 28017, recorded in 1905 (1955).

Nocturne, op. 23, no. 4/Schumann
Welte Corp., Freiburg, Germany: Roll 238.

Notturno/Xaver Scharwenka
The Aeolian Co., New York: 46 note organ Roll 5023.

Novelette/Xaver Scharwenka
Duo-Art: Roll 5519.

On the Beautiful Blue Danube/Strauss
Columbia Phonograph Co.: 10" 78 rpm (mx 36549), recorded on 30 January 1913. (May not have been commercially released.)

Polish National Dance, op. 3, no. 1, in E-flat Minor (1869)/ Xaver Scharwenka

Piano Rolls
The Aeolian Co., New York: World of Music Series: Roll POL 8.
The Aeolian Co., New York: 46 note organ, Roll 2940.
The Aeolian Co., New York: Themodist-Metrostyle, 88 note, Roll 80134/N22.
Ampico Corp., NewYork/Hupfeld, Leipzig, Germany: Rolls 91041, 60001-H (release date 1921).

Apollo Piano Co. DeKalb, IL: Roll 1194, recorded in 1905.

Hupfeld-Phonola, Leipzig, Germany: Roll 50377.

Duo-Art/Hupfeld, Leipzig, Germany: Roll 5637, recorded 8 March 1905.

Perforetur Music Rolls, Germany: 88 note, Roll CR 10009, originally manufactured by QRS, Pianola Recordings, listed as Polish Dance op. 3, no. 2 (for piano 8 hands) (late 1980s).

Wax Cylinders

Everlasting Records, U.S. Phonograph Co., Cleveland, OH: Cylinder 1215, recorded in 1909.

78 RPM Records

Columbia Phonograph Co.: A5260, 12" (matrix 30606), Eng. Col-Rena 251 (UK), recorded 27 December 1910, release date April 1911.

Long-playing 33 1/3 RPM Records

Telefunken, Hamburg, Germany: 10" mono, Welte-Mignon Rolls with Liszt's *Ricordanza-Etude*, WE 28020, recorded in 1905 (1955).

Legendary Masters of the Piano, from Welte-Mignon Rolls (played on a Steinway piano), the Classic Record Library: 12" mono, SWV 6633, recorded in 1906 (1963).

Famous Voices of the Past: Famous Pianists, Rococo Records, Toronto, Canada: 12" mono, RR 2049 (1970s).

Franz Xaver Scharwenka Performs in 1906, Welte Legacy of Piano Treasures, North Hollywood, CA: LP, RTN 685 (1970). (See collected piano music.)

Welte Legacy of Piano Treasures: Great Composers/Pianists Perform Their Own Compositions, Vol. 3, Recorded Treasures, Inc., North Hollywood, CA: 12" stereo LP, GCP 771, recorded in 1906 (1972).

Digital Compact Discs

A Multitude of Pianists' Rare Recordings, from the Harry L. Anderson collection, with *Chopin's Fantasie-Impromptu*, IPAM Records, International Piano Archive at Maryland: IPAM 1206, recorded in 1906 (2000).

Naxos: 8.110 679, from Welte-Mignon rolls, recorded in 1905 (2004).

Piano Rolls versus Discs, from Columbia Records 78 rpm disc, A5260, plus a piano roll excerpt, Symposium SYP1211, recorded 16 August 1904 (2004).

Polish Dance, op. 47, in E-flat Minor/Xaver Scharwenka

Welte-Mignon Corp., Freiburg, Germany: Piano Rolls C-233 and P-233.

Great Masters of the Keyboard, Vol. 4, from Welte Rolls, Columbia Records: 12", ML 4294 (1950).

Rhapsody op. 79/Brahms
Bedeutende Pianisten vergangener Zeiten, from Welte-Mignon rolls, Telefunken, Hamburg, Germany: 10" LP, WE 28023, recorded in 1905 (1955).

Rondo Capriccioso, op. 14, in E/Mendelssohn
The Aeolian Co., New York: Duo-Art Roll 5542, recorded 8 March 1905.
Columbia Phonograph Co: 10" 78 rpm, A5467, (mx 36543-2), recorded 30 January 1913.
Famous Voices of the Past: Famous Pianists, Rococo Records, Toronto, Canada: 12" mono, RR 2049 (1970s).

Le Rossignol, op. 32/Alexander Alabjeff (trans. Franz Liszt)
Hupfeld Phonola: Roll 51033.

Scherzo no. 2 in B-Flat minor, op. 31/Chopin
Nimbus Records: CD, NI 8816, recorded in 1914 (1998).
The Aeolian Co., New York: Duo-Art Roll 5545, recorded 8 March 1905.

Spanish Serenade, op. 63, no. 1
Columbia Phonograph Co.: 12" 78 rpm, A5261, (mx 30611-2), Col-Rena A254 (UK), recorded 27 December 1910.

Tarantella in A-flat (probably Chopin's op. 43)
Apollo Piano Co., DeKalb, IL: Roll 1230.

Valse Brillante, op. 34, no. 1/Chopin
Columbia Phonograph Co.: 12" 78 rpm, A5260, (mx 30609-2), Col-Rena 251 (UK), recorded 27 December 1910, released April 1911.
Famous Voices of the Past: Famous Pianists, Rococo Records, Toronto, Canada: 12" mono, RR 2049 (1970s).

Valse Caprice, op. 31/Xaver Scharwenka
The Aeolian Co., New York: Piano Roll 2988.

Waldszenen, op. 82, no. 7: Bird as Prophet/Schumann
Welte Corp., Freiburg, Germany: Roll 247.

Waltz in A-flat Major, op. 42/Chopin
   Telefunken: 10" LP, WE 28019, from Welte-Mignon Roll recorded 1905 (1955).
   Welte Corp., Freiburg, Germany: Roll 245.
   Franz Xaver Scharwenka Performs in 1906, Welte Legacy of Piano Treasures, North Hollywood, CA: LP, RTN 685 (1970). (See collected piano music.)

Recorded Performances of Scharwenka's Musical Compositions

Historic Recordings

Etude "Staccato," op. 27, no. 5, in E-flat
   Martha Siebold, Welte-Mignon: Roll 1233.

Polish Dance, op. 3, no. 1, in E-flat Minor (1869)

Piano Rolls
   Theodora Sturkow-Ryder (1876–1958), Duo-Art: QRS Autograph Roll 80162. mp3 file:
   www.kunstderfuge.com/_/scharwenka_80162s_polish_dance_%28nc%29 smythe.mid (29 January 2006).
   Harold Bauer (1873–1951), Duo-Art/Hupfeld: Roll 6416 (8 March 1905).
   Marguerite Volavy (1886–1951), Ampico: Rolls 56683H, 37150, and 67311H.
   Jack Blair (?), Welte-Mignon, *Polishola One-Step* (arr. by Fuiks), Rolls 3923, B 3923.
   Le Brun (?), Imperial Industrial Corp.: QRS. Rolls 3745, 1459.

Wax Cylinder
   Edison Concert Band, National Phonograph Co., Edison Record Co., Orange City, NJ: No. 9866 (recorded 1908).

78 RPM Recordings
   Percy Grainger (1882–1961), Columbia Phonograph Co.: 12", A6128 (mx 49639-2), recorded 17 June 1919.
   Harry Thomas (1890–1941), *in A Classical Spasm-Ragtime One-step Based on Scharwenka's Polish Dance*, Victor Records: 10", 18229B (recorded 3 December 1916, released April 1917). mp3 file: www.collectionscanada.ca/obj/m2/f7/10128.mp3 (29 January 2006).

Hans Barth (1897–1956), Victor Records: 2023B (recorded 8 May 1926).

William H. Reitz (ca. 1874–ca. 1928), William H. Reitz Orchestra, Victor Records: 16855B (recorded 9 March 1911).

Rudolph Ganz (1877–1972), Pathé Frères, New York: 59068 (mx E 66500-1-A) and 5382.

B. Walton O'Donnell (1887–1939), BBC Broadcasting Co., Wireless British Military Band, Columbia Records: AX4533 and 50240D.

Edith Lorand (1898–1960), Edith Lorand Orchestra, Odeon Records: 3141.

Toscha Seidel (1900–1962) (violin), Harry Kaufman (piano), Columbia Phonograph Co.: 10", A78747-1-2-3, 78747-4-5-6 (20 October 1919), A78748 (26 March 1920), mxs 30205, 33043.

Charles Kellog (1869–1949) (bird imitator), accompanied by Walter B. Rogers (piano), Victor Records: 45107 (recorded 15 February 1916). See Brian Rust and Allen G. Debus, *Complete Entertainment Discography 1897–1942* (New York: Da Capo Press, 1989).

Tape Recording

Percy Grainger, Bishop's University, Lennoxville, Quebec: sound tape reel (ca. 90 min.), analog, 7 1/2 ips, 4 tracks; 7 (1972).

Long-playing Recordings

Liberace (1919–1987), Columbia Records: 10" LP, CL 6217 (1952), LP, CL 575 (1954), also 45 rpm EP set, B-308, and 78 rpm, C-308.

Anthony Giammatteo (conductor), Manhattan Concert Band, RCA Records: 16" LP, MSO 4558 (arranged for band by Giammatteo). A radio transcription probably recorded in 1937 by RCA for the Federal Music Project, Works Progress Administration.

Charlotte Martin (piano), Educo Records, Ventura Park, CA: International Library of Piano Music, 12" LP, 16 (1967).

Spanish Serenade, op. 63, no. 1

Martha Siebold, Welte-Mignon: Rolls 1235, D-1235.

Waltz

Peter Helm (piano), *Classics of the Ballet*, Vol. 4, Dansounds, Philadelphia, PA: 12" LP Stereo, DSLP 004 (1980–1989?).

Walzer from Ballerinnerungen, op. 54, no. 1, in A-flat

Martha Siebold, Welte-Mignon: Roll E-1234.

Modern Recordings

Orchestral Music

Overture (1869)
Christopher Fifield, Gävle Symphony Orchestra, Sterling 2004, CDS 1060-2, CD, DDD.

Andante Religioso, op. 46a (1881)
Christopher Fifield, Gävle Symphony Orchestra, Sterling (2004),CDS 1060-2, CD, DDD.

Symphony in C Minor, op. 60 (1882)
Christopher Fifield, Gävle Symphony Orchestra, Sterling (2004), CDS 1060-2, CD, DDD.

Concertos for Piano and Orchestra

Piano Concerto no. 1 in B-flat Minor, op. 32 (1876)
Earl Wild (piano), Erich Leinsdorf (conductor), Boston Symphony Orchestra, RCA (1971), 12" LP Stereo, LSC-3190, rec. Symphony Hall Boston, 20 January 1968, rereleased in 1995 by Elan Recordings, CD 82266, ADD.
Seta Tanyel (piano), Yuri Simonov (conductor), the Philharmonia, Collins Classics (1991), CD 12632, DDD.
Laurence Jeanningros (piano), Paul Freeman (conductor), Czech National Symphony Orchestra, Centaur (2001), CD CRC 2500, DDD.
Marc-Andre Hamelin (piano), Michael Stern (conductor), BBC Scottish Symphony Orchestra, Hyperion Records, Ltd. (2005), CD 66790, DDD.

Piano Concerto no. 2 in C Minor, op. 56 (1881)
Raymond Lewenthal (piano), Eleazar de Carvalho (conductor), London Symphony Orchestra, Columbia Records/CBS, Inc. (Finale only, 1970), 12" LP Stereo, MS 7394. A 7" bonus LP, BTS 20, was titled *Raymond Lewenthal Discusses and Illustrates at the Keyboard Rubinstein's Piano Concerto No. 4 and Finale from Scharwenka's Piano Concerto No. 2*, rereleased without bonus recording by Elan Recordings, Inc., Riverdale, MD (1999), CD 82284, ADD.
Michael Ponti (piano), Richard Kapp (conductor), Hamburg Symphony Orchestra, originally issued on Vox/Candide (1972), 12" LP, CE 31046 and STGBY651 (UK), rereleased in 1992 in *The Romantic Piano Concerto*, Vol. 3, on VOX BOX 2, CDX #5066, ADD.

Seta Tanyel (piano), Tadeusz Strugala (conductor), Radio Philharmonie Hannover des NDR, Collins Classics (1997), CD 14852, DDD, rereleased on Hyperion Records Ltd. (2003), CDA 67365.

Laurence Jeanningros (piano), Paul Freeman (conductor), Czech National Symphony Orchestra, Centaur Records (2001), CD CRC 2500, DDD.

Piano Concerto no. 3 in C-sharp Minor, op. 80 (1898–1899)

Seta Tanyel (piano), Tadeusz Strugala (conductor), Radio Philharmonie Hannover des NDR, Collins Classics (1997), CD 14852, DDD, rereleased on Hyperion Records Ltd. (2003), CDA 67365.

Piano Concerto no. 4 in F Minor, op. 82 (1908)

Stephen Hough (piano), Lawrence Foster (conductor), City of Birmingham Symphony Orchestra, Hyperion Records, Ltd. (1995), CD CDA 66790, DDD.

Chamber Music

Piano Trio no. 1 in F-sharp Minor, op. 1 (1869)

Seta Tanyel (piano), Lydia Mordkovitch (violin), and Colin Carr (cello), Collins Classics (1995), CD 1448-2, DDD, rereleased in two-CD set, *The Complete Chamber Music*, Hyperion Records Ltd. (2002), Dyad CDD 22046.

Violin Sonata in D Minor, op. 2 (1869)

Lydia Mordkovitch (violin), Seta Tanyel (piano), Collins Classics (1995), CD 14482, DDD, rereleased in two-CD set, *The Complete Chamber Music*, Hyperion Records Ltd. (2002), Dyad CDD 22046.

Robert Zimansky (violin), Gordon Steel (piano), Genesis Records, Inc. (1975), 12" LP Stereo, GS 1056.

Piano Quartet in F Major, op. 37 (1876)

Seta Tanyel (piano), Levon Chilingirian (violin), Ivo-Jan der Werff (viola), Gargis Atmacayan (cello), Collins Classics (1994), CD 14192, DDD, rereleased in two-CD set, *The Complete Chamber Music*, Hyperion Records Ltd. (2002), Dyad CDD 22046.

Piano Trio no. 2 in A Minor, op. 45 (1878)

Seta Tanyel (piano), Levon Chilingirian (violin), Gargis Atmacayan (cello), Collins Classics (1994), CD 14192, DDD, rereleased in two-CD set, *The Complete Chamber Music*, Hyperion Records Ltd. (2002), Dyad CDD 22046.

Cello Sonata in E Minor, op. 46a (1881)

Colin Carr (cello), Seta Tanyel (piano),Collins Classics (1995), CD 14482, DDD, rereleased in two-CD set, *The Complete Chamber Music*, Hyperion Records Ltd.: (2002), Dyad CDD 22046.

Serenade for Violin and Piano, op. 70 (1895)

Lydia Mordkovitch (violin), Seta Tanyel (piano), Collins Classics (1995), CD 14482, DDD, rereleased in two-CD set, *The Complete Chamber Music*, Hyperion Records Ltd. (2002), Dyad CDD 22046.

Mazurek for Cello and Piano

Hans Meier (cello), Inge Sauer (piano), *Das Cello im Salon*: RBM (1996), CD RBM 463 123. (A transcription of the Mazurka, op. 16, no. 2.)

Piano Music

Polish National Dances, op. 3

Seta Tanyel, *The Piano Works*, Vol. 1, Collins Classics (1992), CD 13252, DDD, rereleased by Hyperion Records Ltd./Helios (2002), CDH 55131.
Evelinde Trenkner, Orion Records (1976), LP Stereo, ORS 76230.

Scherzo in G Major, op. 4

Seta Tanyel, *The Piano Works*, Vol. 3, Collins Classics (1993), CD 13652, DDD, rereleased by Hyperion Records Ltd./Helios (2003), CDH 55133.
Michael Ponti, Candide (1972), LP Stereo, CE 31046 (matrix VS 3646) and STGBY651 (UK).

Erzählungen am Klavier (Legends), op. 5

Seta Tanyel, *The Piano Works*, Vol. 4, Collins Classics (1996), CD 14742, DDD, rereleased by Hyperion Records Ltd./Helios (2003), CDH 55134.
Michael Ponti, Candide (1972), op. 5, no. 2, LP Stereo, CE 31046 (matrix VS 3646) and STGBY651 (UK).

Piano Sonata no. 1 in C-sharp Minor, op. 6

Seta Tanyel, *The Piano Works*, Vol. 1, Collins Classics (1992), CD 13252, DDD, rereleased by Hyperion Records Ltd./Helios (2002), CDH 55131.

First Polonaise in C-sharp Minor, op. 12

Seta Tanyel, *The Piano Works*, Vol. 1, Collins Classics (1992), CD 13252, DDD, rereleased by Hyperion Records Ltd./Helios (2002) CDH 55131.

Barcarolle in E Minor, op. 14

Seta Tanyel, *The Piano Works*, Vol. 3, Collins Classics (1993), CD 13652, DDD, rereleased by Hyperion Records Ltd./Helios (2003), CDH 55133.

Impromptu in D Major, op. 17

Seta Tanyel, *The Piano Works*, Vol. 1, Collins Classics (1992), CD 13252, DDD, rereleased by Hyperion Records Ltd./Helios (2002), CDH 55131.

Two Dances, op. 20

Evelinde Trenkner, Orion Records (1976), LP Stereo, ORS 76230.

Two Pieces, op. 22, Novellette and Melodie

Seta Tanyel, *The Piano Works*, Vol. 3, Collins Classics (1993), CD 13652, DDD, rereleased by Hyperion Records Ltd./Helios (2003), CDH 55133.

Michael Ponti, originally issued on Vox/Candide (1972), Novellette, LP Stereo, CE 31046 (matrix VS 3646) and STGBY651 (UK).

Six Waltzes, op. 28

Seta Tanyel, *The Piano Works*, Vol. 4, Collins Classics (1996), CD 14742, DDD, rereleased by Hyperion Records Ltd./Helios (2003), CDH 55134.

Deux Danses Polonaises, op. 29

Seta Tanyel, *The Piano Works*, Vol. 2, Collins Classics (1993), CD 13522, DDD, rereleased by Hyperion Records Ltd./Helios (2002), CDH 55132.

Valse-Caprice, op. 31

Seta Tanyel, *The Piano Works*, Vol. 1, Collins Classics (1992), CD 13252, DDD, rereleased by Hyperion Records Ltd./Helios (2002), CDH 55131.

Romanzero, op. 33

Seta Tanyel, *The Piano Works*, Vol. 2, Collins Classics (1993), CD 13522, DDD, rereleased by Hyperion Records Ltd./Helios (2002), CDH 55132.

Piano Sonata no. 2 in E-flat Major, op. 36

Seta Tanyel, *The Piano Works*, Vol. 2, Collins Classics (1993), CD 13522, DDD, rereleased by Hyperion Records Ltd./Helios (2002), CDH 55132.

Bilder aus dem Süden, op. 39, no. 2, Allegro molto

Evelinde Trenkner and Sontraud Speidel (pianos), MD&G Gold (2002), CD, MDG 330 1134-2, DDD.

Polonaise, op. 42
Seta Tanyel, *The Piano Works*, Vol. 1, Collins Classics (1992), CD 13252, DDD, rereleased by Hyperion Records Ltd./Helios (2002), CDH 55131.
Michael Ponti, Vox/Candide (1972), LP Stereo, CE 31046 (matrix VS 3646) and STGBY651 (UK).

Zwei Walzer, op. 44
Kölner Klavierduo (Elzbieta Kalvelage and Michael Krücker) (pianos), Koch Schwann (2000), CD 3-1575-2, DDD (recorded in April 1997).

Four Polish Dances, op. 47
Seta Tanyel, *The Piano Works*, Vol. 4, originally issued on Collins Classics (1996), CD 14742, DDD, rereleased on Hyperion Records Ltd./Helios (2003), CDH 55134.

Theme and Variations, op. 48
Seta Tanyel, *The Piano Works*, Vol. 3, originally issued on Collins Classics (1993), CD 13652, DDD, rereleased on Hyperion Records Ltd./Helios (2003), CDH 55133.
Evelinde Trenkner, Orion Records (1976), LP Stereo, ORS 76230.

Sonatine, op. 52, no. 1, in E minor
Seta Tanyel, *The Piano Works*, Vol. 2, originally issued on Collins Classics (1993), CD 13522, DDD, rereleased on Hyperion Records Ltd./Helios (2002), CDH 55132.

Variationen über ein Thema von C.H., op. 57
Seta Tanyel, *The Piano Works*, Vol. 4, originally issued on Collins Classics (1996), CD 14742, DDD, rereleased on Hyperion Records Ltd./Helios (2003), CDH 55134.

Four Polish Dances, op. 58
Seta Tanyel, *The Piano Works*, Vol. 3, originally issued on Collins Classics (1993), CD 13652, DDD, rereleased on Hyperion Records Ltd./Helios (2003), CDH 55133.

Song without Words, op. 62, no. 7 (From Album for Young Pianists)
www.thursdayschild.org/minerva/sounds/scharwenka_songwithout-words.mid (2 February 2006).

Two Pieces: Menuett and Scherzo, op. 65

Seta Tanyel, *The Piano Works*, Vol. 4, originally issued on Collins Classics (1996), CD 14742, DDD, rereleased on Hyperion Records Ltd./Helios (2003), CDH 55134.

Eglantine Waltz, op. 84

Seta Tanyel, *The Piano Works*, Vol. 1, originally issued on Collins Classics (1992), CD 13252, DDD, rereleased on Hyperion Records Ltd./Helios (2002), CDH 55131.

Drei Kavierstücke, op. 86

Seta Tanyel, *The Piano Works*, Vol. 4, originally issued on Collins Classics (1996), CD 14742, DDD, rereleased on Hyperion Records Ltd./Helios (2003), CDH 55134.

Notes

1. Evelinde Trenkner, "Xaver Scharwenka (1850 bis 1924): Ein Pianist der Kaiserzeit," *Das Mechanische Musikinstrument* 15, no. 54 (December 1991): 27–30.

2. Eszter Fontana, *Namhafte Pianisten im Aufnahmesalon Hupfeld* (Dößel, Germany: Verlag Janos Stekovics, 2000), 29.

APPENDIX

~

Compact Disc Contents
Compiled and Transferred to CD by
Robert S. Feigelson

The music selected for this compact disc covers a broad spectrum of Scharwenka's musical output including orchestral, chamber, and piano works. They span a forty-year period from the Trio, op. 1, of 1869, to the Fourth Piano Concerto, op. 82, written in 1908—one of his last compositions. Some of the artists who helped in Scharwenka's musical renaissance perform these selections. The compact disc also contains two examples of Scharwenka at the piano, playing first his own famous Polish Dance and then a portion of a Chopin scherzo. While Earl Wild's pioneering and brilliant recording of the First Piano Concerto could not be included, I am very pleased to be able to provide instead a selection from a stunning live concert performance[1] by Natasha Paremski, a Russian émigré who studied with Wild. At the time of this concert she was only fifteen years old.

Scharwenka Performances

1. Scharwenka: Polish Dance, op. 3, no. 1, off-air tape   3:08
2. Chopin: Scherzo in B-flat Minor, op. 31, Nimbus CD 8816   3:26

Recordings of Scharwenka's Music

3. Lecture on Piano Concerto, no. 2, Raymond Lewenthal (piano), Columbia Records BTS 20/ included with ML7394   7:08

4. Selection from the Adagio sostenuto of the Piano Trio no. 1, op. 1, Seta Tanyel (piano), Lydia Mordkovitch (violin), Colin Carr (cello), Hyperion CDD 22046   3:47

5. Finale—presto agitato from the Violin Sonata, op. 2, Lydia Mordkovitch (violin), Seta Tanyel (piano), Hyperion CDD 22046   5:42

6. Polish Dance, op. 3, no. 2, Evelinde Trenkner (piano), Orion Records ORS 76230   2:52

7. Polish Dance, op. 58, no. 3, Seta Tanyel (piano), Hyperion Helios CDH 55133   3:44

8. Scherzo from the Piano Concerto, no. 1, in B Minor, Natasha Paremski (piano), Jason Klein (conductor), Saratoga Symphony Orchestra, OSR 03-3   7:43

9. Selection from the Andante, Cello Sonata, op. 46, Colin Carr (cello), Seta Tanyel, (piano), Hyperion CDD 22046   2:10

10. Selection from Andante Religioso, op. 46a, Christopher Fifield (conductor), Gävle Symphony Orchestra, Sterling CDS 1060   2:31

11. Selection from the Adagio of the Piano Trio no. 2, op. 45, Seta Tanyel (piano), Levon Chilingirian (violin), Gargis Atmacayan (cello), Hyperion Records CDD 22046   5:26

12. Allegro vivace from the Piano Quartet in F, op. 37, Seta Tanyel (piano), Levon Chilingirian (violin), Ivo-Jan Van Der Werff (viola), Gargis Atmacayan (cello), Hyperion Records CDD 22046   6:38

13. Introduction to the Symphony, op. 60, Christopher Fifield (conductor), Gävle Symphony Orchestra, Sterling CDS 1060   4:29

14. Allegro con fuoco from the Piano Concerto no. 4, op. 82, Stephen Hough (piano), Lawrence Foster (conductor), City of Birmingham Symphony Orchestra, Hyperion CDA 66790   6:38

15–24. Selections from the Theme and Variations, op. 48, 12:34

Theme	0:51
Variation 3	0:22
Variation 5	0:59
Variation 6	1:58
Variation 10	0:43
Variation 15	0:50
Variation 17	1:01
Variation 18	2:19
Variation 19	2:23
Finale	1:02

Evelinde Trenkner (piano), Orion Records ORS 76230

I gratefully acknowledge the following organizations and individuals for their kind permission to use the recordings included on this compact disc:

Track 1. The Yamaha Corporation of America

Track 2. Nimbus Records, www.wyastone.co.uk

Track 3. International Piano Archives, University of Maryland (College Park)

Tracks 4, 5, 7, 9, 11, 12, and 14. Hyperion Records, www.hyperion-records.co.uk

Tracks 6 and 15–24. Orion Master Recordings and G. Cornfield

Track 8. Natasha Paremski, Jason Klein, and Greg Mott, recording engineer

Tracks 10 and 13. Sterling Records and Christopher Fifield

Note

1. This concert performance, which includes the complete concerto, is currently available on a CD from Mr. Greg Mott, P.O. Box 850, Pollack Pines, CA 95726.

Index

~

About the Authors

William E. Petig received his A.B., M.A., and Ph.D. in German from Stanford University and also studied at the University of Hamburg, Germany. He has taught German at Stanford University since 1978, where he served as director of Lower Division German. From 1972 to 1980 he was the managing editor of the scholarly journal *Die Unterrichtspraxis* and served as its book review editor for fifteen years. He has given numerous invited presentations at conferences in the United States and abroad and has published in the areas of eighteenth-century literature, German linguistics, and German-American studies. He is the author of *Literary Antipietism in German during the First Half of the Eighteenth Century* (Bern, 1984) and co-author of *German: A Structural Approach*, 4th ed. (New York, 1989).

He is the past president of the Northern California Chapter of the American Association of Teachers of German, past editor of the *California German Teacher*, and is currently the treasurer of the American Association of Teachers of German. He received the Duden Award for Outstanding Effort and Achievement in German Instruction and the Certificate of Merit for Outstanding Achievements in Furthering and Encouraging the Study of German Language and Culture from the American Association of Teachers of German and the Goethe Institute.

Robert S. Feigelson was born in New York City in 1935. He obtained a B.S. in ceramic engineering from the Georgia Institute of Technology in 1957, an M.S. from the Massachusetts Institute of Technology in 1961, and his Ph.D.

in materials science and engineering from Stanford University in 1974. For over thirty years, he has been on the faculty of the Materials Science and Engineering Department at Stanford University, where he is currently an emeritus professor. He is world renowned for his work related to the science and technology of growing crystals, in particular optical materials and semiconductors. He has published over 250 papers in scientific journals, consulted for many corporations, and delivered numerous invited lectures at national and international conferences.

Feigelson first studied piano with a niece of the well-known composer and conductor Nathaniel Shilkret and later with one of Xaver Scharwenka's students. Although not pursuing a career in music, he has maintained a strong interest in classical music since the age of ten and has a large collection of recorded music and books. He helped with the production of Sterling Records' recent recording of the orchestral music of Xaver Scharwenka and the idea for translating this autobiography came to him during this project. More recently, he organized a premiere performance of an unpublished piano concerto written by Eric Zeisl in the early 1950s. He is married and has three sons and three grandchildren.